DEADLY JEALOUSY

Martin Fido has been writing, lecturing and broadcasting on crime history since he gave up university teaching. He has presented regular broadcasts on murder for LBC Radio since 1987, and is the author of *Bodysnatchers*, *Murder Guide to London* and *Murders After Midnight*, and is one of the co-authors of *The Jack the Ripper A to Z*.

Deadly Jealousy

Martin Fido

HEADLINE

First published in 1993
by HEADLINE BOOK PUBLISHING

First published in paperback in 1994
by HEADLINE BOOK PUBLISHING

10 9 8 7 6 5 4 3 2 1

ISBN 0 7472 4220 8

Printed and bound in Great Britain by
HarperCollins Manufacturing, Glasgow

HEADLINE BOOK PUBLISHING
A division of Hodder Headline PLC
Headline House
79 Great Titchfield Street
London W1P 7FN

For Karen Lynn
with thanks for so many things

Contents

Acknowledgements

Without Keith Skinner, of Causeway Resources Historical and Genealogical Research, this book could not have been completed. To him, first, grateful thanks.

Without the help of the staffs of the British Library, British Newspaper Library, Guildhall Library, Public Records Office, Scotland Yard Library, Metropolitan Police Archives (and especially all in Room 216), LBC Radio Cuttings Library and Penzance Public Library, Keith and I could not have carried out the necessary research. Thanks to them.

Karen Lynn Sandel has supplied recent publications from America and checked up on the availability of scarce material there. Dr Robin Alston helped me trace through the British Library's computer the (extraordinary) whereabouts of one of Brad Steiger's rarer books. Russel Gray generously made available books and extracts from his growing true-crime collection. Richard Whittington-Egan was helpful and warmly encouraging, as he always is to those of us who follow so inadequately in his footsteps. Paul Feldman postponed asking questions about Jack the Ripper when he realized how much they eroded time needed for this book. City Walks and Original Ghost Walks bore with my inability to lead sightseers round sinister places for several months. Correspondents everywhere have been indulgent when I asked them to wait inordinately long times for answers to letters. (Special thanks to Lauri for her patience.) My family and friends accepted less of my company than they usually endure: especially useful were Austin's and Abigail's employment of the time on their own studies, and my Aged Parent's generous agreement to postpone her Imminent Demise until the book was finished. Sarah Hughes of Headline bravely accepted my assurance that I would come in on time with the manuscript, and heroically refrained from impeding composition with the anxious questions about progress that must have troubled her.

And grateful thanks to listeners to *Murder After Midnight* broadcasts. They constantly reassure me that the opinionated pontification, extravagant vocabulary, and recondite references with which I seek to flesh out the semi-fictional character of 'Dr' Martin Fido are acceptable and entertaining additions to the plain tales of murder and grist for the psychologists' mill which the great William Roughead taught us all to serve up with more or less mannered stylistic garnishing.

Introduction: Deadly Jealousy

Except in its subsidiary colloquial meaning of envy — 'They're all jealous of you, darling!' — jealousy is not a sin or even a fault. The books of *Exodus* and *Numbers* in the Bible assure us that the Lord our God is a jealous God, and they assuredly do not mean us to find Him sinful or faulty.

The primary dictionary meaning of jealous is strongly passionate. By extension this becomes strongly passionate about possessions and thence about relationships. It is excellent to be jealous in your care for your children's well-being. It is admirable to be jealous of your good name. But jealousy relates to possessions: *my* good name; *my* wife's love. And it is the error of thinking that the possessive adjective means one is really in some way entitled to *own* another person's affections that leads to murder.

When you let yourself become jealous of your spouse's friendships, you step into Othello's shoes. But even then, your mere feeling need not in itself be reprehensible. It is unnatural *not* to suffer an almost physical pain on seeing a deeply loved partner happy in another's arms. It does not become a vice unless it is dwelt upon to engender hatred. And the hatred may be fed by envy of the rival's happiness or perceived advantages.

So the deadly sins leeching on the natural emotion of jealousy are, surprisingly, avarice (possessiveness) and anger as well as envy — a beastly trio. Give them their head, and they become, as F. Tennyson Jesse observed, one of the five key motives for murder: Deadly Jealousy.

So strong is this motive that, unusually, it may replace almost all physical and circumstantial evidence to secure a conviction. When I started this book, two young sisters, Michelle and Lisa Taylor, were languishing in prison. They stood convicted of murdering Alison O'Shaughnessy in 1991, the wife of Michelle's lover. The physical evidence against them would not have hung a cat: a single fingerprint of Lisa's in the O'Shaughnessy flat. She claimed at first never to have been there, later changing her story to say that she had cleaned the windows there on behalf of her family's cleaning business, and denied it because they all knew Alison would not have liked them doing the work. The circumstantial evidence against Michelle and Lisa was very imprecise testimony by a witness who saw 'two girls' come out of the building at a time when other witnesses said Alison had already returned home. *All* these witnesses could be countered by others who were equally certain that Alison arrived considerably later, and Michelle was definitely at work a mile away by the time her supposed victim reached the murder site.

But how could such pedantic time-keeping compete with the melodramatic evidence of Michelle's jealousy, recorded faithfully in her diary?

'I hate Alison − the unwashed bitch,' she wrote. 'My dream solution would be for Alison to disappear as if she never existed and then maybe I could give everything to the man I loved.'

As is so often the case when a woman feels this kind of jealousy, the man she loved was an unmitigated heel. John O'Shaughnessy seduced Michelle while he was already engaged to Alison. He exploited the eighteen-year-old's continuing passion for him until she felt she was just his 'tart' or 'bit on the side'. Jealousy was the force which transferred that self-contempt over to the rival, in bitter hatred.

Happily, the Taylor sisters' conviction was overturned

on appeal, and they walked free in June 1993.

Men's self-contempt is more likely to relate to their sexual performance. If a woman really wants to bring out the Othello in her lover, I suggest that she tells him in no uncertain terms that she has been sleeping with a better endowed man, blessed with greater staying power and a far more exciting range of erotic techniques. If she throws in for good measure that her normal man has always been a boring wimp, she runs an excellent chance of suffering a rapid fracture of the hyoid bone.

The crime of which Michelle Taylor was convicted often happens, of course. Women may well dispose of other women who stand between them and their men. Couples may unite to get rid of the figure whose irritating bond of matrimony stands between them and their unimpeded union. Men, strangely, are more likely to be genuinely paranoid, and imagine rivalry where none exists, with lethal consequences for unsuspecting and innocent acquaintances. Cassio is as common a victim as Desdemona.

Nobody likes being jilted. But the adolescent's pride in being the one who gives rather than receives 'the brush' when a relationship ends shows how much this murder-inducing situation, too, often reaches its bloody climax as the outcome of misplaced pride and threatened possessiveness.

So here is a collection of true murder stories, clutched together in the claws of the green-eyed monster. We have familiar cases – but readers who think Mrs Barney is old hat may be delighted to learn who the woman was that Michael Scott Stephen was seeing, and why it didn't come out at the trial. And there are new ones. I warrant you've never heard of John Kerr unless you're familiar with Melbourne, and Nicholas Hall's name means nothing to you unless you're from the West Country. We have cases that are sensational, sexy and sad, like Paul Snider's brutal killing of his lovely wife. And

we have sensational sexy silliness, as in the two Miss
Whiplashes who heard a spirit foretell the murder of the
wrong one.

Murder buffs, pray enjoy this new collection.

Martin Fido
Heamoor, 1993

He Done Her Wrong

'He was her man,
But he done her wrong.'
Frankie and Johnny

Elvira Barney

Elvira Barney's jealousy was that of a woman whose looks were fading; whose younger lover was straying, even while he went on milking her for money; who was humiliated by the public attentions he paid to others; who brooded in her lonely apartment while carefree Lothario trolled off to follow his own whims and wills. Such jealousy must surely command sympathy? Not easily in Mrs Barney's case!

Blowzy, raddled, foul-mouthed, drunken, noisy and fat, by the age of twenty-seven Elvira Dolores Barney was squandering her comfortable private means on an empty life of cocktails, night-clubbing, cocktails, bridge, taxis, parties and yet more cocktails. She had contaminated her upper-class heritage of gracious manners; had thrown away much that nature had granted her by way of natural blonde good looks; and forfeited a possible stage career which always owed more to her social standing and personal attractions than to any real talent.

She was born in 1905, the daughter of John Ashley Mullins. An old Etonian, a trustee of the Stock Exchange and subsequently the Chief Government Broker, Mullins was to be knighted in the 1920s, putting the final appropriate gloss on his career as a City gentleman with a town house in Belgravia and a country estate in Haslemere. Tall and gracious Lady Mullins enjoyed the reputation of looking younger than her daughters — and Elvira and her little sister Avril were by no means ill-favoured.

In 1925 Avril married into the aristocracy when she wedded White Russian emigré Prince George Imeretinsky. The bride was just sixteen. Her father gave her a flat in Park Lane, a string of individually matched pearls, and a personal income of £4,000 a year. The treasures of wealth and social standing came automatically to the Mullins girls.

So it should reckon in Elvira's favour that she started by trying to carve out an independent existence for herself as something better than her father's well-dowried trophy to be handed over to a titled taker. As 'Dolores Ashley' – her own and her father's middle names combined – Elvira graduated from Lady Benson's Acting Academy and appeared as an extra in *The Blue Kitten* at the Gaiety Theatre in December 1925. Her part was too small for the programme to list her name. Her social standing, however, secured a full page of pictures in the *Sketch* of Miss Mullins lounging in elegant day pyjamas and a svelte permanent wave. Society journalists preferred a former debutante in a walk-on part to any number of talented girls of unidentifiable class playing leads.

When the play's run closed, so did Dolores Ashley's career. The footlights and greasepaint had seen the last of her, for after a year of the normal dull society whirl – hunt balls, garden parties, Henley Regatta, Ascot week and weekend parties for the mass extermination of pheasants – Elvira made a surprising marriage.

In 1927 she met American song-and-dance man John Sterling Barney. Together with two partners whose subsequent recording and cabaret careers flourished as 'Ross and Sergeant', Barney was a member of the top-hat-white-tie-and-tails hoofing trio 'The Three New Yorkers'. They appeared in *Many Happy Returns* at the Duke of York's Theatre. They appeared in night-clubs. They appeared at society parties which included cabaret. And thus they appeared at a thrash thrown by Lady Mullins.

After performing with Sergeant and Ross, Barney danced with Elvira and, smitten by his terpsichorean charm, she raced into an ill-advised marriage. Just what did Sir John Mullins foresee in this marriage? The vulgarity of wedding an unaristocratic Yank (rather than a princely Russian)? The unwholesome morality of 'the stage' — especially those entertainers who tapped and crooned to lewd 'jazz' music? Or did he just foresee that both his daughter and his new son-in-law were unlikely to bestow on the Mullinses the blessings of stable matrimony and lissom scions?

He certainly foresaw something. For there was no great white wedding at St Margaret's Westminster such as little sister Avril and her Russian Prince had enjoyed; no flat in Park Lane. Just a registry office wedding at Prince's Row, and an allowance for Elvira that ensured they wouldn't live uncomfortably, even if Barney's shufflin' along never brought vast rewards.

In fairness to Barney, he was not, as Sir John might have anticipated, a wedding-ring gigolo, satisfied to live off his wife's unearned income. When the marriage proved unsatisfactory (as it very swiftly did) he took himself off to New York and made no further attempt to contact Elvira or assert his dependency on her.

It is not clear why the marriage went wrong — Barney certainly never said. Elvira claimed he was 'a brute', and showed one friend scars on her upper arms which she said were made by Barney's depraved appetite for stubbing out cigarettes on her. But, frankly, I wouldn't believe anything Elvira said without corroboration. She was an unreliable, self-dramatizing, emotionally unstable woman, and I wouldn't take her word for the state of any emotional relationship in which she was involved.

But, free from John Sterling Barney, Elvira had her wealth and independence. She had her Belgravia flatlet at 21 Williams Mews and she still had her blonde good looks. And she proceeded to dissipate, fashionably. It was the era of the 'Bright Young Things'. Their chroniclers, Evelyn Waugh and Noël Coward, might suggest that their world was one of style, taste, wit and sophistication. Elvira's gamey career, alas, reveals that for the uncreative and untalented it was a world of drunkenness, recreational drugs and stupid rowdiness. She drifted onto the fringes of Brenda Dean Taylor's rackety set and occasionally took cocaine. For intellectual stimulus, Elvira's friends played bridge. This was too demanding for her, but she willingly held bridge parties in her flat, and served whisky, sherry and martinis to those whose brains could cope with remembering what was trumps and who had called them.

By 1930 she had taken an actor called Mervyn Pearce as her main man, and had made her first appearance on a police jotter. She was speeding down Chiswick High Street when she collided with another car. Witnesses unanimously informed PC Gunner and Sergeant Craig, who had been called to take evidence, that she was directly responsible. Gunner told her she would have to be reported for dangerous driving, and Elvira's pettish response was, 'I don't think that's fair'. She then turned to Craig, saying, 'By whose orders is that?'

'By mine,' Craig replied. 'Having read statements as to how this accident occurred, I directed the constable so to inform you.'

He was treated to a torrent of abuse. 'You bloody swine!' the lady shouted. 'I knew Horwood and I'll get you sacked.'

Her boasted acquaintance with the former Metropolitan Police Commissioner (retired in 1928) failed to move the stolid sergeant, who warned her not to create a disturbance on the street.

'I'll shout as much as I like!' yelled Mrs Barney. 'I'll show these bloody swines up! They are all out to get me down.'

Craig again admonished her, but as she stamped past him for a taxi to take her away from the wreckage she had caused she hurled another 'Bloody swine!' over her shoulder. The sergeant informed her that he would have to mention her use of insulting words likely to cause a breach of the peace in his report, which prompted a final flurry of rage as the taxi drew away.

'You bastard,' cried Mrs Barney. 'How I hate you!
I will always remember you.' The outcome of that
little incident was a fine of £10 plus costs for the society
'lady'.

Shortly before Christmas 1931 Mrs Barney made the
fatal friendship that was to bring her to the dock at the
Old Bailey. 'Michael' Scott Stephen (his real forenames
were William Thomas) was a couple of years younger
than Elvira. A good-looking man, he had worked briefly
in insurance before describing himself as a dress-designer
in Paris. Nobody has ever traced any dresses he designed,
and he might better have been described as a sponger and
almost, if not quite, a bi-sexual gigolo. His father, a
respectable bank manager and JP, cut off his allowance,
disgusted by his irresponsibility. So Michael borrowed
money shamelessly from his mother and friends. He slept
with men and women alike in that age when ignorance
about contraception, a silly chivalric attitude to 'ladies'
and the sexually segregated education of the upper classes
meant that extraordinary numbers of young gentlemen
experienced little or nothing but homosexuality in their
late teens and early twenties, despite the essentially
heterosexual natures of men such as Rupert Brooke and
Evelyn Waugh. It seems likely that Stephen's real
predilections were also heterosexual, but he couldn't
afford to turn down a man's invitation to bed if it
promised the hope of a little loan.

Stephen's circle tended simply to view him as bi-sexual.
Mrs Barney introduced him to the screaming queen Brian
Howard, an essentially uncreative self-publicist, whose
capacity to produce pastiche of Edith Sitwell's verse won
him the enthusiastic endorsement of that lady — always
over-generous in her estimation of younger people who
admired her. Howard made a striking undergraduate
reputation as a 'poet' at Oxford, and Evelyn Waugh
combined him with the far abler Harold Acton to provide
elements for his outrageously camp characters Ambrose

Silk and Anthony Blanche. But Howard's progress after graduating was a steady decline into drinking, night-clubbing and living off his wits. Elvira Barney and Michael Scott Stephen would not have been probable friends for a young man who showed any real promise.

However, Howard was the brightest light to find Stephen's company tolerable. Beverly Nichols — another homosexual undergraduate who launched himself in the world with an Oxford 'intellectual' reputation for loung-ing among Siamese cats in a silk dressing-gown — called Stephen 'a very unpleasant little gigolo who once offered me cocaine'.

But to Mrs Barney, Stephen was a wonderful discovery — a man she loved 'more than all the others', by her own account. And the whiff of perversity surrounding him was undoubtedly part of his attraction. The perversity Michael and Elvira shared, however, was sado-masochis-tic. An erotic painting over the cocktail bar in her Williams Mews flat would shock police. Pornographic books in her library shocked them still more. And the presence of flagellation and bondage equipment in her bedroom was the greatest shock of all. Ladies were not expected to enjoy such things. In his final report on the case, Detective Inspector William Winter flatly informed his approving superiors, 'not only (Mrs Barney and Mr Stephen), but the clique in which they moved, indulged in almost every sexual vice it is possible to imagine, and one can only think that Mrs Barney is indeed a very fortunate person to be at liberty at the moment.'

It would have been happier for both of them if they restricted their pleasures to tying each other up and lashing each other silly. Unfortunately, they both enjoyed the self-dramatization of building up real rows to the point where screaming matches degenerated to blows. Michael was seen with a black eye his inamorata had given him. The neighbours started complaining.

At 4 a.m. on 17 February 1932, a taxi-driver sum-moned PC Robert Campbell from his beat in Knightsbridge, saying he'd been asked to send a policeman to Williams Mews where there was said to be a lunatic at large. Campbell found three men and two women quarrelling in the doorway of number 21. All were drunk, and Mrs Barney (whose name he misheard as Mrs Burnett) said she had called the taxi to get rid of her unwelcome guests who refused to leave. The following morning at half-past ten, Mr Elverton from 11 Williams Mews made a formal complaint to PC Richard Francis that the constant noise and shouting at night from Mrs Barney's flat was making it impossible for the neighbours to sleep. PC Francis promised to give the matter his attention, and did nothing further.

On 3 March, Mrs Barney called the police out at 2 a.m., saying a man had smashed her window and assaulted her. Sergeant James Barnes found a small ground-floor window smashed from the inside and Mrs Barney nursing some red weals on her arms and chest. She said she knew the man responsible but did not wish to give the police his name. What she wanted was a policeman left to guard her through the night. Sergeant James contented himself with finding out that a road-sweeper had seen the man leave in a taxi, after which he ordered the beat constable to keep a general eye on the premises.

Towards the end of April, Mrs Barney had an altercation with a taxi-driver, whom she first cursed and then tried to seduce. She had arrived at Waterloo on the early evening Bournemouth train and took Edward Coles' cab from the rank. He drove her to the wrong mews at first and was called a bloody fool who wasn't fit to hold a licence. His passenger continued to scream at him as he followed her directions to Williams Mews until at the flat she asked him to come inside with her. Coles demurred, whereupon Elvira said she would not pay him if he didn't join her indoors. In the end he had to fetch a policeman to recover his fare.

Mrs Barney's drunken scenes were starting to feature a

new element. She occasionally threatened suicide if she couldn't get her way. Her twittering circle of Bright Young Things knew that one of the obstacles to her happiness was 'Another Woman' whom Michael insisted on seeing.

Early in 1932, Terence Skeffington-Smyth and a couple of friends went back to Williams Mews after dining with Mrs Barney. When they all went in, Elvira declared herself tired and upset and locked herself in her bedroom. Her friends became alarmed when total silence ensued and she made no response to their calls. So they went outside and hunted for a ladder so they could peer in at the bedroom window. While they were thus engaged, Mrs Barney popped downstairs and slammed the door shut on them, leaving them locked out.

After this event, there were several occasions when Mrs Barney telephoned Mr Skeffington-Smyth in the small hours of the morning, asking him to hurry round as she was about to kill herself. Knowing the extent of her drunken self-dramatization, he wisely refused to leave his bed.

On 15 April Mrs Barney combined a suicide threat with a call to the police. PC Albert Sewards was sent from Gerald Road police station after she made an alarming telephone call (from a lone woman) that there was a man in her house. Sewards found Michael Stephen, quiet and sober, leaning against the mantelpiece. Mrs Barney, noisy and drunk, said, 'That is the man. He refuses to leave my house. Will you see that he leaves the house?'

Stephen said to Sewards, 'Before I go, would you like to know who her father and mother are?' Sewards couldn't have cared less if they were the Man in the Moon and Queen Mary. And, as if to rub in the complete waste of the policeman's time, the couple were quiet and amicable as he departed.

'You'll promise me, darling, won't you?' Stephen asked on the doorstep. Mrs Barney responded affectionately, 'Yes, I promise, dear,' and made no complaint when

Stephen had to call her out again to fetch his hat which he had forgotten.

As he made his final departure from Williams Mews, Stephen quietly told Sewards that the promise he had exacted was that Elvira should not try to kill herself with poison or a revolver, as she had threatened.

The most notorious of Mrs Barney's nocturnal scenes involving taxis and Michael Scott Stephen occurred toward the end of the first week in May 1932. Mrs Dorothy Hall, a chauffeur's wife who lived opposite number 21, was aroused in the small hours by raised voices. A taxi-driver was complaining vociferously about damage done to his vehicle, and Elvira, for once, was apologizing instead of cursing him. Placated, the taxi left while Mrs Barney went indoors. But before long, another taxi drew up and deposited Michael on his lady-love's doorstep. He needed her to pay his fare for him and this Elvira refused to do. 'Go and fish for it!' she yelled, and Stephen briefly went away and somehow made his peace with the cabman.

He was soon back, provoking Elvira's worst public exhibition yet. Looking out of her window as the noise levels rose again, Mrs Hall saw Mrs Barney leaning out of her own bedroom window, stark naked, pointing a pistol at Stephen.

'Laugh, baby, laugh for the last time!' she cried, and with B-picture melodrama she fired the pistol in his direction.

Stephen, a young man of some insouciance, told her not to be so foolish as everybody was watching. Elvira promptly keeled over as though in a dead faint. Then, belatedly recalling the good manners Shrewsbury School had instilled in him, Stephen looked up at Mrs Hall and apologized for being such a nuisance in the mews. She confirmed that he really was a perfect nuisance, and told him to clear off. He explained courteously that he was afraid to leave as he feared Mrs Barney might try to kill herself, and after pacing up and down the mews for some

time, he got quietly into a greengrocer's van parked there
to pass an uncomfortable night.

The fatal rumpus took place on the night of 30 – 31 May
when Mrs Barney threw a party.

Despite the constant unneighbourly noisiness of her
social life, this was only a monthly occurrence. It was
more usual for her to entertain two or three friends
intimately, or keep the drinks flowing for a bridge four,
than to invite a large body of people in to stand around
consuming whisky and martinis and sandwiches while the
gramophone played. She and Stephen often went together
to other people's cocktail parties (in between going to
night-clubs and first nights, football matches and the
greyhounds). And they might bring a few people back to
the flat for drinks and gramophone records after they had
all been night-clubbing. When Mrs Barney threw larger
formal invitation cocktail parties they were in the early
evening, running as a rule from about 6.30 to 9 p.m.

Residents of Williams Mews sighed as cars and taxis
arrived, carrying between twenty and thirty people in for
Elvira's party on 30 May. And they watched the action as
the party went on. Michael Stephen arrived in a taxi with
another woman. Mrs Barney went out at one point with
another man and came back bearing more drinks and
syphons of soda water. But the hour was reasonable and
there was no noisy quarrelling; it was altogether one of
the more civilized moments in Mrs Barney's life.

Brian Howard and his German boyfriend Alton
Altmann were among the guests, as was Terence
Skeffington-Smyth's brother Dennis. The first to leave
was musician Hugh Wade who had an engagement to
play the piano at the Blue Angel night-club in Dean
Street, Soho. The last arrival was Arthur Jeffress who
came so late that the party was almost over. In
consequence, he stayed on alone with Elvira and Michael
for some time, and at about half-past ten went with them
to the Café de Paris for a light dinner.

Having eaten, Jeffress invited his companions to go on with him to the Blue Angel, where he was a member. Both had been there before, usually as his guests or Terence Skeffington-Smyth's. Earlier in the year, Mrs Barney had attracted the attention of the cloakroom attendant by hiding in the lavatory and getting the attendant to tell a gentleman who came looking for her that she had gone home. This was certainly not Stephen – the gentleman was older and taller. He was definitely anxious to see Elvira, who was equally anxious not to see him, and stayed in hiding while he made three or four return visits to the cloakroom inquiring after her. Neither of them revealed to the attendant what it was all about, but one may be reasonably sure from the lifestyle of the Bright Young Things that it was some trivial nonsense.

At the Blue Angel, the trio greeted Hugh Wade, who was busy at the keyboard. And around midnight they invited Terence Skeffington-Smyth to join them when he dropped in. He had not been at the party in Williams Mews as he had only arrived back in London from Paris at 7 p.m. that night.

As a nightcap, the party had a pair of kippers apiece, washed down with whisky. After their pleasant and tranquil evening, the party split up and Elvira and Michael went back to her bed where they made love – not to Michael's satisfaction, however. He felt Elvira was wilfully unresponsive, and said so. He believed he knew why she was not responding too. She objected to his friendship with Mrs Dora Wright, a lady known to her friends as Peggy, whose flat in Park Street was close to Michael's lodgings.

Elvira's objections to Peggy had a respectable reason for public consumption. Michael played a lot of bridge with Peggy (he did not play it at Elvira's flat) and Peggy encouraged him to back his play. But Elvira feared that he was losing money by gambling. Since Michael fancied himself as a card player and nursed private hopes that he might make a living at the tables, she was right to be worried — especially as he expected her to pay his gambling debts. But all their circle took it for granted that Elvira's distaste for Michael's friend was really plain, straightforward, old-fashioned jealousy.

Some of them thought her jealousy focused on Marion Carstairs of Mulberry Walk, Chelsea. As that lady told the police she did not know either Mrs Barney or Mr Stephen, they were presumably wrong. But their error subsequently confused the prosecution and kept much of the jealousy motivation obscure at Mrs Barney's trial.

Michael was foolishly content to provoke Elvira's jealousy during their quarrels. He sometimes told Elvira that he preferred Peggy to her. Not that Peggy thought there was anything in this. As far as she could see, Michael and Elvira were tightly bonded to each other. None of their social set acknowledged that this bonding was cemented by the screaming, histrionic rows. None of them seemed to be aware that Mrs Barney feared that Michael might be jealous of her own flirtatious conduct, and pleaded with him in a letter to be 'broadminded'. Nobody knew of the existence of this unsolicited apology for offence Michael never seems to have taken, so nobody could reflect that it looked an excellent way of starting a row for which there was no real reason at all. Nobody seems to have put together Elvira's constant complaints that Mr Barney had been 'a brute' to her, with her frequent lament that Michael had been 'unkind'.

But looking back on their relationship with benefit of hindsight, it seems safe to suggest that, at a very deep level, Mrs Barney actually enjoyed the situation of being an ill-used woman. The cultural and ethical climate of the early twentieth century encouraged Rudyard Kipling to make a heroine of an East End street prostitute in *The Record of Badalia Herodsfoot*. And her tragic nobility lies in the equanimity with which she suffers the brutal treatment of a husband who ultimately kills her. The lachrymose introductory poem, *Mary, Pity Women*, adds to Kipling's general suggestion that females are angelic creatures with a fine capacity to suffer the assaults of the brutal male.

Now there is copious evidence that Mrs Barney substituted unstable role-playing for self-knowledge and integrity. And it seems that the tragedy queen's role which she particularly favoured was that of the loyal and doting, but badly abused wife or mistress. Poor old Michael Stephen, whose consistent good manners to the general public contrasted so favourably with her infantile tantrums, was willy-nilly cast as the villain as soon as he yielded to Elvira's charms. He might not have wanted to hurt her. Not a shred of real evidence has been produced that he ever seriously tried to, except, possibly as part of sado-masochistic bedroom games. But Elvira needed lovers' rows to prove to herself that she was a loving and forgiving woman, and so she simply provoked them!

It is notable, too, that neither of them seems to have had any deeper genuine attachment to the other than their erotic attraction. I may be unfair in this – though the police report made the same point. But it is not without significance that Michael complained when Elvira was not as passionate a sexual partner as he wanted that night – at 4 a.m. after a hard evening of partying and night-clubbing! A lover who was truly close to her would surely have allowed that she was justifiably tired and appropriately grateful that she managed any response at all! But Stephen sulked. The row started. Michael Scott Stephen, however, did not resort to violence to bring his mistress to heel! He did not put Elvira in the desirably haloed position of brutalized victim of his rage. He simply got out of bed, dressed and prepared to leave.

After that we have only Mrs Barney's word for exactly what happened. But we have the neighbours' testimony that the mews was once again treated to the nocturnal sound of Mrs Barney's uplifted voice, and a shot was fired around 4.30 a.m.

The first disruption of Mrs Hall's slumber came from Stephen shouting. Then she heard Mrs Barney say, twice, either 'I'll shoot' or 'I'll shoot you'.

There came a shot. Stephen cried, 'What have you done?'

Now Mrs Hall heard Mrs Barney break into wailing, 'Chicken, come back to me! I will do anything for you.' A little later she heard Mrs Barney telephoning the doctor to say that someone had shot himself.

A little further down the mews, another chauffeur's wife, Mrs Kate Stevens, was awakened by what she took to be shots.

'That is Mrs Barney firing her pistol,' she said sagely to her husband, having looked out of the window and seen nothing. Then she returned to bed and heard another much louder shot. She heard quarrelling voices from the bedroom of number 21. A man's voice – she could not recognize it as Stephen's – said, 'What made you do it?' And Mrs Barney wailed incessantly, 'Michael, Michael, come back. I love you.'

Possibly the first shots Mrs Stevens thought she heard were noises made by Mrs Barney's next-door neighbour, William Kiff, who threw a piece of gas iron at a cat in the mews during the night. His missile skidded across the street to strike a dustbin after clanging off a manhole cover. Mr Kiff heard Mrs Barney screaming at 4 a.m. – then a single shot at 4.35 a.m.

Certainly Mrs Barney was very busy summoning a doctor. Her GP, Dr Thomas Durrant of Westbourne Terrace, was aroused by the telephone at about 4.30 a.m. His wife took the call, but received no coherent message to pass on. Three minutes later the telephone went again, and the doctor heard Mrs Barney crying hysterically and demanding that he come at once as a gentleman had shot himself. Before the unfortunate medic had finished dressing, she called again.

'Why haven't you come? Come at once! Jump into a taxi! He is bleeding,' she urged.

At the flat, Dr Durrant found Michael's body lying at the top of the stairs. Elvira was babbling incoherently,

and saying, 'Is he dead? He can't be dead. I love him so.'
The doctor ordered her into the bedroom (where he
observed with mild distaste the evidence of Michael's and
Elvira's love-making earlier in the night) while he
examined the body and confirmed that Michael Scott
Stephen had expired.

Now, in fragmentary sobs and bits and pieces, Mrs
Barney poured out her tale to the doctor. With a few
additional details after the police had questioned her it
was to remain her story from start to finish. She never
altered it. She never obviously embellished it. And it was
certainly a strong point in her favour that her recollections did not undergo the sudden 'improvements' to cover
fresh evidence that have embarrassed so many murderers
under cross-examination.

She told the doctor that Michael had been most anxious
for him to arrive before he died, so that he could explain
that it was not Elvira's fault. This might have been a self-
serving invention. But Mrs Barney produced it instantly
after the shooting, at a time when she hardly seemed in a
state to use her imagination to good effect.

She said that Michael and she had words over Mrs
Wright at the party, and the quarrel revived more
seriously after their rather unsatisfactory love-making.
She said that when Michael dressed and declared his
intention of leaving, he even threatened to go to the other
woman. Mrs Barney thereupon made her by now
customary threat to kill herself if he left.

'Don't leave me! Don't leave me! I'll shoot myself,' she
claimed to have cried. Which led Michael to go straight to
the chair where she kept her pistol under a cushion,
saying, 'Anyway, you won't do it with this.' And he
started out of the bedroom with the gun in his hand. She
ran after him and struggled to take the gun away. And in
the course of their struggle the gun went off.

She denied that Michael said, 'What have you done?'
By her account he said nothing until he went into the
bathroom, where she called to him from outside, 'Come

back to me, Michael. Come back'. She was quite unprepared for his opening the door and saying to her, very seriously, 'Go quickly, fetch a doctor'. And from then until he lost the ability to speak, he kept hoping the doctor would arrive soon, so that he could explain it was not Elvira's fault.

As he collapsed on the landing, she took pillows from the bed to put under his head. She loosened his collar and thrust a towel under his shirt to staunch the bleeding. And she summoned the doctor.

So the great jealous melodrama of Michael and Elvira reached its catastrophe. Only instead of a tragic heroine lying on the floor in a pool of blood for all to weep sympathetic tears over her sacrificial passion, a totally drunk Mrs Barney was raving around her flat in her underwear, hardly covered by a negligee. At the top of the stairs lay the body of a lover she seemed to have killed herself. And a resolutely prosaic medical man who prudently took command of the murder weapon so that she could neither destroy herself nor any vital evidence, insisted that the police must be called.

Their arrival brought her to her senses. *Her* senses, that is, not those of a rational person. Detective Inspector Winter asked her what she could tell him about the tragedy. She shouted at him and ordered him out of the house. Inspector Campion suggested that she take a warm coat for questioning in the cold police station. She punched his face, saying, 'I will teach you to say you will put me in a cell, you vile swine.' And when Lady Mullins telephoned the flat to see what was going on, Mrs Barney gloated at Campion, 'Now you know who my mother is, perhaps you will be a little more careful what you say and do. I will teach you to say you will take me to a police station.'

Fortunately, Sir John and Lady Mullins persuaded her to behave decently when they arrived, and she went lamb-like to Gerald Street police station to make her statement. Indeed, she was quite uncharacteristically well behaved from then until the end of her trial.

In addition to the neighbours' statements, the police and forensic scientists felt that the physical evidence was not compatible with Mrs Barney's story of an accident and she was swiftly charged with murder. The wound in Stephen's chest which had punctured his lung was not one he could have inflicted himself. His hand would have had to be bent backwards at an impossible angle. That hand, moreover, showed no staining with gunpowder, as would be expected if he had actually been holding the weapon while Elvira tried to wrest it from him as it went off.

The pistol was a loaded five-chambered revolver. Two shots had been fired from it, but they did not come from consecutive chambers. The one loaded chamber between the two that had been discharged presented a puzzle. But the discovery of a second bullet in the room that had hit the wall and ricocheted into the wardrobe suggested something more deliberate than the single, accidental explosion Mrs Barney claimed.

Furthermore, gunsmith Robert Churchill testified that the ·32 calibre American-made pistol was one of the safest weapons on the market. It didn't have a safety catch because it didn't need one. A single finger on the cylinder would prevent it from revolving, thereby stopping a bullet from being chambered and rendering the gun harmless. Moreover, the trigger required a 14 lb pull to fire it — and that's an awfully strong spring to pull back with one finger, as anyone may find out by trying to lift a weight or depress a bathroom scale as if squeezing a trigger. It seemed absolutely impossible that the accident Mrs Barney described could have made her gun go off.

It seemed equally impossible that Mrs Barney could establish her innocence before a jury and rescue herself from death on the gallows. But she was saved by extraordinary chance. Her former nanny, who remembered her affectionately as little Elvira of the golden curls, was now employed by the barrister Sir Patrick Hastings. Silver-tongued Hastings was certainly the outstanding figure at the bar between Sir Edward Marshall Hall and Sir Norman Birkett. Though he had failed resoundingly in politics, his lack-lustre parliamentary performance and poor political judgement as Attorney-General contributing signally to the fall of Ramsay MacDonald's first Labour government, he rarely failed to persuade a jury of the excellence of his case.

But Sir Patrick, society's favourite advocate, preferred not to soil his record with sordid criminal cases. Mrs Barney's was just such a brief. Had he declined, he would have lost his most famous victory, and she might well have lost her freedom to die of dissipation in a hotel room of her own choosing, enduring instead an appointment with a rope and trapdoor at Holloway.

It was the nanny, remembering the sweet little girl of yesteryear who saved her. Distressed at the thought of Lady Mullins' grief, and knowing the Mullinses pinned their hopes on persuading Sir Patrick to take the case, the good nurse went to work tearing at Lady Hastings' heartstrings. Lady Hastings went to work on Sir Patrick, and Sir Patrick accepted the case and saved Mrs Barney. He did so by three brilliant forensic tricks; by the great good fortune that the most damaging prosecution witness changed her story by the omission of a single word; and the advantage that Mrs Barney changed hers not a whit.

Sir Patrick's first move was a casual, almost negligent request to the judge that all witnesses be asked to leave the court – including the expert witnesses. Now it is a normal and proper rule that witnesses to the facts do not hear evidence before they have given their own, lest their memories be contaminated and their stories change to harmonize perfectly with other people's recollections. Police witnesses may be allowed to remain in court if they are testifying to little more than the finding of the body, though their exclusion may be requested by the defence if it seems necessary. But as Sir Patrick made clear, diffidently and courteously offering to withdraw if the judge preferred, he was actually referring to expert witnesses: witnesses who would be asked to give their opinion on professional questions only. Quite simply, Sir Patrick wanted the great pathologist Sir Bernard Spilsbury to be prevented from hearing the testimony.

There was good reason for this. If Sir Bernard heard the defence case expounded in court, the prosecution would be entitled to ask him whether, in his opinion, it was compatible with the wound he had examined. And it was quite certain that Sir Bernard, with all the magisterial weight of his great reputation and newspaper following, would assure the court that it was not. He had already told the magistrate's court that Stephen must have been shot by another hand – that his own hand could not have gripped the gun that killed him.

But if the eminent witness never heard the theory of accidental shooting put forward as evidence in court, he could not be asked to offer any opinion on the matter. Sir Patrick knew better than to argue with the pathologist, whose experience of the courts had made him as expert in his role of witness as he was in his profession of pathologist. Many a defence counsel had made the case against his client worse by striving, unsuccessfully, to wring a favourable reservation from Sir Bernard.

Hastings, on the other hand, ran no risks. He let the direct examination elicit from Sir Bernard the height and angle of the bullet wound, and the cause of death by shock and internal bleeding in the lung. He heard Sir Bernard confirm that Stephen could not have shot himself: the wound was incompatible with suicide. And never a word of accident was proposed.

Sir Patrick cheerfully confined himself to the most perfunctory cross-examination. Had Sir Bernard made his measurements on Stephen's actual body as well as a laboratory skeleton? Yes. And didn't all skeletons differ slightly? Yes. Thank you, Sir Bernard. That was all. Mrs Barney had been saved from the weightiest possible declaration that her story was impossible.

The other great expert witness to be defused was

gunsmith Robert Churchill. His testimony that the 14 lb
trigger pull could never have been fired accidentally in a
mêlée had to be refuted. Churchill couldn't be accused of
lying. And the point that the pistol had no safety catch
was two-edged in view of Churchill's clear opinion that it
didn't need one.

In cross-examination, Sir Patrick skilfully elicited the
fact that the unfired bullet in the chamber between the
two that had been fired must have been the result of the
cylinder's being spun round after the first shot; and that
such revolution of the cylinder was rather easily achieved,
and might well have been the result of a struggle. And he
distracted some attention from the damaging significance
of Churchill's testimony that a struggle might equally
have prevented the cylinder from chambering any bullet
by staging a histrionic mock-struggle with his junior,
Walter Frampton. It can't have proved much one way or
the other, but it had the useful effect of being far more
memorable than the quietly damaging evidence uttered by
the gunsmith.

But Sir Patrick's great demonstration and refutation
was saved for the notorious 14 lb pull on the trigger,
which Churchill was sure no woman could effect accidentally. Languidly pointing the empty pistol at the ceiling,
Hastings remarked that it seemed to him to fire very
easily — and he clicked it casually and repeatedly with
each finger of his right hand. In best Noël Coward
manner he implied that it didn't really matter very much,
and the jury would be able to make up their own minds.
But the theatrical spectacle of the gun's hammer clicking
and striking repeatedly in answer to the gentleman's
effortless pull made an overwhelming impression.

It was all around the Temple the next day that Sir
Patrick's fingers needed treatment after he had so abused
them in simulating ease for the difficult and exceedingly
painful pull! His daughter said, later, that his hand nearly
required surgery for the damaged tendons, but her father
felt he was fully justified, as someone had told him that

the gun actually fired quite easily until the mechanism started to rust while in the hands of the police.

The prosecution's dangerous witness from the neighbourhood was also dealt with in part by a theatrical trick. Mrs Hall's claim that she had heard Mrs Barney say 'I'll shoot you', coupled with her evidence that Elvira had shot at Michael once before, was fully as damaging as the experts' testimony. Sir Patrick needed to cast serious doubt on her reliability.

For the worst part of the evidence he had a remarkable stroke of luck. Whereas in the magistrate's court Mrs Hall had unequivocally given Mrs Barney's words as 'I'll shoot you!' now, for no obvious reason, she reduced them to 'I'll shoot'. Sir Patrick made no big issue of this while she was in the witness box, relying on his final speech to draw the jury's attention to the similarity with the words Mrs Barney confessed – 'I'll shoot *myself*'.

But he wanted to shake that story of the early May night when Elvira's less than sylph-like naked loveliness screamed, 'Laugh, baby, laugh for the last time!' before firing at Michael in the mews. Not only did the defence want to cut out the sinister suggestion that she made a habit of shooting at her errant lover, they actually wanted to use the incident to eliminate the alarming implication that the second bullet hole in the bedroom showed that Mrs Barney had taken two shots at Michael to finish him off on 31 May.

Mrs Hall was allowed to give her whole stories with little serious challenge to her memory except the pointer that Mrs Barney pretty certainly called Stephen 'Mickey', and not 'Chicken'. (No doubt Mrs Barney was right about this: the young man signed his letters to her 'Mickech' and called himself 'Mickums' in the course of them.) Sir Patrick also elicited a repetition of Mrs Hall's well-reported observation that Mrs Barney had held the pistol in her left hand when she hung out of her window and fired.

When it came to Mrs Barney's turn to go into the

witness box on her own account, she gave a vastly cleaned up version of the 'Laugh, baby, laugh' incident. She had been wearing a dressing-gown, not exposing herself in the street lights. She had said, 'Smile, baby, smile', because Stephen had been smirking annoyingly about the place all evening. She had not used the words 'for the last time' at all. Her threat had been to shoot herself. And to persuade Stephen she had done so, she fired into the room, not out into the mews — hence the second bullet found in the bedroom wall. And she had not either fallen or simulated falling after the shot; simply betaken herself back to bed.

So there it was. A minor public nuisance for the neighbours, of course. But not at all the dry run for a murder that the prosecution made it seem. But why should the jury believe self-interested Mrs Barney rather than disinterested Mrs Hall? Sir Patrick encouraged them to mistrust Mrs Hall's memory with another brilliant piece of theatricality. Calling for the gun, he had it placed on the ledge in front of Mrs Barney. Then, after a pregnant pause, he suddenly shouted at his client, 'Pick it up!'

Manifestly startled by the unexpected order, Mrs Barney snatched up the weapon. In her *right* hand. Triumphantly, Sir Patrick pointed this out to the jury. Triumphantly he elicited from Mrs Barney that she was right-handed and would never have held the pistol in her left hand.

Since her main story about the events of 30—31 May had never changed, he was entitled to point out her consistency. He was lucky, too, in her answer to the prosecution's two-edged question: whose hand was on the trigger when the gun went off? 'Mine' could look like a confession of responsibility. 'Michael's' could have looked like a self-interested evasion.

'I have no idea,' said Mrs Barney — a claim that rang absolutely true in the circumstances of the drunken dispute.

And so Sir Patrick saved his client. We may doubt

whether he would have done so had the jury taken the gun with them for their deliberations and tried the pull for themselves. We may doubt whether he would have done so had the shrewdly cynical Mr Justice Humphreys heard the case without benefit of jury. His summing-up constantly showed his doubts about the defence case: 'It would be absurd to suppose that if she deliberately fired the revolver at and into the body of the deceased man at the distance of a few inches she desired to do him grievous bodily harm and not kill him.'

'There is really very little dispute that Mrs Barney was the person who fired the shot.'

'You saw (Mrs Hall) and might have formed the opinion that she was a sensible, quiet, composed person.'

The judge, unlike the jury, had Sir Bernard Spilsbury's depositions to the magistrate's court in front of him. But he could only hint that it was obvious Sir Bernard didn't believe in the accident theory. The pathologist had not been given a chance to say so to the jury.

In fact, the only witness who seemed to the judge favourable to Mrs Barney was Dr Durrant. He reported the defendant as making the same statement, in essence, when drunk and hysterical with a dead body in the flat, as she now made in court on trial for her life. (The police were far more cynical about him, and believed that he formulated his story to save his patient from the outset!)

I suspect Mr Justice Humphreys thought a conviction for manslaughter would have been appropriate, Mrs Barney having accidentally caused the death of Michael Stephen while attempting or simulating the felonious act of suicide. As it was, he had to content himself with referring her on to Westminster Police Court for possessing an illegal firearm, and remonstrating with her friend Captain Coler who had given her the gun for rabbit shooting in Devon some years previously.

Mrs Barney walked free and dropped her pretence of good behaviour. She was soon boasting drunkenly in night-clubs of being the notorious defendant in a murder trial.

And in 1936, with another marriage to another adventurer imminent, she was found dead in a hotel room in Paris. Oddly, at the end of it all, the widely despised gigolo William Thomas 'Michael' Scott Stephen emerges as a marginally more admirable figure than his killer. At least he always seems to have been well mannered.

Ruth Ellis

The similarities between Mrs Barney and Mrs Ellis are truly remarkable. I do not know of another pair of notorious murderers whose crimes and situations so closely parallel each other.

Both women were in their late twenties and both feared or were facing the loss of youthful looks by which they had set some store. Both made a prominent feature of carefully shaded and coifed blonde hair. Both were married, but had divorced or separated from their husbands after a very short time. Both were promiscuous by the standards of their times.

Both also had quick and violent tempers and used markedly profane language by the standards of their times and classes. Both were unduly concerned with class. Both were under-educated, or rather, made no particular use of their education. Both acquired some elementary training in the hope of starting some sort of career in show business. Both failed.

Both found their major recreation in raucous drinking parties. Both had noisy confrontations with the police when drunk. Both were heavily dependent on alcohol by the time of their crises, and both were under its influence when wielding the five-chambered handguns that shot their lovers.

Both were charged with murdering their lovers, after quarrels that sprang from their jealous accusations that the young men were sleeping with other women. Both lovers were good-looking men, a few years younger than their respective women. Both lovers were unable to hold down responsible jobs to earn a living, and both sponged off their women. Both were sleeping with more women than the ones who shot them, though neither seems to have been actually guilty of the precise infidelity that triggered their final quarrels.

Both men were charming idlers, whose friends were limited to those who found their charm outweighed their obvious defects. Both were gamblers — Michael Stephen in the obvious sense of playing cards for money; David Blakely in the Micawberish sense that he ventured his patrimony on the inadequately assessed project of making a fortune by designing and building a perfect racing car. Both were habitually drowning their sorrows in drink by the time they died. And, the biggest coincidence of all, both young men were old boys of the same public school, though I don't believe Shrewsbury remarks on the fact in its prospectus.

Although similar in so many ways, Mrs Barney and Mrs Ellis suffered diametrically opposed fates from the moments they were found beside their lovers' bullet-riddled bodies. Mrs Barney abused the police roundly, consistently denied any guilt or responsibility for Stephen's death, and only started to behave sensibly when her parents procured her the best possible legal advice. From then on she sailed through her trial, modestly dressed and with a deferential manner that successfully counteracted the evidence of her outrageous excesses presented in court.

Mrs Ellis behaved with becoming quiet and dignity when she gave herself up to arrest and confessed her guilt immediately. But her legal advice was atrocious, and she was permitted to appear in court looking preposterously tarty, even though counsel kept evidence of her actual practice of prostitution out of the case. Her courtroom manner was one of despairing uninterest, and nobody advised her that this would look to the jury like the cold detachment of an unfeeling murderess.

Every possible item in Mrs Barney's favour was presented to the court, and she was acquitted on the

grounds that her lover had been shot by accident. None of
the main points that might have won Mrs Ellis a
recommendation for mercy appeared in evidence, and she
was convicted after her counsel conceded that she had no
defence to make.

Mr Justice Humphreys, who tried Mrs Barney,
appeared to think that she should at least have been
found guilty of manslaughter. Mr Justice Havers, who
tried Mrs Ellis, later believed that if all the evidence in her
favour had been properly brought out, she should have
been given a reprieve.

Elvira Barney was given a small fine for possession of
an unlicensed weapon. Ruth Ellis was hanged.

Ruth Neilson was born in Rhyl in 1926. She was not
Welsh: her father lived there because it was convenient
for Liverpool, whence he frequently shipped on cruise
liners, playing his cello in their orchestras. He also took
engagements around the country playing in cinemas.
Ruth's mother was a Belgian immigrant, devoutly Catholic, but so poor a household manager that before long,
Ruth's five-years-older sister Muriel was the Dickensian
'little mother' taking care of her home and siblings.

The first ten years of Ruth's life were tranquil. Her
father's frequent absences did not cause domestic instability, and the spindly short-sighted little girl went to the
local school and attended Catholic Sunday school with no
premonition of a garish life in the big cities.

The coming of the talkies combined with the
Depression to wreck Arthur Neilson's career. Regular
engagements dried up. His repeated absence on tour
yielded to his surly presence. In the end he moved with his
family to Basingstoke for menial work in a mental
hospital. His temper was frayed by his impecuniosity and
lack of status, and he took it out on his wife and Muriel
with frequent beatings. The family's insecurity increased
as they moved from house to house to escape the
neighbours' criticism of their domestic life. Ruth's early

adolescence accustomed her to male violence and the uncertain feeling that anywhere she hung her hat might have to be home.

At fourteen she left school. Her educational standard was abysmal: her spelling was erratic, her reading negligible. Her taste in music was confined to syrupy pops and torch songs. She plunged into a succession of undemanding dead-end jobs: waitressing, factory work and the like.

When Arthur Neilson was offered work as a live-in chauffeur in south London, she accompanied him there while the rest of the family stayed in the country. Ruth worked in a munitions factory and in the Oxo factory on the Thames, and discovered a taste for going out dancing in the evenings. This was given official sanction when a bout of rheumatic fever kept her in hospital for eight weeks — an experience she would later dramatize as 'a year on my back eating boiled fish!' — and she was advised that exercise would speed her recovery, and dancing would be an appropriate exercise.

She made some dodgy friends. A crude girl of Ruth's age known as 'Mac' earned Arthur's instant disfavour, but later wheedled herself into residence with him and Ruth; a situation from which she was summarily discharged when Mrs Neilson paid an unexpected visit to find Mac in bed with Arthur!

Ruth began to envisage herself as a professional dancer and actress. She took movement, singing and elocution lessons, mastering the 'aitch' when she remembered to use it; developing a lamentable off-key crooning voice for her favourite melodies; bringing her dancing to the awkward pitch of an undemanding ballroom shuffle. She just wasn't very talented.

When the rest of the family came to London and joined Arthur and Ruth, however, Muriel discovered that her little sister had acquired some back-street sophistication. When the two went waltzing at the Palais together, it was Ruth who spent long periods kissing and fumbling in darkened doorways on the way home. It was Ruth who asked Muriel to cover for her when she spent nights out. It was Ruth who confirmed, truthfully, that she might be the younger sister, but she was ten years older in experience than Muriel. And it was Ruth who carried her sadly limited view of female prospects to the point of finding a man to marry.

He was a Canadian soldier by the name of Clare. Ten years older than Ruth, he was forceful, better paid than his British counterparts, and casually generous with his money. He gave Ruth red roses and carnations and met her family. They approved − until the seventeen-year-old Ruth found she was pregnant.

Clare was all propriety and consideration. He would marry her, of course. Only he needed his commanding officer's permission. Mrs Neilson wrote to the commanding officer, and received the shattering reply that Clare was already married, with a wife and children in Canada.

Despite Clare's assurance that he would divorce his wife and marry Ruth, despite his definite provision of an allowance of £4 a week for her and the expected baby, he was suddenly shipped off back home, leaving Ruth with a bunch of red carnations and a big belly.

Ruth went north to have her baby. She named him Andria Clare ('Andy') and pretended his father was an American who had been killed in action. She came back south and let Muriel and her parents take care of the child, whom she saw regularly while she went out to earn money for his keep.

A small advertisement in the evening paper seeking photographic models, without necessary experience, was Ruth's gateway to the primrose path. She found herself working in a West End 'Camera Club' where she posed nude for leering men whose cameras usually contained no film, as they encouraged her to adopt more and more revealing postures. Ruth didn't mind. The money was fair enough. The work was easy. And she was sufficiently street-smart to know how to handle unwelcome propositions and advances. And thus she came to Maury Conley's attention.

Maury Conley did not visit the Camera Club out of a desperate need to goggle at naked women. He could lay his hands on plenty of them on his own account. Maury came as a talent scout. And he liked the talent he saw in Ruth: the blonde hair and well-formed bust, rendered just a little fuller by Andy's birth; the slim legs and pointy-chinned cat-like face. And, above all, the confident ability to take care of herself if men tried to push their luck. Maury could use Ruth in his business.

The pre-war generation would have called him a White Slaver. Of course, the pre-war myth of men with hypodermic syringes who doped unwilling girls and shipped them off to a life of shame in Buenos Aires was just that — a myth with no foundation in reality. The modern legend of the brutal pimp who picks up a runaway from a big city station, rapes her, and forces her into his stable on the streets is likewise an extreme exaggeration of the more normal pattern of seducing lonely girls, and then 'turning them out'.

But the vital recruiting agent for the prostitution industry is the plausible man who can persuade girls from respectable families that accepting presents from casual lovers is an absolutely normal thing. And then lead them imperceptibly across the line where the presents are *expected*, and increasingly take the form of gifts of money (perhaps as a generous free-will 'contribution' to the expenses of nursing an imaginary aged parent or orphaned little sister). And at last the fee is negotiated before any love-making takes place.

And *still* a foolish girl may not grasp that she has joined the sisterhood who sell their sexual favours! Stephen Ward managed this trick brilliantly with Christine Keeler and Mandy Rice-Davies, telling them that prostitution was 'an attitude of mind', so that, with what Miss Keeler now recognizes as fatuous naïvety, they simply regarded themselves as 'good-time girls' who accepted presents from the friends to whom he introduced them. Even though they learned to solicit the gifts for themselves with phoney stories of their family responsibilities! Even though they knew that Ward entertained, liked and used street prostitutes whose occupation was open and undisguised and honest!

Maury Conley didn't have Ward's charm and class and circle of upper-crust friends to lure girls into his world. He was ugly as a toad, and most of his friends, from the pushy worlds of gangland crime and get-rich-quick downmarket business, were equally unprepossessing. But Maury could offer girls money. Lots of it.

He made his original pile by gambling and a fraudulent bankruptcy, for which he spent a couple of years in jail. He revisited prison when he was found to be fixing one-armed bandits beyond limits the law could tolerate. But in the post-war years he discovered that a combination of property development and night-club interests offered access to the golden millions of poncing. After Ruth's death he would be sent down for this crime, accused by the Sunday papers of being London's biggest vice lord. No doubt this was the usual exaggeration, but as police had watched eighty-two men (and two women) go into one of Maury's properties in the course of three days, somebody was making an awful lot of money (at the risk of some soreness and fatigue), and Maury was skimming a fat cat's share of it.

He protected himself from the law by registering much of his house property in his wife's name; by creating a tangle of companies to disguise his own interests; and by letting the 'hostesses' in his night-clubs work quasi-independently.

The deal Maury offered Ruth was pretty clear-cut. He paid her £5 a week to work as a hostess at the Court Club. This was emphatically not a disguised brothel. Her job was to sit with customers and persuade them to buy her (and themselves) drinks for as long as possible. Her orders were champagne or gin, for which the mark was charged. Her glasses contained cider or water. She got a commission on the amount spent at her table. Maury provided evening dresses for her to wear.

In addition, she got a flat where she could entertain customers after the club had closed. While the rent might reflect the fact that the bedroom should prove a nice little earner, there was no immediate pressure on her to take 'friends' back there. Except for Maury's. If he wanted her to put out for his friends and business associates, she should do so. If he wanted her himself at any time, she had to be available to him. If she let him down in this respect, he would use his own key to get into her flat and slash her clothes. Maury Conley didn't beat up his stable but he kept them in line.

Ruth took to this life like a duck to water. She enjoyed the company of other hostesses and learned from them to peroxide her hair, which retained the brassily unnatural tint she took to be Gentlemen's Preference until the end of her life. She loved the clothes and spent the money as fast as it came. She accepted sexual relations with Maury and his oafish friends as something that went with the job. And while she still vaguely hoped to break into show business, she was less self-deceiving than many of her colleagues. Ruth had little doubt that she was now a prostitute. It was class (she believed), not morals, that raised her above the prostitutes lining Piccadilly and Shaftesbury Avenue.

I once overheard a snatch of conversation between two prostitutes in the entrance to a popular Barbados bar-cum-brothel, which ran, 'I still hopin' that Mr Right come by.'

'Up *them* stairs, darlin'? *Never!*'

Ruth might have been realistic enough to share that healthy cynicism. But drunken dentist George Ellis accidentally made an appeal to her quite well-developed sense of moral responsibility. She accepted a date to go on from the Court Club when it closed, and meet him at the Hollywood, another of Maury Conley's clubs, which remained open till 3 a.m. and where he liked his girls to keep business going and champagne flowing.

Alas, Ruth met a nice American and stood Mr Ellis up. George came out of the Hollywood alone to get into a fight with some petty criminals who jeered at him and slashed his face with a razor.

Ruth felt guiltily that she was responsible for an innocent customer getting a scar on his face. And so she started drinking with Mr Ellis and accepting dinner dates with him. She heard his tale of sorrow since his wife had left him. She put time into cheering him up, and went on a long three-month holiday to Cornwall with him: a holiday on which Mr Ellis and the skipper of a fishing boat they rented got so drunk on a cruise from Newquay that they were incapable of doing anything useful when one engine expired and their fuel ran out. Ruth took effective command as they jilled around in fairly heavy seas until a French crabber gave them fuel, and they limped into St Ives.

Despite this warning of Ellis's limitations, Ruth consulted with her fellow hostesses and accepted their view that a dentist was a good catch and she would do well to marry George Ellis. When the two were surprised together by his mother (and Mr Ellis revealed the further problem that at forty he still could not handle her), Ruth consented to being passed off as his registry office wife. After extracting a promise that Mr Ellis would go into a hospital to dry out, she made a reality of the fiction. She was happy that her husband knew all about her disreputable career in Maury's clubs and didn't object. She was always a snob, and felt that being the wife of a fully qualified dental practitioner made her someone far superior to little Miss Neilson of Brixton. She looked forward to a secure life on the south coast when Ellis accepted a junior partnership in Hampshire.

The idyll was smashed quite quickly. An unexpected aspect of Ruth's personality was uncontrollable rage provoked by paranoid suspicious jealousy once she was

apparently safe in a stable or marital relationship. She
suspected Mr Ellis of affairs with his patients, his dental
nurse and almost anyone he might come across. She made
violent scenes.

Mr Ellis went back to the bottle, and enjoyed the
dedicated alcoholic's furtive disappearances to get drunk.
Ruth, ludicrously, ascribed them to sexual liaisons.

They separated periodically. Mr Ellis lost his Hampshire job, lost another in Cornwall, and went back to dry
out again. Their daughter Georgina was born while he
was actually in a mental institution being treated for
alcoholism. The treatment was not helped by Ruth's
raving appearances accusing him of infidelities with
fellow patients, a lady doctor and his nurses. She was
given tranquillizers, but they did little for her. And Ellis's
tendency to call her 'the bitch from Brixton' in their rows,
revealing his true conviction that he had married beneath
him, did nothing for her shaky sense of social status.

The marriage came to an end, and Ruth went back to
Maury Conley. He was happy to see her. It was widely
known among their acquaintances that he fancied her
strongly. He also recognized her ambition, strength of
mind and reliability. He soon had something better to
offer her than hostessing at the Court Club (now named
Carroll's). She could become manageress herself of one
of his clubs: the Little Club in Knightsbridge.

This, as its name suggested, was too small to have
Conley's usual complement of a middle-aged manageress
directing fifteen or twenty hostesses around the place,
and out on 'calls'. Ruth would have just three girls
working under her, and might be expected to put out for
punters herself from time to time. She would also have a
rent-free flat above the premises. Two other flats there
were occupied by working prostitutes but they did not use
the Little Club. As was usual with Conley's ventures, the
club was emphatically not a brothel; not even a disguised
brothel. The hostesses' job was to encourage members to
drink up. They might take them home after the place

closed, but this was technically their own private arrangement.

Ruth was in seventh heaven. She had £15 a week salary and £10 a week entertainment allowance. Andy and Georgina could live with her in the flat. She could drop the crude trappings of professional prostitution which accompanied her life as a hostess at Carroll's: pornographic pictures to amuse clients, and advertisements for kinky rubberwear firms which paid an introduction fee if she sent men to them. Her sexual entertaining was now a discreet supplement to her wages, undertaken at her own volition in the afternoons when the club did not need her attention and Georgina and Andy were not around.

The club itself, with flocked wallpaper and little gilt electric candelabra-ed mirrors seemed to her the acme of sophistication. It was in the posh West End, easily accessible from Mayfair and Belgravia. She was the boss: it was *her* club. Ruth felt she had made it.

The serpent entered Eden almost as soon as Ruth acquired it. Later she would say that David Blakely was the first person to whom she served a drink in the Little Club, but truthfulness was never one of her virtues, and she always embellished stories for dramatic effect.

Certainly the young racing driver lounged into the place soon after Ruth took it over in October 1953. She had encountered him a few weeks previously at Carroll's, and disliked his arrogant manner, saying she hoped she never saw that little shit again.

But Ruth was determined to be a good manageress. She could not set herself up against members as she might when she was just a hostess. She served David politely, and kept her temper beautifully controlled when he sneered at the cheap tawdriness of her watering hole and its tarty hostesses. Good old Ruth could always take a joke would be the view of her club's patrons. They never dreamed of the potential passions burning under her calm exterior.

David was three years younger than Ruth. He visited the Little Club as one of a group of motor racing drivers who hung around the champion Mike Hawthorn, and wanted a place for continued imbibing after the Steering Wheel Club had closed. Most, like David, were well-heeled middle-class amateurs, who hoped they might one day make a full-time living by driving, while recognizing that such success was only open to the few. David was a promising young driver in the 1500cc class, which was dominated by his friend Cliff Davis.

When he first joined the Little Club, David was supposed to be training in hotel management at the nearby Hyde Park Hotel. The work was not much to his taste, except insofar as his lustrous-eyed, long-lashed, dark good looks gave him frequent opportunities to be seduced and pampered by wealthy older women on their vacations. David was unashamedly willing to sponge off women. Moreover, as a young man whose nanny still looked after him (now employed by his stepfather to be housekeeper for David and his brother in their Mayfair flat), he would always feel more at ease playing the spoilt little boy with older women than trying to be a commanding male presence with women of his own age.

Before long he spent so much time skiving off to the Steering Wheel and the Little Club that the Hyde Park Hotel fired him. He took a job with a piston making firm near Penn in Buckinghamshire, where his indulgent stepfather Humphrey Cook had moved. David retained the flat in Mayfair and another flat in Penn. He continued to socialize in London, in addition to enjoying a liaison with an older married woman in Penn.

In 1952 his natural father died — David's parents had divorced in 1940 — and David inherited £7,000. Immediately, he abandoned gainful employment and hurled his money into an attempt to develop a perfect racing car, which he called the Emperor. His engineering assistant on the project was another ex-public schoolboy, Anthony Findlater.

'Ant', four years older than David, was equally obsessed with racing cars and a first-rate mechanic. Rashly, he accepted David's offer of £10 a week to work full-time on the Emperor, although he was married and soon to be the father of a little girl. David's undercapitalized venture was shaky financial support for a family, and Ant's journalist wife Carole was really the family breadwinner.

As if his independent life were not precarious enough, David enjoyed a brief affair with dark, intelligent, commanding and vivacious Carole. It came to an end, apparently, because Carole jibbed at his suggestion that they should elope together. It is not clear whether she confessed to Ant, bringing down David's immature wrath for jeopardizing his relations with the vital mechanic – designer of the Emperor. But in any case, the affair came to an end and the tie between the two car-mad men was stronger than that between either of them and any woman. The Findlaters remained David's close friends.

By the time Ruth met him, David's sexual partners included a tall American model, a fluffy little cinema usherette and the married woman in Penn – all older than himself. He was also engaged to a nice plump girl of his own age, Linda Dawson. As the daughter of a prosperous Huddersfield manufacturer, she was an entirely appropriate fiancée. David, typically, seems to have been more impressed by her father's possession of a private petrol pump on his grounds than anything else!

It was Ruth who initiated the affair with the young almost-ne'er-do-well. Though she did not use the club for business sex – her afternoon punters were largely businessmen from the call-girl list she built up in her Carroll's Club days – she was not averse to taking a nice-looking young Little Club member to bed with her if the prospect appealed. Cliff Davis has recalled how the boozy, boastful, bawdy companionship of the racing drivers could lead to a night in Ruth's bed. They all teased each other coarsely, and he often said lightly to the cheerfully foul-mouthed manageress, 'I think you'd make a real good fuck, Ruth'. One night she responded, 'Come on then, let's go', and she proved him right.

There was no charge for such casual encounters, and no promise of any repetition. They simply enhanced the Little Club's reputation as a good place of essentially masculine companionship.

We don't know whether David enjoyed Ruth's bedroom techniques as much as Cliff Davis, who rated her the very best bedfellow of his life. She seems to have given Cliff a version of the prostitute's classic 'round the world': a sort of all-over oral sex.

Other lovers who passed nights with Ruth were less complimentary, one saying she was 'too mechanical'. But there was a deep lack of respect between the club hostesses and their punters. One punter once told Ruth that 'screwing the girls was like sticking it into a bowl of rice'. The girls equally despised the men who, they felt, only used their services because they were such inadequate lovers that they could not satisfy their wives and girlfriends.

There is copious evidence of David's sexual inadequacy. He looked greedily for his own pleasure, apparently unaware that women, too, might have physical needs for something more than his penetration and self-satisfaction. He was unable to sustain his potency over long periods with the same lover. He needed changes of partners to keep up his sexual interest and amyl nitrite to delay his emissions.

But Ruth may not have expected any profound physical pleasure for herself from sleeping with men. Always lurking hazily in the background are rumours that her real joys were lesbian. There is no real evidence, but we should bear in mind that the intimation is there doing its bit to undermine the occasional suggestion that Ruth and David were bonded by pure sexual obsession.

Of course, no outsider can ever tell what really happens between two people in bed. Couples do or don't work together magically or adequately or disastrously on a quite unpredictable basis, with a total disregard for the supposed skills of one or inhibitions of the other. Still, it seems that extra-cubicular attractions were the real cement between Ruth and David.

Cliff Davis describes David's attractions well enough: 'He was a charming, good-looking, well-educated, supercilious shit.' It should be noted that Cliff liked him very much. His charm and good-fellowship comfortably outweighed the supercilious shitfulness.

We know Ruth was well aware of the drawbacks too. We must assume that the charm and Old Salopian manners, added to the undoubted good looks, persuaded her to invite him into her bed. And thereafter persuaded her that he made a very desirable escort to squire her around. We know from her own account that his initial coolness was also part of the attraction. David represented a challenge, and Ruth deliberately exercised her skills to manipulate him into her bed. She succeeded within a fortnight.

And what did David get from this liaison? Another older woman, obviously. Someone else to scold him and forgive him and pet him. But also a blatantly obvious sexpot: a woman whose stiffly permed, unnaturally coloured hair declared her wish to be noticed by men; a woman whose uneducated accent and profane vocabulary declared her to be one of the whores and not one of the Madonnas; a woman whose very appearance at his side signalled to the world that David must be screwing her. Why else would he be seen with her?

And, indeed, with childish ill manners, he boasted about her to his friends as 'the best fuck in London'. Not that bed-hopping, popper-taking, inadequate David would have known, let alone realized, that different men and women find different 'best' companions in bed.

No harm need have been done if the two had simply enjoyed a liaison and broken up. Both had plenty of experience of such things. But there was a third party to their association: a necessary third side to the triangle which ensured that jealousy would motivate all three.

Desmond Cussen was the oldest of them. At thirty-three, he was also the most stable, respectable and financially secure. He was a director of his family's chain of tobacconists and had a comfortable flat in Goodwood Court, to the north of Broadcasting House. A motor racing enthusiast, he was a fringe hanger-on of the Mike Hawthorn crowd at the Steering Wheel and not a promising driver like David.

What he did share with David was the quality of being a bit of an outsider among the racing men. In appearance, the stocky, heavy-jowled Cussen, with a pencil moustache and receding brilliantined hair, was more like one of Ruth's gooseberry-eyed business punters than the young, sporty, boozy circle of drivers. He didn't go down awfully well with them. He rather sat on the edge of things and only came into the conversation when sexual boasting became the topic. His idea of wit was to put on a funny voice and say, 'Yais!'

But then, David Blakely, too, failed as the life and soul of the party. He enjoyed schoolboy horseplay, squirting soda syphons at other people or putting ice-cubes down their necks. When this was resented, he became a whingeing coward, hiding behind furniture or women's skirts to escape the fisticuffs he provoked. Some of the drivers enjoyed his boyish high spirits. Others despised him. And David and Desmond disliked each other. Each could see the social failings in the other that are fully confirmed from other sources.

They were sufficiently well-mannered to try and conceal this hostility. David even invited Desmond to accompany him as co-driver on one occasion. But there was hostility lying underneath, waiting for something or someone to light the fuse.

The fuse was Ruth, for Desmond fell helplessly in love with her. She may not even have noticed to start with. He was a shy man; rather gauche with women and, like many mother-dominated men, diffidently inhibited about making passes at those he fancied.

But he loved Ruth's energy; her style; her wit; her self-possession in the company of swaggering clubmen; her raunchy and profane capacity to keep up with their bawdry. He loved, and he watched, as more and more of her attention became drawn to the good-looking supercilious little shit.

Ruth and David were brought unexpectedly close in December 1953. Almost as soon as they started sleeping together, Ruth became pregnant. She was always careless (or vestigially Catholic) about contraception, and it was not the first time she had sought an abortion. But David's reaction was surprising. He expressed deep regret at the loss of the child and said he would have liked to marry Ruth. Of course, this was quite out of the question. Her divorce from George Ellis had not been completed. David was still engaged to Linda Dawson, and nobody who knew him could imagine that he would ever have the strength of mind to break off a socially acceptable engagement – or even relinquish the last hope of inheriting a private petrol pump! But Ruth was naturally touched by this display of concern. She spent more and more time with him in the Little Club bar, and David manifestly felt more and more bound to her.

At this stage, he was the one who inclined to jealousy. The manageress's habitual flirtation and raunchy chat with other customers seemed to detract from what he thought was his and he made no secret of his wish that she would let other people go and manifest herself as his woman. (Not that he was giving up his liaisons with the usherette and the married woman in Penn, of course!)

The miasma of jealous possessiveness was fuelled by the Findlaters. Carole and Ant were not impressed by David's new conquest. A brassy blonde tart with a south London accent was not acceptable in their middle-class circle. Ruth's first appearance on David's arm at a motor race meeting was a social disaster as she wore an inappropriate black sheath dress. Though she learned quickly to assume plain tweeds, heavy coats and sensible shoes for these occasions, and brought generous picnic hampers, she still appeared *malapropos* to the Findlaters.

Carole felt affronted that her ex-lover should replace her with something so tawdry. Ruth thought Carole was stuck up. Carole loftily excused Ruth's bad manners as inevitable, given her background. Ruth gave Carole a £30 christening robe for baby Francisca — something the Findlaters' rather straitened circumstances could never have risen to. Carole put it away unused and later handed it over to collectors for a white elephant stall.

David was far too weak to sort out this contretemps between those who loved him. Like a certain nineteenth-century politician, he was like a cushion who would take the imprint of the last person to sit on him. And so Ruth and the Findlaters each accepted the assurance that they held the real key to David's wavering affections.

A succession of events in 1954 ignited the slow fuse. Linda Dawson learned about one or more of David's infidelities and broke off the engagement. David, now definitely free to marry Ruth, again offered to do so. Ruth, delighted, abandoned all claim to maintenance and rushed through her divorce from George Ellis. Georgina went into her father's custody, but Ruth still had Andy to feed, clothe and educate. Desmond Cussen stepped in. The only one of Ruth's close circle who could afford it, he offered to pay Andy's school fees, thus giving himself a central and permanent position in her life. In the summer, when David was thrilled to be included on the Bristol driving team at Le Mans, Ruth slept with Desmond while her main man was away.

On David's return, passions increased in a soured situation. David was despondent because the Emperor was giving trouble. He had hoped to race it at Le Mans. But its connecting rod broke in a practice run, and he was left contemplating the increasing expense of spare parts and the diminishing prospect of making his fortune by having a superb rally-proven, custom-built vehicle to put on the market. Ant had to go back to work as a car salesman and could only work on the Emperor in the evenings. David was running out of money and started sponging off Ruth.

She let him run up an enormous tab for drinks and cigarettes at the Little Club. She bore with his increasingly morose temper and drunkenness. They drifted into a situation of mutual recriminations and screaming rows. David knew he was wasting time in an alcoholic stupor at the Little Club and he blamed Ruth. She was jinxing his car. She was leading him into unprofitable dissipation when he should be helping Ant. She must give up the Little Club and its entourage of flirtatious men who came between them.

In the event, Ruth did not have to make this sacrifice voluntarily. Another jealous figure intervened. Maury Conley. Maury didn't like having the manageress he fancied commandeered by a drunken and handsome young member with a superior class manner. He hadn't given Ruth a free flat for David to spend night after night in it. He started charging her rent.

But even this warning didn't halt Ruth's decline into impassioned self-destruction. The situation between the two had reversed. It was now Ruth who was possessively jealous of David. He had dangled before her the hope of matrimony – and with it a station in society even more secure than that of West End club manageress. Yet he was still ashamed to introduce her to his mother.

He spent most of his time and much of her money drinking – often for hard cash at neighbouring clubs – so that she was all too often out keeping an eye on him instead of minding Maury Conley's business. Furthermore, he still slept with the usherette and the lady from Penn. When he was in the Little Club he created drunken rows and messed up the place with soda syphon battles. Ruth had to clean up after him and watch regular customers abandon the place where they could no longer anticipate a peaceful evening's jollity. Yet he blamed her for destroying his prospects. And when the club's takings fell from £200 – £300 a week to £70 – £80, Maury Conley stepped in again. He fired Ruth.

Now she was in real trouble and she started to behave really badly. She needed somewhere for her and Andy to live. Desmond Cussen came forward, and she accepted his offer to live with him at Goodwood Court. But she still slept with David behind Desmond's back. Sometimes she made the excuse that she had to go away and visit Georgina, while she actually spent nights with David in a hotel in Kensington. Sometimes, when Desmond was away, she brought David into his bed. And she lied to Desmond unconscionably about all this.

Ruth strikes many people as a fundamentally decent, if limited, woman, whose chosen occupation and impassioned social climbing led her into situations where she behaved badly. And the worse she behaved, the more her internalized fury with herself was taken out on other people. David became the focus of her jealous rage. Whatever she was doing wrong, it was because she loved him and he was running her around. Their relationship grew stormier and stormier.

At last, even Desmond could take no more. He came home once too often to find Ruth missing – a note pinned to the door, Andy left on his own, and his cohabitee off on a jaunt with her irresponsible boyfriend. Desmond politely put Ruth out of his flat and placed her in a bedsitting room in Egerton Gardens.

Ruth behaved worse. Her rows with David had degenerated to fisticuffs. David, maddened by her tongue, would beat her. Ruth defended herself with fingernails and possibly knives. Another girlfriend found David's back scored with wounds which he said Ruth had inflicted.

Desmond repeatedly helped Ruth cover heavy bruises with makeup. And he continued to support Ruth's unrealistic ambitions. She went to a modelling school, blindly unaware that the slender ankles on which she prided herself made her legs look spindly and that there was no future for her in front of the cameras. She took a few French lessons, thinking this would help her to become a model. But all the time she knew she had lost the best job she had ever had, and one for which she was superbly suited. And she had lost it because that bastard David had promised to marry her, and now he was chickening out and sleeping with other women.

Desmond wanted to marry her. He said so over and over again. But Ruth had learned something from the past. She had been through one marriage with a heavy-set older man whom she didn't love. The social status it offered hadn't made it satisfactory. And she wasn't prepared to repeat the experience. Instead she used Desmond cruelly. Her life as an upmarket prostitute had left her with a moral code that suggested it was perfectly all right to milk men for all you could get, provided you honestly put out sexually in return. Their emotions could be assumed to be quite detached from their lust. And so, in the teeth of Desmond's constant declarations of love, she used him as a chauffeur to drive her on wild journeys to Penn and parts of London, spying on David.

She caught David drinking with his married lover at the Crown in Penn and made an outrageous public scene. She went to his parents' home in Penn, and to the young man's terror made a scene outside. Once Desmond tried to get David to fight him, but David was always a physical coward.

In the end, David wanted out. He didn't know how to give up any of his women. But he wanted someone to rescue him from Ruth – the one of them who made violent difficulties about the others.

At Easter 1955, David's wimpish dependence on other people to sort out his emotional crises came to a head, as he turned to the Findlaters for help. It was not only Ruth who was reducing him to despair. His great ambition was collapsing. It was increasingly clear that the world would never enjoy the sight of leading racing drivers steering 'David Blakely's Emperor' to success on the world's circuits. He just couldn't afford the parts and the amount of Ant's time it needed for the pilot model to be brought to perfection. He wanted a weekend to get away from it all.

The Findlaters offered him sanctuary. They invited him to spend Easter weekend with them at their flat in Tanza Road, Hampstead. They promised to shield him from Ruth. They would not admit her if she came to the door. They would field her telephone calls and tell her he was not there.

Ruth brooded with Desmond. David skulked with Ant and Carole. That was the miserable, alcoholic, depressed combination that unexpectedly exploded in a hail of bullets on Easter Sunday.

Ruth was sure David was with the Findlaters, and disbelieved their denials over the telephone. As she sat drinking with Desmond and calling the flat over and over again, she became furious that Ant and Carole started putting the phone back on the hook as soon as they recognized her voice. She got the long-suffering Desmond to drive her out to Tanza Road to spy on the house. The Findlaters had recently employed an au pair girl, and hearing giggling from inside the flat, Ruth jumped to the conclusion that she had been hired simply to provide a distraction for David: a sexual lure to ensure that he finally dropped the brassy tart he had met in Conley's clubs.

She was quite wrong. But jealousy made her totally irrational. Nor was her continuous consumption of pastis, tranquillizers and cigarettes, with virtually no sleep over the weekend, conducive to rational thinking. She spied on a party the Findlaters gave on Saturday night and saw David come out to see the au pair girl to the car. This completely convinced her that there was a liaison between the two.

She went back to the house in the small hours of the

morning and telephoned and beat on the door to bring
Anthony Findlater out to stop her from rousing the
neighbourhood. She made yet more noise, using a rubber
torch to push in the windows of David's car.

Ant called a policeman, who tried, unsuccessfully, to
persuade the drunken termagant to go home. Since she
insisted that she had partly paid for the car, and it was her
property to do what she liked with, he could not charge
her for wilful damage. The policeman left, not wanting to
be involved in a private domestic dispute. He had to be
called back again as Ruth continued to disturb the night,
and at last she was persuaded to let Desmond drive her
home.

Easter Sunday was a dreary, drunken, deadly day.
Ruth sat around in Desmond's flat, pitying herself and
raging at David. David didn't call. Ant put down the
phone on her terse message, 'I hope you've enjoyed your
holiday, because you've ruined mine.'

According to Andy, who must have had a gloomy day
with two sullen adults sunk in despondency, Uncle
Desmond fetched a pistol, oiled it, and showed Ruth how
to use it. Desmond has denied this.

In the evening, he drove her back to Egerton Gardens
at half-past seven to put Andy to bed. By his own account
this was the last time he saw her that day. Other people
have speculated that he, as usual, was the chauffeur who
took her out to Hampstead. It really isn't as important as
they suggest.

Ruth was back in Hampstead that night, and seeing
David's car missing from outside the Findlaters' flat,
walked down to the Magdala Tavern on the corner with
Parliament Hill Road and found, as she expected, the
car outside. David had gone out with his friend Clive
Gunnell to fetch some more beer and cigarettes. Now
the two were enjoying a drink inside the pub before
returning.

Ruth was wearing her spectacles. Jealousy outweighed
vanity at this point in her life. She peered through the

distorting moulded glass of the pub windows to confirm that her quarry was inside.

When the two men came out, she called, 'David'. Her lover pretended not to hear. So she screamed it at him again, and when he looked round he saw that she had a pistol pointing at him.

David rushed to Clive for cover. Ruth chased him around the car, screaming 'Get out of the way, Clive!' before she fired, felling David as he ran down the hill.

She fired two more shots, then went over to the injured man and lifted the pistol to her own temple. But in the end she couldn't bring herself to die on the spot. She turned the gun on David, and at pointblank range discharged the lethal bullet into his back that punctured his lung. Then, despairingly, she shot her last bullet into the pavement, from which it ricocheted and slammed into the thumb of Mrs Gladys Yule, walking with her husband for a peaceful drink at the Magdala.

An off-duty policeman who was in the pub came out when he was told that the series of reports was not a car backfiring, but a woman shooting a man. Ruth said tremulously to him, 'Will you call the police and an ambulance?'

'I am the police,' said PC Anthony Thompson, who had quietly and bravely approached this apparently armed and dangerous woman. And he took the gun from her and made it safe in his pocket.

The short remainder of Ruth's life has evoked considerable admiration in hindsight. The Catholic girl turned prostitute lived by the simple morality she had learned. She had done wrong. She knew it. She accepted the certainty of punishment – even the punishment of the gallows. Her full statement to the police almost opened with the words, 'I am guilty'. When lawyers were engaged for her, they had difficulty in persuading her that a plea of not guilty was morally in order. Only an appeal to think of Andy persuaded her.

But she was desperately unlucky in her leading counsel.

Mr Melford Stevenson was to become a famous conservative hanging judge. He made a perfunctory and disastrous defence for Ruth Ellis, which wound up by being no defence at all.

There was a problem in law. Ruth had shot David deliberately, in full view of the public, with a full awareness of what she was doing and a complete understanding that it was both illegal and wrong. And in saying so, she abolished any insanity plea.

Mr Stevenson decided to set up a novel defence: that jealousy in a woman so over-powered her reason that she was incapable of forming a premeditated intention to murder; that women, unlike men, are so made that jealousy constitutes overwhelming provocation and therefore Ruth's crime was manslaughter. A comprehensive search of British and American cases failed to find a single precedent for this proposition, which ran dangerously close to the continental concept of *crime passionel* – something the British courts resolutely deny.

But Melford Stevenson ploughed on with it. The outdated psychology on which he relied was evident in his opening speech when he said, 'The effect of jealousy upon that feminine mind can so work as to unseat the reason and can operate to a degree in which a male mind is quite incapable of operating.' His attitude to women was further illustrated when he misquoted Byron. The poet, commenting fairly on a society in which the only career open to women was marriage, said:

> 'Man's love is of his life a thing apart –
> 'Tis woman's whole existence.'

In Mr Stevenson's mouth, this became, 'A man's love is a man's boast, a woman's is her whole existence.' How well the learned jurist would have fitted in with the raunchy racing drivers and their crude talk about 'the best fuck in London'! Ruth was employed, loved and ultimately defended by men who couldn't see her as much more than the ego-trip she offered to any male who wanted to brag that he'd bedded a blonde.

In concentrating on this view of Ruth, Mr Stevenson totally ignored points that might have won Ruth a recommendation to mercy. He did not make the point that she had found herself pregnant by David again in the spring of 1955. That David had hit her hard in the abdomen at that time, possibly causing a miscarriage. That the manageress of the Steering Wheel Club could have testified to numerous occasions when David publicly hit Ruth in the weeks before the murder — once beating her so fiercely that he was ejected from the club. That a doctor who had been treating Ruth ever since George Ellis's hospitalization could testify that she had long been prone to unbalanced jealous rage — as an aspect of her own individual psychological illness, not some imaginary female condition! That she had been on medication for this trouble ever since. And that her medication, coupled with alcohol and sleeplessness in the forty-eight hours leading up to the murder would have seriously reduced her capacity to think clearly.

All these points, Mr Justice Havers later remarked, would certainly have swayed him and the jury had they been heard in court. A recommendation to mercy and a reprieve would surely have followed. But they were not heard. A brief bench conference produced the judge's ruling that Mr Melford Stevenson's peculiar ideas about female psychology could not possibly constitute a legal basis for a plea of manslaughter. Whereupon Mr Melford Stevenson sat down and declined to offer a final speech for the defence. There was, he remarked, no defence now.

Mr Christmas Humphreys, prosecuting, equitably refrained from making a closing speech either. Indeed, his private remark to the judge that Blakely's undoubted abuse of Ruth's devotion might be a matter for consideration elsewhere may have represented a personal belief that Ruth should receive the Home Secretary's reprieve, despite her unquestionable legal guilt.

But it didn't happen. Ruth Ellis was hanged, to the horror of continental Europe, which recognized a clear case of *crime passionel*. And today, nearly forty years later, the case still weighs on our collective conscience.

Jean Harris

'Miss Buss and Miss Beale
Cupid's darts do not feel'

And quite right too. We certainly don't expect an elegant,
intelligent private school headmistress with a *summa cum
laude* degree from Smith College to burst into her man's
bedroom and fill him full of lead, like Frankie 'gettin'
back' at Johnny for 'doin' her wrong'. Nor do we expect
an eminent millionaire medical practitioner, approaching
his seventieth birthday, to have his bedroom and bathroom littered with knickers and nighties left behind by
several of his thirty or more girlfriends – including the
elegant headmistress.

The love of Jean Harris and Herman Tarnower was
certainly not conducted by following the etiquette-book
principles that governed their social lives. He was as crude
and blatant a heel as one might come across. She, the self-
assured headmistress known to her pupils as 'Integrity
Jean', enjoyed Hy's *money* as shamelessly as the most
blatant prostitute.

They met at a dinner party in 1966. They gravitated to
one another as good conversationalists with excellent all-
round taste (except in music – Hy was tone-deaf and
Jean loved golden oldies). And they rather needed one
another. Hy had just lost his favourite lover. A pretty
nurse receptionist, some thirty-odd years younger than
he, had gone and married and removed herself from his
bed. He was ripe to fall for a new charmer. And Jean,
nearer his own age and better educated than lost Lynne,
seemed a perfect healing substitute.

Jean's needs were more complex and grew stronger as time passed. Like Dr Tarnower, she needed a boost for her ego for within four years of meeting him, she had succumbed to the Peter principle and accepted promotion beyond her level of competence.

Jean Harris was — is, for she still finds opportunities to practise her skills in prison — a talented teacher. Married, mother of two children, bored as a housewife, divorced in 1960 and not really strapped for cash, Jean could afford to teach in the private sector. In America, unlike Britain, this entails a lower salary than that offered in the maintained school system. Indeed, even college teachers in the smaller American institutions are less well paid than classroom secondary teachers in big municipal high schools. But private school teachers enjoy greater freedom to exercise pedagogic skills, smaller classes, less interference from school boards. They are less vulnerable to the chilly blasts of criticism from under-informed, over-confident politicians. Jean thrived in a system where she was encouraged to do her best for her pupils, instilling high academic standards and slightly old-fashioned lady-like character building. She did well, so that by her late forties she found herself headmistress of the classy Madeira School for Girls in Virginia (as well as lady friend — sometime fiancée — of classy Dr Herman Tarnower in New York).

But at this point Jean's life began to suffer more professional frustration than satisfaction. A head teacher is not first and foremost a teacher. The ability to inspire and instruct a roomful of pubescent and adolescent children comes second to the need for administrative ability, the right use of authority and, above all, political skills. Political skills in dealing with difficult parents and worldly governors. Political skills of self-presentation as Sovereign and Fount of All Grace in the microcosm of the school.

Frankly, Jean was out of her depth. Shifted from the classroom she handled so well, Mrs Harris slipped to

'Integrity Jean' as the school's figurehead of authority. She found no joy whatsoever in dealing with parents' stupid demands that pot be ruthlessly suppressed, without *their* daughters ever suffering suspension, or that riding be given its proper prominence in the lives of young aristocrats at the expense of, say, maths. She was not an expert at handling governors who wanted to know why the school didn't continue to reflect the sort of drilled manners and antiquated deportment that had proved so valuable in their own younger days. She did not enjoy the drab task of balancing educational needs against budgetary possibilities. Perhaps the only group that wholeheartedly admired Jean's leadership were her teaching staff. The best of them at least shared her aims and ideals for the school.

Mrs Harris struggled on with her task of raising standards and updating the institutional ethos without abandoning anything she thought essential to good schooling. But she lacked the rhinoceros hide that a politician needs. A leadership role inevitably attracts criticism, and this needled her. She was probably unhappier than she had ever been in a generally successful career of high achievement.

And she would hardly have been human if she had not resented the wealth of those who criticized her. An American private school headmistress is a long way from the breadline. But she is a pauper compared with the parents and governors. And in America money talks. A man whose business skills enable him to have five bathrooms in his house and drive three Cadillacs really believes this makes him more able and *intelligent* than the threadbare genius who can make Mr Moneybags' unpromising son understand and appreciate Homer. Jean was despised by people who, by her standards, were barely fit to converse with her. And their contempt had the backing of a materialist society.

So she revelled in her relationship with a rich doctor who fully appreciated her as a well-preserved woman with a fine mind. She was flattered that the founder of the prestigious Scarsdale Practice accepted her as an equal and someone whose company he sought out keenly. She put Miss Buss and Miss Beale right out of her headmistress's mind and delightedly pursued an acquaintance which started with presents of red roses, then an engagement ring the following year. If Miss Harris had ever become Mrs Tarnower, she could have wished all the fat cats of Virginia and their bratty, catty daughters to hell and Cerberus!

Money talked for Hy, too. It talked as loudly as it could for the crudest one-armed bandit dealer or soft-core porn promoter. Hy came from a poor, ambitious Jewish background. He used his education, industry and ability to buy himself class, and to the extent that class in America rests on money, he made damn sure he possessed it!

In naming his group the 'Scarsdale Practice', Dr Tarnower displayed his skill. Scarsdale is a very upmarket residential area close to New York. Murderess Carolyn Warmus's lover, Paul Solomon, was delighted to own an apartment using the name, though it was actually just outside Scarsdale's true, unaffordable boundary. Like 'Mayfair' or 'Belgravia' in London fifty years ago, the name 'Scarsdale' in your address conveys its own assurance of class and wealth.

Dr Tarnower's dependence on the appearance of success suggests some self-doubt on his part. His genuine pleasure in good books and fine art, and his love of trees and Oriental sculpture were qualities which are not universally admired in America. He was lucky to live on the Europeanized east coast, where good taste and intelligence are less likely to prove boring and suspect social handicaps than in the mid-west or west.

So a lover like Jean Harris who genuinely appreciated the value of his non-tangible assets was a welcome addition to the umpteen bimbos who would bound into his bed on hearing the beautiful sound of a gold pen nib scratching across a thoroughly unbounceable cheque book.

One assumes that Dr Tarnower could look in a mirror and see that his bald, blotchy, thin-lipped, pock-marked, rather cruel features were not what attracted young women. His angular skinny frame no turn-on for a healthy young woman. Brainless women were attracted by his money and status, so it was a relief to be engaged to an adult woman who genuinely loved his wit, charm and taste. Only the engagement didn't ripen into marriage. There were always excuses allowing Hy to postpone taking the plunge, until Jean realized he never would. He simply could not face a new lifestyle of permanent committed domesticity.

Unfortunately, by that time she had become hooked on the expensive pleasures he offered: the joy of foreign holidays in exotic places, or just weekend breaks from school in his luxurious surroundings in New York. The foreign holidays were particularly exciting. Dr Tarnower had a sharp nose for fascinating destinations that hadn't yet become part of the standard tourist trail. Mrs Harris saw Bangkok before it became the world capital for cut-price commercial sex; Jiddah when the Gulf was not associated with crises and wars; Khartoum before Sudan fell to Islamic fundamentalists and devastating civil war.

Then there were the more conventional fair-weather short breaks: Florida, Mexico, the Caribbean. No school teacher's salary could have afforded the travel and top-price holidays Hy dished out. No over-stressed headmistress, feeling a constant need to get away from or get even with her snotty opponents among parents and governors could have resisted the habitual call of five-star hotels in faraway places.

One other thing that Hy dished out would raise more serious eyebrows today. When Mrs Harris complained of overwork and stress, Hy prescribed medication for her. Fair enough — he was a doctor. No doubt, you think, he gave her a mild tranquillizer? Not a bit of it. Hy liked his women peppy, and he gave Jean uppers rather than downers. In fact, he had her on speed for ten years without telling her what it was!

Foreign tours revealed to Jean that she was not alone in Hy's affections. He bought cards and presents for other women, even using her taste to select their headscarves for him. She could live with this. Hy had been a wealthy bachelor for years before she had known him. He had become accustomed to filling his bed as and when he pleased. As long as the other women were just bimbos, Jean was not stirred to outrageous jealousy.

It had a mildly depressing effect on her, however, which she handled with self-deprecating wit. She would introduce herself to new friends of Dr Tarnower's as 'one of Hy's girls', or 'the broad Hy brought along'. This restored a touch of self-esteem, showing that she was confident and sophisticated enough to tolerate Hy's philandering; a cut above the breathless little floozies who were overwhelmed at being dated by the great Dr Herman Tarnower. But it depended on her certainty that she really was the one who was different; the one who was valued for her mind; the one he had wanted to marry in 1967 and who was adult enough to realize that such commitment lay beyond Hy's immature emotional range.

Unfortunately, her attitude also permitted Hy to become careless and casual. He stopped bothering to clear out other women's forgotten undies and toiletries when Jean was coming to stay. Good old Jean could take them in her sophisticated stride.

But that tolerance took a heavy fall on New Year's Day 1977. Jean and Hy were taking a break in Palm Beach, Florida. When Jean was scanning the *New York Times* personal column, she found the message, 'Happy New Year, Hi T. Love Always, Lynne.' Ouch! Now Hy's dilatory failure to go through with the engagement in 1967 was explained.

Mrs Lynne Tryforos, his former lover, had not disappeared from his life. She had presented herself at the door again some time after her marriage. For ten years Hy had kept this secret from Jean. Jean was furious. Lynne Tryforos was not an easy-come, easy-go, one-night stand. She was nearly twenty years younger than Jean, and much as Jean might affect to despise her class and educational attainments, she was clearly necessary to Hy. Jean was not the unique emotional partner her lover required. Lynne was a serious challenger for his affection.

Yet at this point, while it seemed that Hy might even prefer Lynne to Jean, he also needed Jean. He needed her for a project that was important in his life. She was helping him with his book, *The Scarsdale Diet*.

For years, Hy had handed his patients a simple list of foods to enjoy and foods to avoid. As a doctor (and a good one) it was his job to steer his patients clear of debilitating obesity. As a gourmet, he appreciated the love of good food which led many of his circle into gross over-indulgence. As a man who was as thin as a rake, despite his pleasure in preparing entrancing little sauces for his dinner guests, he knew how to recommend a healthy diet that didn't have all the appeal of a spartan soya-bean-and-orange-juice health farm. And Dr Tarnower's diet sheet had acquired a considerable reputation by word of mouth from its grateful recipients. Now a publisher had asked him to turn it into a book.

This was not a simple task. A diet sheet covering a few cyclostyled pages isn't easily transformed into 60,000 words. Professional writer Samm Sinclair Baker was called in as co-author to supply jokes, anecdotes and a running text.

Unfortunately, Mr Baker's association created its own problems. Even when two writers enjoy a perfect understanding, co-authorship is more laborious than writing a book independently. Every word has to be checked and considered to make sure that each writer is happy with the matter which will go out under his or her name. When one writer is motivated to meet the publisher's commercial requirements and the other has a professional and scientific reputation at stake, there are bound to be differences of opinion. The commercial author may sacrifice accuracy to readability; the scientific author may be unaware that general readers are easily bored by mere facts.

Dr Herman Tarnower was not the most diplomatic figure to work in such a partnership. And so Jean worked on the book for him. She wrote or rewrote parts that needed accommodating to the popular style. She studied proofs. She checked Samm Baker's input. Yet all the time she had the feeling that Hy might have dropped her in favour of Lynne Tryforos had she not been so useful. Bitter jealousy was the inevitable result.

It seems to have been felt on both sides. The two women came to identify each other's abandoned clothes dropped around Hy's love-nest, and they took to cutting them up. According to Mrs Harris, she began to be harassed by obscene phone calls. It was an intolerable situation for both of them, which Herman Tarnower should have resolved firmly by deciding which lover was to keep her place in his life and gently making this clear to the other.

Hy did no such thing. He had managed to deceive Jean successfully for ten years. He now took on Captain MacHeath's impossible task of trying to be 'happy with either While t'other dear charmer's away'. It was his willingness to enjoy all the advantages of two lovers in the teeth of their miserable rivalry that is most indefensible. It is to the credit of both Mrs Harris and Mrs Tryforos that Hy's sudden acquisition of immense wealth with the successful publication of *The Scarsdale Diet* does not seem to have played a major part in their hostilities. When figure-conscious Americans bought the book in such numbers that the doctor became a multi-millionaire and a national celebrity, he was, to that extent, a more desirable property. But for his warring Polly Peachum and Lucy Lockit he was essentially what he had always been: the charming lover and companion over whom each wanted to exert the prime emotional hold.

Once the book was completed, Jean was losing. Hy lacked the strength and courage to tell her he definitely preferred Lynne. But that seemed to be the case. It meant that Hy's home in New York, which had once been Jean's perfect bolt-hole into peace and tranquillity when school got on top of her, was transformed into a torture chamber where everything intensified her frantic jealousy to the point of anguish.

The breaking point came on 10 March 1980. After a hard day at school, Jean decided she needed the solace of a break with Hy. She telephoned him to say she was coming up from Virginia for the night. Hy tried to fob her off tactfully, but his evasiveness only convinced her (correctly) that he was having her hated rival round in her absence. 'Integrity Jean' then demonstrated the ease with which a commitment to frank truthfulness, fully integrated with one's emotions by self-knowledge, may be turned into obstinate self-assertion. If Hy had put her off for business reasons or family concerns, she would have accepted it gracefully. If Lynne Tryforos was going to be there, Jean was definitely going to drive the 500 miles to New York. She might convince herself it was to face the situation openly and boldly. Most people would assume it was to spoil her rival's night with their lover.

Before leaving Virginia she did three things which cast an entirely different light on her intentions. She made three attempts to write a will, indicating a determination to do something pretty drastic. She took her amphetamines to give her courage and energy. And she loaded her ·32 pistol — very awkwardly, so that she left one chamber empty — but she loaded it and took it with her.

No one knows whether Hy intended to sleep with Lynne that night. He had her over to dinner with another lady friend, but I don't know if Hy ever played three-in-a-bed games. If he had hoped that Mrs Tryforos might stay behind after dinner, that hope was abruptly thwarted when Jean's telephone call confirmed beyond doubt that she was driving to New York forthwith. While she drove the 500 miles north, raging, the dinner party came to its civilized end. Mrs Tryforos and the other guest went home and Dr Tarnower went to bed.

Jean was angry when she arrived to find that the courtesy light had not been left on over the door for her. But she knew her way round Hy's place. She put her car away in the garage and went up to Hy's bedroom by the lift.

She has said that her intention was to force Hy into a showdown about their relationship and then, fuelled by the amphetamines, persuade him to shoot her if he didn't need her. She has also said she wanted to talk gently and lovingly to Hy and then, if it was clear he really didn't want her, walk out into the still night air in his beautiful garden and shoot herself beside the pond.

One thing that's consistent in her stories is that she wanted Hy to talk.

Hy was distinctly less than thrilled by her appearance in his bedroom after he had gone to sleep, and when she tried to rouse him for frantic conversation he just said, 'Jesus, Jean, go to bed!'

Jean went into the bathroom instead, where she found Lynne Tryforos' nightie. This provoked positive action. Jean screamed curses as she tore it to shreds. Hy leapt out of bed and slapped her hard. Whether this was an attempt to cure hysterics or sheer bad temper at being disturbed, I don't know − probably the latter, using the former as an excuse. It appeared to work, for Jean sat morosely on the bed and then drew her pistol out of her handbag.

Hy rushed at her and batted the weapon from her grasp. As he did so it went off, injuring his hand. With superb civilized aplomb, Dr Tarnower simply said, 'Jesus, Jean, now look what you've done!' and padded off to the bathroom to rinse away the blood.

On his return, Mrs Harris claims, he found her trying to gather herself together to shoot herself. He struggled with her to wrest the gun from her grasp. As they tussled she realized the muzzle was jammed into her abdomen, so she pulled the trigger. The shock was intense but there was no pain and she wondered why she had not killed herself before. Then she realized Hy was staggering away from her, bleeding. It had been the butt, not the barrel that pressed into her.

So she pointed the pistol to her head and pulled the trigger again. A hollow click was the result: the empty chamber had come round. She pointed the gun away from herself and fired repeatedly to bring the gun back to try to make it work properly again. Only one shot fired among a succession of clicks, and that shot flew through the window.

That's what Mrs Harris says happened before she realized that Herman was seriously hurt and went to his aid. The housekeeper, on the other hand, said she heard Dr Tarnower shout, 'Get out of here! You're crazy!' before four shots sounded.

Rescuers discovered Herman with bullet wounds in his hand, chest and back, as well as the broken window. One of the four bullets fired has never been found. Mrs Harris has never accounted for shooting her lover in the back.

She has an explanation for being found by the police, preparing to drive away from the house. She says the servants did not answer the buzzer and she could not get Hy out of the room on her own so she was going to look for a call-box to summon the police and an ambulance. The police say the housekeeper called them, and on arrival Mrs Harris appeared to be about to make her escape.

None of this evidence did her so much damage when she came to trial as 'the Scarlet Letter' she had written to Hy from Virginia a couple of days previously, and which had not made its way through the infamous US mail to his hands by the time she killed him. In this letter she laid bare that deep jealousy which was still so unassuaged that she barely mentioned, and would not name, Lynne

Tryforos when she came to write her memoirs several years later.

In writing to Hy, she didn't hide her contempt. She called her rival 'a dishonest adultress', a 'slut' and a 'psychotic whore'. Commenting on a testimonial dinner to which Hy proposed taking Mrs Tryforos, Mrs Harris declared her determination to be present herself, 'even if the slut comes – indeed I don't care if she pops naked out of a cake with her tits frosted with chocolate'.

Thus did Mrs Harris's jealousy pop naked out of her cool, controlled exterior, its fangs frosted with hatred. The jury concluded that she might indeed have reached a valid moral judgement that Hy Tarnower was a pretty awful man, but this didn't entitle her to kill him. She was sent down for second degree murder.

Betty Broderick

The wedding took place in April 1969 at a Catholic church in Bronxville, New York. The bride was a tall, pretty girl of Italian descent with long, thick blonde hair. She taught in a Westchester elementary school.

The groom was a skinny, gangly student with granny glasses and long meagre sideburns. In terms of good looks he was marrying way out of his class. But inside he felt himself to be a natural dandy. He loved clothes — his new wife sometimes called him 'Dapper Dan'. He saw himself as Rhett Butler in *Gone With the Wind* and kept a framed picture of Clark Gable costumed for the part.

He had a BA from Notre Dame University (a natural stopping point for a good Catholic boy from an Irish background) and was pursuing medical studies at Cornell. His wife would keep house and be the breadwinner while he earned his MD, and would still support him as he went on to add Harvard Law School to his qualifications.

They were totally unrepresentative of the 1960s generation. Their aspirations were mixed 1950s and 1980s. Like good little Eisenhower years' homemakers, they wanted a large Catholic family housed in suburban comfort. Mom would devote herself to waxing the freezer and polishing the stair-rods and being den mother to the cub scouts and doing all the other time-consuming things that Betty Friedan showed belonged at the centre of household product commercials and not at the heart of any adult's life. The young bride was committed to a 'feminine mystique' that was almost twenty years out of date by the time she married.

Her husband, Daniel Broderick III, prefigured the yuppies of the 1980s. His ambition was to be extremely rich and well regarded by the bourgeoisie of his immediate circle. He would be a lawyer, but he was not inspired by a vision of justice or dedication to the proper ordering of society. Able and intelligent, Dan Broderick would devote his talents to swelling his bank balance and his local importance. His duty to his family, he believed, was met by bringing home the bacon. He explicitly described being a nice attentive husband and father as a 'luxury' that had to wait until he was earning enough money to give his family holidays in Europe and a swimming pool.

Later, both Brodericks would minimize or maximize the love either had felt for the other as suited their interests. Neither had their emotions well integrated with their personalities, though they seem quite a good match: two ambitious kids, determined to claw their way into upper-middle-class prosperity and a stupefyingly conventional glamorous lifestyle. Betty was intelligent, witty and could be fun to be with. Her children could expect a good time on formal picnics and celebrations. Dan was intelligent, industrious and an admirable colleague. His children could expect to keep out of his way when he had work to do — which was practically all the time.

The first six years of marriage were given over to establishing a secure basis for the great goal of bourgeois beatitude. Dan secured his legal qualifications which, added to his MD, gave him a wonderfully strong position for taking on medical malpractice suits. The couple went to San Diego, the southernmost coastal city in California, where Dan joined the old-established law firm of Gray, Cary, Ames and Frye.

Hitherto Betty's teaching had earned the daily bread: loans had supported Dan's continuing education. The game plan was to make him so highly qualified that he could hardly avoid earning well, whereupon Betty would get her washing machines and other kitchen robots and step back into graceful *kirche, küche, kinder* matron-hood.

The game plan also meant that postgraduate student Dan had his military draft deferred. He quietly skipped the Vietnam War without ever raising a peep of principled or antipatriotic objection to it.

Nor were he and Betty touched by the sexual revolution. While all around them rejoiced in the new freedom of the contraceptive pill and questioned the traditional family structure that tried to protect women and children against the drawbacks of unwanted offspring, Dan and Betty just got on with making babies in the good old married Catholic way.

Kimberley was born in January 1970, conceived on the very boundary of matrimony. (Later Kimberley would tell the world that Betty had one abortion before she wed, somewhat besmirching the picture of Catholic chastity Betty liked to paint of herself.)

In 1971 another daughter, Lee, followed Kimberley. Betty Broderick, teacher, housewife and mother, supporting her young husband through college and prentice years, deserves all the credit she claims for the hard work of this period. With no washing machine and no car at one point, she had to take baby clothes and dirty nappies to the launderette by bus. She invested her time, energy and personality in the luxury future, and the shallowness of her dream existence cannot detract from the fact that she earned it fully by her efforts throughout the difficult years. Had she and Dan been twenty years older and enjoyed the support of a society that shared their vision of the good life, they would probably have made it to a financially secure old age together, wondering vaguely why they weren't enjoying perfect contentment and probably putting it down to the universally unreasonable nature of the opposite sex.

The ties between them should also have been strengthened by shared natural sorrows. A third child, a little boy, died two days after his birth, while Dan was still at

Harvard. And there were to be two more miscarriages.
But in San Diego, with Dan earning at last and material
possessions starting to accumulate, Daniel T. Broderick
IV was born. And in 1979 came their fourth and last
child. Another boy, he was named after Dan's fictional
idol, Rhett.

After that Betty knew she had enough children. Once
again, she dropped her boasted Catholic principles
without a qualm in her own interest and had an abortion
when she found herself pregnant. Then she had her tubes
tied.

The professional demands on Dan were growing. He
made the bold decision to leave Gray, Carey and set up
independently. He kept his overheads low by sharing
part-time secretarial help with other lawyers. But he
still had his own office costs to meet and he was taking a
risk.

He also took a mortgage. For the first time, the
Brodericks bought a house of their own. They put down a
deposit on a house in the Coral Reef section of La Jolla
– the most upmarket suburb of San Diego. They had a
three-car garage and Betty had her own washing machine
and dryer at last, though Dan's outgoing expenses meant
that they were still acquiring furniture gradually. Betty
still worked to contribute to the family budget, serving as
a restaurant's evening cashier.

It's a mark of Betty's intelligence that she realized
something was wrong. Her horizons did not embrace the
new feminist vision of women's potential, but she
persuaded Dan to go with her for marriage counselling on
a Catholic Marriage Encounter weekend. She complained
that their new possessions did not include a sofa. She
wanted furniture on which they could cuddle up in the
evenings and enjoy real physical 'togetherness'.

Dan acknowledged that he was devoting so much time
to getting on professionally that he was not a close and
caring husband and father. But he still saw these qualities
as 'luxuries'. Realistic and responsible manly love, to his

cold and inhibited mind, was supplying the material goods of life. Later his daughter would report that he was always emotionally constipated. He could only bring himself to say 'I love you' if he was drunk. But what did that matter to him when he found he was prospering enough to put a swimming pool in his back yard?

As the 1980s opened, the Brodericks were at last a wealthy and successful couple. They belonged to exclusive country clubs in La Jolla. Their children went to expensive private schools. They took holidays in Europe and the Caribbean and Dan went skiing and owned a power boat. He also started indulging his taste for 'Dapper Dan' clothes, adding a top hat and cape to his wardrobe of custom-made suits.

In his late thirties, Dan Broderick had filled out and grown good-looking. The scrawny student whom Betty's friends had seen as a real geek was left far behind. With the thrusting jaw and confident demeanour of a man who tried and usually won the meatiest medical malpractice suits in south California, Dan had made it. The goal was achieved, and he had only to watch his income climb to the million dollars a year mark.

But there were unexpected drawbacks for Betty. She was the rich and beautiful wife of a handsome and successful husband in one of the most golden parts of the sunbelt, but her social life was still restricted to Dan's law circles. Though she now bought expensive couturier clothes and jewels, her public identity was submerged in her husband's. She experienced many of the discontents Betty Friedan had analyzed years before, yet her own conservative pre-feminist attitudes prevented her from recognizing them and building her own personality through evening classes or a new and demanding job. Instead she tried harder at the old, failed pattern.

She chauffeured the children everywhere; she became the organizer of children's parties and outings – the life and soul of groups of other wives and mothers. Deep discontent left her insecure, but she had no idea why.

That was until 1983. That year fully opened Betty's eyes to the fact of her unhappiness. It was the year that, she came to believe, signalled the end of a life of perfect, idyllic happiness.

Early in 1983, Betty overheard her husband remark, 'Isn't she beautiful?' at a cocktail party. The object of his glance was not his wife. It was Linda Kolkena, the receptionist he shared with other offices in the building where he had hung his shingle. Betty didn't think too much of it at the time, though it was the strongest expression of admiration she had ever heard her husband make.

In the spring the Brodericks went on an expensive European holiday. Dan seemed tense and unhappy all the time.

In the summer Betty took the kids camping. Dan never seemed to be home when they called him.

In the autumn Dan offered an explanation. He didn't find life fun any more. He thought their house was tacky. He thought their friends were tacky. He thought Betty was 'old, fat, ugly and boring'.

Who can blame Betty for remembering this outburst with resentment? The joyless workaholic life was of Dan's choosing. The house was of his choosing. Their whole social circle of friends, for heaven's sake, was of his choosing, selected to help Dan in his ambition of becoming President of the San Diego Bar Association!

And how on earth could Dan Broderick expect any woman to forgive those four adjectives? Inevitably Betty was fourteen years older than she had been when they married. In those days she was a more sophisticated city person than him, but she never, as she might have done, accused him of being a tasteless, skinny, hick swot in his student days. She had flattered him as 'Dapper Dan' before he deserved it.

Ugly, Betty was not and is not. A more confident, independent woman would have observed the deliberate insult and known it was time to start splitting off emotionally from Dan. Betty ingested all the pain of the verbal assault, and tried to win back her husband's lost affection.

After Betty killed Dan, a juror at her first trial wondered, 'What took her so long?' The autumn of 1983 was the first moment at which one feels Dan Broderick was asking for retribution. He instantly made things worse. He told Betty he was taking on an assistant. She was pleased. She hoped that some of the burden of his work would be lifted and he might become less of a grouch around the house.

It was a shock to discover that the new assistant was Linda Kolkena. Not only had the twenty-two-year-old no legal qualifications, she hadn't even got secretarial skills. What assistance could the blonde, with looks that reminded some people of the young Betty, possibly offer?

Obvious, isn't it? But Betty Broderick blinkered herself and resolutely avoided the inescapable truth that her husband was having an affair with Linda. She could hardly fail to suspect it, but it was such a deep threat to her self-image as part of a happy, pre-feminist, home-centred family that she greedily swallowed Dan's lies and evasions; willingly accepted his insistence that he was still faithful to her; listened to his claims that her jealousy was irrational, her doubts about his fidelity all horrible imaginings.

However, 1983 undoubtedly shifted the Brodericks from boring wedlock to a straightforward unhappy marriage. Dan lied, grumbled about the house and accused Betty of mental instability when she raised the topic of Linda Kolkena. Betty became a shrew and a termagant. She and her friends laughed at Dan's 'mid-life crisis' – his purchase of a red Corvette and ever more dandiacal clothes. When he sported designer sunglasses and silk scarves, Betty jeered that he was trying to return to his twenties. And she persuaded herself that he was only exhibiting the middle-aged discontent some of her friends were encountering in their spouses.

On Betty's thirty-sixth birthday, Dan didn't come home. Betty put the kids to bed, took a mild overdose of sleeping pills and slashed her wrists lightly with Dan's razor after putting herself to bed in the spare room. She woke to find Dan shaking her awake, after which he bandaged her wrists for her (he was, after all, a doctor as well as a lawyer).

Two weeks later came Dan's thirty-ninth birthday. Betty baked a chocolate cake and took it to his office at 4 p.m. by which time he should have finished work. Indeed he had! Two champagne glasses showed that he had already celebrated, and the receptionist told her that Dan and Linda had gone out together before lunch and never returned. Betty went straight home, took all Dan's prized suits from the wardrobe and burned the lot in the back yard.

As she later acknowledged, she ought to have known her suspicions were justified when Dan swallowed her vandalism, but claimed that he had been out all afternoon taking a client's deposition. An innocent husband, who placed such store by his threads, would have accepted Betty's offer of his car keys, chequebook and invitation to get out of her life.

Toward the end of 1984, Dan decided they needed a bigger house. Without consulting Betty, he shifted the family into rented accommodation on the Pacific at La Jolla while the foundations of the family home were repaired before selling it and buying another. It had been an unhappy year in which rows between the couple built up. Three days after his birthday in February 1985, Dan walked out of Betty's house, hoping he had walked out of her life.

He returned to the old family home at Coral Reef where, six weeks later, Betty handed over the first of their children to him. Kim and Lee had been squabbling. Betty lost her temper when Kim asked to be driven to a friend's house, and dumped her on Dan's doorstep instead. The following day Kim was joined by Dan Jr, though the little boy was frightened and arrived screaming and clinging to his mother.

Betty claimed that the house on La Jolla shores was rat-infested and she had to get the children out. She said four children were too much for her to manage singlehanded. But within a few weeks she had turned them all over to Dan and was leaving him to learn the art of single-parenting.

He did so surprisingly well. He hired a housekeeper, and for the first time in his life started devoting time to his family in the evenings. He was firmer and stricter than his mercurial wife, so that sometimes some of the kids felt they'd rather be with Mom. But Dan Broderick made an unpredictably successful move into the world of *Kramer vs Kramer*.

Betty now lost her cool completely. Thinking of the Coral Reef house as her family home (it was the only piece of property the Brodericks held jointly) she went there as she felt inclined, taking the children food and clothing. When she found her husband genuinely didn't need or want her back, she started taking cans of spray paint to vandalize the walls and implements to smash mirrors and an answering-machine.

Dan responded by putting down a deposit on another house for her in Calle de Cielo and filing for divorce. He was voluntarily paying her $9,000 a month maintenance, so she was not suffering financially. But Betty wanted everything she had previously enjoyed: her house, her husband, her children, and a life without Linda Kolkena at the edges.

Linda Kolkena — the shadowy woman in the Broderick case. Dan was such a jerk he didn't confess to Betty she'd been right all along about the affair until they'd been living apart for several months, and word filtered back that Linda had accompanied Dan to a Broderick family pre-Thanksgiving get-together in Colorado.

What was Linda's great appeal to Dan? Friends said

she was a bouncy, bubbly personality, who could make him laugh and let his hair down. Linda had been a stewardess with Delta Airlines until she was sacked for having a few drinks too many and using profane language about a passenger who got fresh with her. Linda took this in her stride, remarking that she always used strong language. And she took the receptionist's post that brought her into Dan's orbit.

If she really swore habitually, some of Dan's grievances against Betty look hypocritical. For Betty's obscene profanity over the next four years became one of the great points at issue between them. When Betty discovered Dan couldn't stand her swearing at him, especially in front of the children, she made a point of doing so. Sometimes she would swear into the answerphone, and claim that she was having enormous fun in leaving dirty words around for anyone to pick up. Her classic answerphone message, left when she heard Linda's voice deliver the taped outgoing ran: 'What's this, "*We* can't come to the phone", cunt? *You're* not supposed to come to the phone at the house. You're supposed to fuck him at the house and answer the phone at the office.'

As a father, Dan was furious that his children might pick up comments like that. But as a lawyer he was delighted — Betty was leaving taped evidence that she was harassing him illegally.

Betty's harassment also involved coming into the house to pick up the children as and when she pleased. She returned them, too, without warning Dan. Prissy, punitive, legalistic Dan set about curbing this misconduct by a tariff of fines. She was fined for each expletive; fined more for each unheralded visit to the house; fined yet more for each unarranged removal of the children. A couple of times, Dan sent no maintenance cheque, saying her fines were so heavy she owed him money!

But he always carefully remained within the law. He paid her maintenance before the courts ordered it. And apart from the deductions he unilaterally imposed, the money came through punctually at the beginning of each month. Betty Broderick, while complaining that her husband was keeping her in penury, spent more on clothes in 1986 than most of us earned!

Dan used his legal skill to blitz Betty with the snowstorm of court orders and injunctions and summonses that had always been the hallmark of his legal aggression. Betty was driven wild by the perfectly legal harassment that came through her letterbox and responded with ever more frenzied personal harassment which, in turn, attracted yet more court orders. Dan persistently refused to speak to her face to face, retreating behind communication through lawyers.

In 1985 Dan moved out of the Coral Reef house and bought a new home in expensive Cypress Avenue, north of Balboa Park in downtown San Diego. He also set about doing up the old family home for sale.

Betty tried to block him by refusing her legal assent. She ignored her lawyer's advice that she would have to appear in court or Dan would be given leave to sell it over her head. To her absolute fury this happened, whereupon she went round to the house and threw petrol over the hall in a vain attempt to block the sale of the only joint property of her marriage. Then she went to Dan's house on Cypress Avenue and drove her car through his front door. She was taken to a mental hospital in handcuffs for that little escapade.

More ill-advised refusals to attend court allowed lawyer Dan (the personal friend of most San Diego judges) to get the divorce entirely his own way. He was given his freedom without final arrangements about the children and maintenance being made, though he did appeal against the $16,000 a month he was ordered to pay Betty. (She agreed it was wrong. She thought it should be more!)

By staying away, Betty had brought on herself a complete loss of custody, care and control of the children. She wasn't even given access rights! When court-appointed counsellor Ruth Roth assured her in

1987 this could be altered, and she could get the children back, Betty made the declarations that lost her the sympathy of many separated spouses who had never wanted their families broken up: 'I'm not going to be the single parent of four kids,' she said. 'He'll die first . . . The less I see of them the better. No bother, no kids.'

She wanted her worthless man, her status and her house back – probably in that order – with the kids a poor fourth, to be used by both parents as a weapon in their increasingly public battle.

'I'm not letting go that easy,' Betty told Dr Roth. 'The little fuckhead was mine and he'll stay mine.'

She even managed the difficult task of creating sympathy for Dan by calling him 'the fuckhead' and Linda 'the cunt' to their children, and demanding that they use the same terms.

The great Broderick divorce attracted attention all over California as Betty appealed to the press and the feminist organizations for support, putting the apparently good case that she was a mother who had been denied access to her children while her vengeful husband savaged her with legal threats and exposed his innocent Catholic offspring to his immoral life with a live-in girlfriend.

Dan was forced to answer as pressmen asked for his side of the story, and the quarrelling couple became a popular subject of dinner-table conversation. Almost anybody who had been through a divorce could see echoes or caricatures of their own bad behaviour or injuries, spite or suffering, anger, frustration, jealousy and helplessness. It remains the great fascination of the case that Dan and Betty seem to have taken common experience and raised it to new and unforgivable levels.

When it was announced that Dan and Linda were to marry, Betty broke into their house and stole the guest list. Linda, for once, conversely stole some papers from Betty's house. The couple's worst moment was a half-hour phone call to young Dan Jr, in which Betty reduced him to helpless tears, while Dan coldly taped it as useful potential evidence instead of putting an immediate stop to the emotional cruelty. Betty was cursing the 'fuckhead' and the 'cunt', calling Dan a 'slimeball' and 'scum', and demanding her half of the property. The little boy sobbed that he wanted to be with his mother, but wouldn't be allowed to while she used bad words. And the self-obsessed parody of a mother just cursed the more furiously and called her child a 'little monster'. Linda seems to be the only person who tried to intervene, but she had no option but to get off the line when little Dan Jr screamed at her.

The last straw for Betty came on 3 November 1988. It was another legal injunction against her visiting Dan's house. She didn't really need to by now. The girls were big enough to visit her when they chose. Kim was away at college in Tucson. Lee had attracted her father's chilly, authoritarian disfavour when she got kicked out of school for possessing drugs. The pompous patriarch disowned her and cut her out of his will! So Lee was often at Betty's.

Betty had a boyfriend, too: Brad Wright. She swore that she retained her virtue and moral superiority by not sleeping with him. But worse for Brad than her frozen chastity must have been her white-hot ongoing obsession with Dan and Linda. It came to a climax on Sunday 5 November. Provoked beyond endurance by the last legal threat, Betty arose quietly before dawn and took one of Lee's keys which she rightly suspected opened Dan's door. She drove over to Cypress Avenue, let herself in through the back door and made her way into the master bedroom through the adjacent bathroom.

Somebody stirred in the darkened room as she entered. Betty had the impression Linda's was the body in the bed nearest to her. She shot her immediately.

Then she shot Dan: she shot him again and again as he scrambled from the bed toward the telephone. When he fell, she ripped the telephone from the wall and dropped it at the top of the stairs. In some confused way she got home and told one of her friends and Lee what she had done. She seemed proud or relieved that it was all over.

Her defence was that she took the gun to force Dan to listen to her grievances. That she intended to kill herself and blow her brains over his bedroom if she got no satisfaction. That she really couldn't remember how she came to fire, except that she thought Dan was going to call the police and have her arrested again.

None of this probably convinced anybody. She'd murdered him all right, but Dan Broderick was such a jerk that it was understandable — so the hung jury felt at her first trial.

The jury at her second trial, which found her guilty of second degree homicide, probably reacted to her unshaken egocentricity; her lasting incapacity to understand or care how her own actions, from start to finish, have hurt her children; and her selfish belief that everyone else and every other consideration should yield to Betty Broderick's title to live the life of a glamorous soap powder commercial. Instead, she will live a large part of her life in prison.

She Done Him Wrong

'But fare thee well, most foul, most fair! farewell,
Thou pure impiety, and impious purity!
For thee I'll lock up all the gates of love'
  William Shakespeare *Much Ado About Nothing*

Above left: By the age of twenty-seven, glamorous debutante Elvira Mullins had declined to drunken overweight Mrs Elvira Barney *(Popperfoto)*

Above right: 'Michael' Scott Stephen *(Hulton Picture Company)*

Mrs Barney's flat in Williams Mews, with one of her succession of expensive cars outside *(Popperfoto)*

Ruth Ellis with her protector and occasional lover, Desmond Cussen
(Syndication International)

David Blakely, motor racing enthusiast *(Press Association/Topham)*

Headmistress and doctor's mistress Jean Harris *(UPI/ Bettmann/Hulton Picture Company)*

Dr Herman Tarnower, a charming, witty, wealthy heel *(Associated Press/ Topham)*

Dorothy Stratten, *Playboy* Playmate of the Year 1980, with Paul Snider, the hustler husband who killed her *(Press Association/ Topham)*

Betty Broderick smiles as she and her attorney listen to Judge Thomas Whelan declare a mistrial *(Bettmann/Hulton Picture Company)*

Dr Geza de Kaplany under arrest, looking unusually open-faced and innocent without his tinted spectacles *(Topham)*

Beautiful model and murder victim Hajna de Kaplany *(Topham)*

Above left: Stanford White, millionaire architect and stage-door Johnny *(Hulton Picture Company)*

Above right: Harry Kendall Thaw – mad, bad and dangerous to know

Evelyn Nesbit Thaw, the girl in the red velvet swing *(Popperfoto)*

Frederick Emmett-Dunne with Mia *(Topham)*

Reg Watters *(far right, grinning)* and Mia *(second woman from the left)* partying in the sergeants' mess at the British Army barracks in Duisburg, Germany *(Topham)*

Thomas Ley

Back entrance to 5 Beaufort Gardens, where young Buckingham and Lil Bruce brought John Mudie to be murdered by Ley and Smith *(Topham)*

James Snook, Joe Lippart,
Leonard Tyburski and
Nicholas Hall

The victims of women's jealousy seem, by and large, utter bounders. Michael Stephen, David Blakely, Herman Tarnower and Dan Broderick didn't deserve death sentences, but surely they behaved abominably to their women and made a positive contribution to their own murders. Their persistent lies, cheating and jiggery-pokery with the money they either scrounged or doled out like a favour when it suited them, created tense quarrelling scenarios and their women were bound to snap when they felt especially down. Like Betty Broderick's juror, one wonders 'What took them so long?'

But the courts have been uniformly stern with killer women, unless, like Mrs Barney, they could establish doubt about the facts.

By contrast, men who kill their wives after similar provocation may be subject to more lenient treatment. When the justice system sees a man crack up after long and obvious cruelty from an unfeeling, exploitative woman, he may well get a gentle tap on the knuckles from a judge who would almost like to pin a medal on him. Joe Lippart and Nicholas Hall benefited from this legal gender bias.

More frequently, jealous men's women get killed for telling an unacceptable truth. Often one finds the woman killed by a jealous husband or lover meets her doom at the moment when she reports that some rival is better in bed. Jealous men kill in the rage that comes from learning − truly or falsely − that their beloved prefers somebody else's embraces, and makes odious, disparaging comparisons about their pathetic sexual stamina or puny equipment. One might distort Byron's tag (as Mr Melford Stevenson did at Ruth Ellis's trial) to propose that:

'Woman's sexual pride's but part of self-esteem —
For man, 'tis *the* essential.'

Professor Snook and Leonard Tybulski illustrate murder as explosive sexual assertion. Both show, too, how (unlike the killer husband who has suffered long-running abuse), the man who murders in defence of his manhood will lie and wriggle and evade when he's caught. The man who could stand no more cruel shrewishness has less difficulty in admitting exactly what he's done.

James Snook

James Howard Snook was born in 1880 on a farm near Lebanon, Ohio. He had a country boy's skill with rifle and shotgun; a young farmer's expertise in handling animals. When he finished high school, he went to Ohio State University, where he was to spend the whole of his career.

He entered the College of Veterinary Medicine, graduated, gained his doctorate, was appointed instructor, and rose steadily to reach the rank of full professor.

When he was forty he added a little colour to his life, travelling to the Olympics as a member of the American pistol-shooting team. His marksmanship didn't win any medals, but his sportsmanship didn't do him any harm.

Snook was married. He and his wife Helen were a gracious host and hostess when entertaining colleagues, and until 1926 there were few more respected professors on the OSU Veterinary faculty. Then suddenly, at the age of forty-six, James Howard Snook plunged into a mid-life crisis. He began staying out and leading a social life that no longer involved his wife. He began taking note of the attractive young women around him on campus.

For a happily libidinous man, employment as a

university teacher is rather like the proverbial good fortune of the alcoholic working in a brewery. Not only is he surrounded by nubile women (which in itself only means marriageable), they are actually at that pleasant stage of nubility when the more daring of them wish to experiment with sex. And a professor is placed, by virtue of his occupation, on a podium before them – marked out as a man enjoying the aphrodisiac qualities of power and public attention. He is likely to be richer than many of his pupils.

James Howard Snook added to all this the genuine personal attractions of grace, charm and good looks, all of which swiftly got him into hot water. For the first time in his career he was summoned before Dr Brumley, Head of the Veterinary College and Dr White the Dean. He was reprimanded for publicly associating with women other than his wife. (It wouldn't happen today, but the 1920s still treasured some Victorian myths about maidenhood and chastity.) He was also called in to explain why he had given narcotics to a woman student. (That *would* happen today, and the professor's resignation would be demanded. But the 1920s still treasured some Victorian liberal principles about the individual's right to harm his own health if he wants to.)

Snook's past good reputation stood him in good stead. His superiors deplored his fallen standards, but hoped he would recover moral stability after enjoying a mid-life fling. They reckoned without Theora Hix.

She was twenty-three years old in 1926. A true child of the jazz age. Her father was a retired college professor, and Miss Hix was working her way through OSU Medical School on an allowance of $600 a year. It wasn't a fortune, but it didn't stop her from having a good time.

Theora particularly enjoyed her classes with Dr Clayton Smith, the Professor of Pharmacology and Physiology. She learned that the pharmacopoeia included cocaine, whose effects she found extremely pleasant. She found out how much pleasure her own physiology could yield to both herself and a male partner, with the help of William Miller, a thirty-five-year-old instructor in the College of Agriculture. Agriculture plus physiology equals veterinary science – Theora added Professor Snook as a second string to her bow. She became closely acquainted with him when the professor employed her as a part-time secretary. And she cultivated the acquaintance.

The professor was overwhelmed. 'She was a good companion in a different way than my wife,' he remarked, with unconscious irony. She introduced him to cocaine. And she confirmed that he was the nicest man she knew. Only she didn't drop Bill Miller.

In 1927 Snook introduced his new beloved to the sport of pistol-shooting, and gave her a ·41 calibre derringer. Theora took to carrying it around in her handbag. And, in return, she introduced Snook to the sports of ingesting cocaine and making love in motor cars. She got him to sterilize her so that her sex-life might be completely uninhibited. She also foolishly used the spice of induced jealousy to keep him up to the mark. She would occasionally hint that Bill Miller was a younger and better lover.

By March 1929 the besotted professor wanted more undisturbed nights with Theora. He rented a room in Columbus from Mrs Margaret Smalley, using the slenderly disguised name 'Howard Snook', and describing himself as a salt company representative. Theora, he claimed, was his wife and she would stay with him from time to time.

It was a hot and humid day on 14 June 1929 – the sort of day that threatens thunder without ever producing it and clearing the air. James' and Theora's emotional tension matched the weather. They quarrelled on and off during the day. Theora resented James' preparing to go away for the weekend with Helen and their baby daughter. She threatened to kill Mrs Snook and the baby if they went ahead with their trip. Snook reproached her for interfering in his private affairs and Theora resorted to comparing him unfavourably with Miller.

It's hardly surprising that the two didn't feel inclined to stay in their stuffy love-nest in the city that night. They prepared some beef sandwiches, spiced with cocaine, and took off in Professor Snook's car for his golf club. Unfortunately it was crowded (a tournament was in progress) and Snook did not wish to be seen escorting Theora when he had already been reprimanded for womanizing. They ate their sandwiches in the car near the links and then drove to a rifle range the veterinarian marksman patronized.

The New York Central Rifle Range was neither in New York nor centrally located in Columbus, Ohio. It was on the city's outskirts, and when Professor Snook's new blue car drew up it was deserted. The professor parked happily and, like a randy student, immediately started making out.

This was a mistake. Theora, like him, was stoned and uninhibited. She squawked that the car was a cramped and uncomfortable venue for sex and she didn't like it. She told the professor he was a rotten lover anyway and she'd rather have Bill Miller.

Professor Snook lost his cool. It would appear that he said, 'I'll kill you!' For Theora's undoubted response was, 'And I'll kill you, too!' She didn't get a chance to try it. The professor seized a hammer that he kept in the car and hit her lightly across the face. Theora pulled away and tumbled out of the car, but her lover was after her at once and smashed the hammer brutally over her head. She dropped her handbag and key-ring and lay on the ground moaning. Snook, under a hazy impression that he was putting her out of her misery, beat her over the head twice more with the hammer. Then he drew his penknife and cut her throat. He was never able to offer an explanation for that final act. Nor did he understand how her body came to be found face down – she had been lying on her back when he killed her. He came to as he sat on the running board of his car, looking in a dazed fashion at the shattered head of his mistress. He didn't stay long.

At dawn, two small boys found the body. Theora was identified and Bill Miller was pulled in for questioning. He made a poor impression, seeming awkward and evasive. But he did not own a blue Ford coupé, and Miss Hix had been seen being driven in one on the evening of 14 June.

The blue Ford led to Snook's being questioned. He did his best to cast suspicion back on Miller, but broke down when Mrs Smalley identified him and his recently dry-cleaned suit showed traces of blood under analysis. He confessed the story, much as told above, only adding the suggestion that Miss Hix reached for her handbag as she cried, 'I'll kill you, too!' so that he feared she was going to draw her pistol and shoot him. He also remarked that his defence would be temporary insanity.

After making his statement to District Attorney John Chester, Snook repeated it in an interview with Columbus journalists James Fusco and William Howells of the Cleveland *Plain Dealer* — which was imprudent. He was later to claim that Chester had beaten the confession out of him and it was false. Chester's response was to blandly replace Snook's signed statement with the journalists' sworn testimony to the identical account they had heard.

The statement's self-serving nature is most clearly shown in Snook's recollection of four blows — two of them delivered with benign and merciful intent. The pathologist found that Theora died under a frenzied battery of seventeen blows!

Snook's defence was hydra-headed. His attorney, E.O. Ricketts, carefully studied the recent case of Cincinnati bootlegger James Remus, who was acquitted of murdering his pretty wife Imogene after being found temporarily insane. It cost him a few months in an asylum, but no doubt Mr Remus thought that a light price to escape the electric chair. Temporary insanity was, as Professor

Snook had predicted, the first claim he put forward. He would not suffer the inconvenience of the asylum because the insanity could be attributed in part to the beef and cocaine cocktail he had eaten before going to the rifle range.

Self-defence was the second proposition. If Theora really went for her derringer, Snook was entitled to use force to stop her, and perhaps might be forgiven for having got a little carried away.

Learned psychiatrists were also called in to suggest a more permanent imbalance: the male mid-life crisis which had led to his carpeting by the Dean and the College Head. Helen Snook, who stood by her husband loyally, testified that he had not really been himself for three years. And even old Mrs Abner Snook, the professor's aged mother, hobbled in from the farm to say what a good boy he'd always been back in the 1880s and 1890s!

If his reason couldn't be blamed, perhaps the cocaine could. Ricketts tried a hopeful suggestion that Snook was too stoned to know what he was doing, with the added gloss that it was all Theora's fault as she had introduced the professor to recreational drugs in the first place.

Finally there was the claim that the police had questioned Snook till he was frightened and exhausted, and Mr Chester had slapped him to force out the confession.

None of it did Snook a blind bit of good. He exhibited slippery evasiveness from the outset of the trial. He claimed a different debilitating illness every day, until the judge had him examined by a court appointed doctor each morning, whereupon Professor Snook's maladies gave no more problems. He was convicted and sentenced to death.

The trial enjoyed a good deal of attention because of the spicy letters the professor had written to his love in the days of their happy passion. These were all read out in court, but the respectable newspapers of the time refused to print their lurid contents. Happily, sub rosa publishers were less bashful, and booklets giving the 'complete' proceedings circulated around Columbus and must, today, rank among the valuable murder ephemera sought by collectors.

Helen Snook was perhaps a little quietly triumphant that her man had been forced back to her with his tail between his legs. He had punished naughty Miss Hix severely enough to satisfy the most vengeful wronged wife, though, regrettably, at the cost of his own life.

Helen saw to it that Snook left the prison with a bang rather than a whimper. Four chefs prepared a magnificent banquet for the veterinarian's last night on earth. Mrs Snook and he graciously entertained two dinner guests for the last time. And only the prison authorities slightly spoiled the occasion by refusing Snook permission to wear his dinner jacket in place of his convict uniform.

Joe Lippart

The unposted note was in Mrs Betty Lippart's writing. Its purport was unmistakable:

> Dear Kenny,
> I miss you so much . . . I love you. Nobody has ever made me feel the way you do when you kiss me and make love to me, not even Sonny . . . I wish we could be together all the time. I feel I belong more to you than to Sonny.

Sonny was Mrs Lippart's truck-driver husband, Joe. He stared with horror at the document he had found and he knew the object of his wife's infidelity.

Kenny Childress was the boy next door, in Gaithersburg, Maryland. Big, bearded, but only seventeen years old, he had been enjoying a steamy liaison with twenty-nine-year-old Betty, the mother of four children, ever since she admired his buns at a poolside party.

I don't know what Sonny said or did to Betty. But he

told Kenny's mother that he'd kill the boy! Not that he actually attempted or intended it. Mr and Mrs Childress were almost equally horrified, in any case. They acted firmly to restrain their errant son and put a stop to his precocious adultery. Kenny's car was confiscated, his movements were restricted and he came under a curfew.

Kenny skipped school to go on seeing Betty while everybody else was out at work. When this truancy came to the Childresses' attention they didn't mess about. They took their son down to the State Attorney's office and asked the law to intervene. He might be forgiven for extreme and extraordinary adolescent straying, but Mrs Lippart had to be stopped from encouraging him to miss school and jeopardizing the peace of the neighbourhood.

Public attorneys worked out a formula that Kenny and Betty both signed. They accepted a legally binding injunction against seeing each other. Kenny may have sulked a bit with his parents. But Betty was 'mean as hell' with Joe.

'All she cared about was saying mean things,' he complained. 'She'd cuss me out before I went to work and when I got to work I couldn't work. I was sick on my stomach. My nerves got to me, she'd been so mean and nasty. She'd say, "Love it or leave it".'

Nor was Joe's sickness imaginary. On a hot day in June 1976 he suffered cramping stomach pains and found it impossible to think of going to work. He asked Betty to take him to the doctor. 'I begged and begged and begged and she wouldn't do it,' he reported. Betty had quite another idea about how to spend the day. She was going next door, she said.

And so Joe suddenly realized that the injunction was being ignored. Betty was still playing with her toy boy and her pleasure counted for far more than his health. With that, Joe snapped. He grabbed the loaded shotgun he kept beneath the bed and fired both barrels into Betty's chest. After which he telephoned the police to report his murder, and promised that he would be waiting outside his house for the arresting officers and he would come without making any trouble.

Joe went on trial in Montgomery County Circuit Court and was convicted of second degree homicide — intentional murder, but with no premeditation. He was sentenced to twenty years' imprisonment. But evidently Judge Thomas Mitchell felt he had been sorely tried. He suspended eighteen and a half years of the sentence, and Joe only had to spend four months behind bars before becoming eligible for parole.

I don't know whether the Childress family were still living next door to him when he came out.

Leonard Tyburski

Leonard Tyburski was less lucky. He, too, was convicted of the second degree murder of his wife. But none of his twenty- to forty-year sentence was mercifully suspended. Leonard had shown just a bit too much calculation after the crime; varied his story once too often under cross-examination.

Dorothy Tyburski disappeared on 2 October 1985. Leonard, the Dean of Students at Mackenzie High School in Detroit, reported her missing to the police. He added the information that she had been very depressed following her sister's death the previous year and he feared she had just wandered off in a state of emotional confusion.

After two years they shelved the file on Mrs Tyburski. They couldn't find a trace of her, and there's no law against wandering off and starting a new life under a new identity if the old life is unhappy.

Leonard accepted the police closure of the case, and started proceedings for divorce so as to lead his own life without ties to the past. But his daughter Kelly was uneasy. Kelly was a student in Michigan State University in East Lansing. It is the largest single-campus university in America, with its own farmlands rolling away from the tree-shaded and lamplit grassy slopes around its main buildings and running south for miles. Three huge generator buildings overhang the campus centre, initials on their chimneys marking the institution's three stages of development: from the Michigan Agricultural College to Michigan State College and finally to Michigan State University. Between the generators, labyrinthine, spooky underground tunnels were used by students in the 1980s for especially exciting games of Dungeons and Dragons.

But real life spooked Kelly. She was always dreaming about her mother – dreaming that she was tied up and imprisoned somewhere in the family house at Canton Township, Detroit. She couldn't shake off daytime thoughts reverting to the dreams. She couldn't get out of her mind the padlocked cabinet freezer in her dad's basement: a freezer like the secret chamber in Bluebeard's Castle.

Murders solved by dreams are far from unknown. The most famous case is Maria Marten in the Old Red Barn: killed by her fiancé William Corder in 1827, and discovered when her mother dreamed that her body lay buried in the barn. Eric Tombe was found at the bottom of a well in 1922, where his mother had dreamed he lay. His fraudulent partner, Ernest Dyer, had murdered him and subsequently killed himself when he was about to be arrested in connection with another confidence trick. In one extraordinary case in the Wild West, a miner recognized four complete strangers as figures he had dreamed about the previous night killing a friend of his. And they had done just that!

Kelly Tyburski presents us with rather less mystery. She lived on the spot with her father. She knew about the locked freezer in the basement. Her dreams and premonitions seem likely to be the astute working of the subconscious mind, not mystical clairvoyance.

On 2 January 1989, Kelly's suspicions were put to the test. She succeeded in forcing the freezer open. There lay her mother's battered body, frozen and preserved for over three years. Kelly and her younger sister went straight to the police, ignoring their father who passed them as he hurried home.

Tyburski's evasive action in reporting Dorothy's disappearance told against him; so did his self-control in seeking divorce from the woman he kept on ice in his basement. His story of how she died was quite unexpected, too.

Kelly was in for more shock than the loss of her mother. She was to learn that Dorothy Tyburski had betrayed both her husband and her daughter back in 1985. The Tyburskis were a modern family, and Kelly had a live-in boyfriend, Craig Albright. Dorothy, it transpired, had seduced her daughter's lover — twice.

The third time Craig refused her. It was 28 September 1985, and the frustrated female turned her wrath on her husband. She told him all about Craig, made derogatory comparisons between Craig's manliness with his own and infuriated Leonard by calling him a wimp.

When he attacked her in jealous rage, she picked up a steak knife and stabbed him. Then she fell into the freezer. Yes, fell in, just like that. That was Leonard's first story.

Pressed by disbelieving lawyers in court, he eventually admitted that he had thrown her in. It still didn't seem to explain why her head was so savagely battered. Leonard could account for that. He had been so blind with rage that he bashed her head against a beam before tossing her into the freezer.

His final and complete story painted the most preposterous picture of Dorothy's end. Apparently she was not concussed by his manhandling, and as she lay in the freezer where her husband was about to lock her in and freeze her to death she continued to scream 'Wimp! Wimp!' at him, and call for Craig to come to her aid as the lethal lid closed over her.

Nicholas Hall

In the same year that Dorothy Tyburski was playing Potiphar's wife, twenty-seven-year-old Nicholas Hall met and fell in love with a most unsuitable young woman.

Thelma was a nineteen-year-old drop-out drug addict. She had fluffy blonde good looks, but she was also filthy, disorderly and abandoned. She had two children and no idea how to look after them properly.

Hall was a dustman. He was a very good-looking young man, whose spectacles, open face and close-cut hair gave him a surprisingly intellectual look. He was also caring, reliable, serious and methodical. He took Thelma in hand. He taught her basic hygiene. He showed her how to look after the children. He gave her marriage, respectability and a decent home in Exmouth.

He was, alas, too naïve to understand that character is character: that people don't change radically unless they suffer from hysterical instability. He didn't realize that the dream of a louche, egotistical, self-indulgent, deceitful young woman growing up to attain moral responsibility was not going to be fulfilled.

The Halls had two more children. And then Thelma reverted to her bad old ways. The house became filthy and the children were untended. Thelma rediscovered her drug suppliers and did a little dealing herself to support her habit. She compensated for her growing grubbiness by wearing the shortest of skirts to allure men, with whom she casually slept.

Nicholas was a deeply responsible young man. No matter how unhappy he and Thelma might be, the children came first. It's an oddity about men who murder their wives that they often reveal a tightly self-controlled and responsible character under atrocious provocation – until they snap. In their very different ways, educational administrator Leonard Tyburski and truck-driver Joe Lippart were both far more respectable citizens than the light-skirted spouses they murdered. Nicholas Hall carried the pattern still further.

It's a pattern, too, which seems to encourage the wives to behave worse and worse. Certainly Thelma did. She slept with other men without disguising her promiscuity from Nicholas. She taunted him with his sexual inadequacy compared with her casual lovers. And in one final, humiliating episode, she openly took a man in the Cat and Fiddle pub at Clyst St Mary and made love to him in the lavatory, letting Nicholas know this was going on.

Nicholas could take no more. He threw her out of the house. He gave up his job to look after the children full-time − and he did it extremely well. Neighbours noticed at once that the Hall kids were cleaner, better turned out and better tended once Dad took charge of them.

Thelma showed every sign of wanting to go on injuring the ex-spouse who could manage so well without her. Unfortunately, she found allies in the social workers. She went to the social services and demanded their help in recovering custody of the children. The child care authorities are often hideously blinkered in their reaction to fathers taking over the traditionally maternal role. Some of the early child psychology of John Bowlby and Maurice Winnicott can be misused to suggest that mothers should always retain their offspring, even when the children themselves know full well they are better off with their fathers. Thelma looked as though she was about to break up the happy home that Nicholas was straining to keep together.

He became deeply depressed and was given tranquillizers by his doctor. Thelma's true motivation seemed to be a selfish wish to regain the house, which she could only do by presenting herself as the proper custodial parent for the children.

On 15 August 1991 she came round to scream at her husband and insist that she was going to oust him and take the children away. She behaved like a cartoon shrew, hitting him over the head with a frying pan. Nicholas Hall snapped. He picked up a piece of lead pipe and hit her back, battering her across the head. He strangled her with some flex and a piece of webbing. Then he sat crying beside his dead wife until his mother came round in response to neighbours' anxious summons.

'I think I've killed Thelma,' said Nicholas Hall.

At Truro Crown Court in April 1993, Mr Justice Buckley gave Hall three years' probation and released him at once to go back to looking after his children. 'You were goaded beyond anyone's endurance,' he told the defendant, observing that he had been led 'a dog's life'.

The judge knew many people would be surprised that he imposed no heavy custodial sentence for the crime of taking a life. But he willingly accepted Hall's plea of guilty to manslaughter, his responsibility having been diminished by Thelma's misconduct. Hall, said Mr Justice Buckley, had lifted his wife out of the gutter and had been repaid by deliberate and monstrous incitement to jealous rage. And, to his children's delight, Nicholas Hall is again free to do what he does so well: caring for them.

Geza de Kaplany

In the summer of 1962 Dr Geza de Kaplany courted beautiful Hajna Piller — through her mother. For the doctor was Hungarian with old-fashioned aristocratic manners.

Widowed Mrs Piller, another Hungarian, was an absolutely fearful snob. She accepted the doctor's proposal of marriage to her daughter avidly. As a compatriot of vaguely aristocratic lineage and a well-paid anaesthesiologist, de Kaplany was everything she wanted for Hajna. The couple were married early in August. Neither Hajna nor her mother seem to have included in their calculations the fact that the doctor was the most irredeemably odious man in the not very prepossessing upper-class Hungarian emigré community of San Jose, California.

Dr de Kaplany was one of three sons of a supposed baron. Brought up on the family estate in a remote part of Hungary, the boy was almost untouched by the Second World War. The worst suffering of his childhood was caused by his father's autocratic severity. He was blinded in one eye as a result of paternal chastisement, and wore rose-tinted rimless spectacles in adult life to conceal the defect. But this suffering ended after his father's death when the boy was twelve.

Somehow, the family ingratiated themselves with the post-war Communist regime and Geza acquired training as a doctor. But he fled the country after Imre Nogy's ill-fated uprising of 1956 and went to America. He wrote a book of memoirs describing his adventures and escape which other Hungarians perceived as totally phoney.

Indeed, they calculated from the time of Dr de Kaplany's flight that he was among the notorious Communist sympathizers and secret police informants who took to their heels when the brief flowering of democracy allowed mobs to lynch the worst persecutors of the Stalinist regime. Naturally Dr de Kaplany didn't allow any such blemish on his credentials to be known in McCarthyite America.

He was astoundingly arrogant and self-important. He was outraged that his central European qualifications were not instantly acknowledged in the USA, and (like any immigrant doctor) he had to sit state examinations before being allowed to practise. He was distinctly ungrateful when he was permitted to study for the anaesthesiology exams in Boston. The doctor saw himself as a heart specialist and despised anaesthetics as too humble a branch of the profession for a man of his talents.

In Boston, in 1959, he embarked on an American love-life that was to be extensive and consistently revolting. He seduced a Swedish bank clerk named Ruth Krueger. She quickly became pregnant and the doctor took decisive steps to rid himself of the embarrassment.

He told Ruth he could not marry her as he had a wife who was, tragically, incarcerated in an insane asylum and could not be divorced. It was a bare-faced lie. He told Ruth he would provide for her and her unborn child through a valuable insurance policy which he took out, naming her as beneficiary. He encouraged Ruth to go back to Sweden to have her baby, and as soon as she was out of the way, he altered the policy to name his mother and an aircraft engineer friend in Seattle as beneficiaries.

His real and explicit reason for not marrying Ruth (though he did not tell her this!) was that she was too plain for the doctor's refined aesthetic taste. The man wanted formal moral approval for his wickedness, however, and he consulted a Catholic priest in Boston. The good father proved that either he or his Church's

policy was, under duress, only marginally less immoral
than the doctor. He solemnly assured the penitent that it
would be quite wrong for him to make an honest woman
of Ruth Krueger as she was a Protestant! Ruth out of
sight became Ruth out of mind. She was far, far luckier
to be rid of Geza than she could ever have imagined.

Once properly qualified as an American medical
practitioner, de Kaplany accepted the appointment as
anaesthesiologist at San Jose hospital. The west coast was
a fine and hospitable setting where he easily found a
comfortable flat. The doctor's income was handsome. He
had $5,000 deposited in a savings account, the mysterious
origins of which the 'penniless' refugee never explained.
He could now set about one of his life's preferred
activities: pursuing women.

He enjoyed good looks as well as prosperity and status.
In a thin-lipped rather cruel way, the slender, well-
dressed, dark and wavy-haired doctor was handsome.

At the time when he started paying court to Hajna
through her mother, the doctor was actively pursuing, or
more or less terminating, no less than five other
relationships. The most important to him was with a
Protestant Irish divorcee called Yvonne Sinagoglu. She
was extremely beautiful and the doctor repeatedly proposed to her – in person, too, and not through any
relatives. She, equally repeatedly, refused him. This was
not because she detected his detestable qualities, but for
the genuine reason the doctor had so hypocritically used
when his ghostly father in Boston put it to him. She
would not marry a Catholic. The affair began in
November 1961 and came to an end in June 1962.

While avidly courting both Yvonne Sinagoglu *and*
Hajna Piller, the doctor proposed to yet a third woman,
and was accepted! Beautiful Margaretha Herbst was a
nurse at the hospital, and marriages between attractive
nurses and handsome doctors are a familiar part of soap
opera folklore.

Yet the course of this true love was not running

especially smoothly. Margaretha had no idea there were other women in the doctor's life. She was, however, acutely aware that he blew hot and cold to the extent that she started accepting dates with other men. But it was still a complete surprise to her when, two days before his wedding, the doctor told her he was about to marry Hajna. Happy Margaretha, who had kept other, less frayed strings for her bow!

Klara Gabriel was another beautiful nurse at the hospital. She accepted dates with the doctor, but never considered him as a marriage prospect. With cynical honesty, he assured her that if they did marry he would certainly go on sleeping with other women. So she accepted him merely as a casual beau.

Geraldine Smith was less lucky. The twenty-one-year-old hospital clerk went to plays and concerts with the doctor, and accepted dinner invitations. She also accepted his invitation to accompany him on a skiing trip in April 1962. Perhaps she was naïve, but she thought skiing meant skiing. When they reached Yosemite and she discovered that he had booked them into a double cabin and expected to sleep with her, she was shocked and refused (as was her right). The disappointed fornicator immediately packed his bags and walked out on her, leaving the poor girl stranded without the money to continue the holiday on her own or make her way straight home.

Hajna Piller – the name, pronounced 'Hoyna', is presumably the Hungarian form of Hannah – came to America as a teenager under circumstances that made international headlines. During the Melbourne Olympics in 1952, the entire Hungarian fencing team defected *en masse* to the West. Hajna's father was the team coach.

Life in southern California suited Hajna, who was a tall blonde beauty with a creamily tanned complexion. She had been a beauty queen and was a model, often displaying distinctly revealing and sexy clothes, when Dr de Kaplany's whirlwind courtship commenced.

Her acceptance of the doctor (assuming her mother allowed her any say in the matter) seems to have been quite loveless. She already had a lover — another Hungarian who was an engineer. However, he was married, and Hajna slipped quite easily into the apparently fickle commitments of this emigré circle, accepting the doctor's money and status without any intention of giving up her main squeeze.

I don't think the doctor deserved any better. They made a lovely couple at the wedding and it might have been assumed that their life would always be one of glamorous civilized surfaces and coldly self-interested interiors.

But less than three weeks after marrying, de Kaplany went to San Francisco and stayed overnight with Mrs Jane Hajdu. This forty-year-old woman, four years older than the svelte doctor, proceeded to make trouble in a big way. She said she felt a deeply maternal concern for Geza. Perhaps she fancied him. She certainly behaved as though she were consumed with jealousy of the lovely Hajna.

Mrs Hajdu told the doctor about Hajna's engineer lover. The news apparently came as a shock to him and the following day he let Mrs Hajdu take him to see Berkeley attorney Scott Anderson. The newly wed doctor wanted a divorce. He wanted it on grounds of adultery and he didn't want to pay a penny in alimony.

The lawyer told him it couldn't be done. Not right away. He would have to go on living quietly with Hajna while more evidence of adultery than Mrs Hajdu's word was collected. On the other hand, he could start divorce proceedings immediately on grounds of mental cruelty. And he would be assured of unpublicized proceedings and the certainty of being granted his freedom. The doctor loftily refused. Hajna would escape without being severely criticized, and he might still have to pay alimony.

The doctor returned to San Jose immediately with his own plans boiling in his head. The following day, 29 August, hospital workers were a little surprised to see Dr de Kaplany bustling around the place clad only in bermuda shorts, sandals and a rubber apron. True, southern California tolerated a relaxed informality of dress. But snooty Dr Geza de Kaplany did not normally lower his sartorial standards so far.

At 7 p.m. the doctor was back at home. He started playing classical music very loudly on his hi-fi and went to various neighbours apologising for any disturbance. As another resident in the block of flats was playing pop music almost equally loudly, the cacophony was unpleasant. But most of those to whom the doctor spoke were quietly impressed by his courtesy. They also reported that he wore only bermuda shorts and sandals.

At 7.20 p.m., Hajna was seen alive and well, moving around in the flat. After that, she and the doctor made love. Their congress was not a success. It is suggested that the doctor found himself impotent. It is also suggested that Hajna taunted her husband with his failure, comparing him unfavourably with her engineer lover.

The blaring music continued unabated and at 9 p.m. a couple enjoying the last of the evening sun on the patio outside the block of flats became aware that there was an additional sound of constant running water from the de Kaplany residence.

At 10 p.m., a curious undertone of moaning rose to a terrible wailing that pierced the sound of music and water. It continued unabated, attracting a small gathering of anxious listeners on the patio, until at 10.18 p.m. the police drove up. The doctor himself had telephoned the emergency services. He greeted the constables with a self-satisfied smirk. He was still wearing his shorts and sandals and was sweating profusely. At 10.45 p.m. the neighbourhood saw him led away under arrest, now smartly clad in a suit, collar and tie.

The police had found a horrific spectacle. Hajna was

tied, naked, to her bedposts, spread-eagled across the bed. Her face, breasts and genitals were hideously mutilated. After their unsuccessful coupling, the doctor had tied her down and warned her to make no sound if she hoped to survive. Then, donning rubber gloves and his rubber apron, he had taken a scalpel and made small cuts on her face and body. He had a quantity of bottles of acid – nitric, hydrochloric and sulphuric – in the bedroom, and he daubed the acid into the incisions with swabs.

Hajna was slowly and inexorably tortured and defaced. Her moans rose to the piteous keening the neighbours heard. And by the time the police arrived, the acids' corrosion had left nothing but frightful raw wounds and skinless flesh exuding water, where there had once been beauty. The wretched woman survived for two weeks in hospital, before succumbing horribly and grotesquely scarred.

There were fireworks at the doctor's trial the following year. His lawyers wanted him to plead not guilty by reason of insanity – and well they might, given what he had done and expected the police to accept as his prerogative when he telephoned them. But the doctor refused this advice out of hand. He was certainly not insane, he insisted. He knew perfectly well what he was doing and he was entirely justified in doing it. He was deliberately destroying Hajna's beauty so that no other men might ever be tempted and humiliated by it as he had been.

He was a difficult client, arrogantly trying to interfere with the proceedings of the trial from the defence table. He was particularly adamant that the prosecution should not be allowed to show the jury photographs of Hajna's mutilated body. When he was overruled and the photographs were produced, the doctor staged an amazing scene. He stormed across the courtroom, seized the offending pictures and changed his plea after looking at them.

'I am a doctor,' he screamed, 'and if I have done this, then I must be mad!'

So a new line of defence emerged. Dr Geza de Kaplany now claimed to suffer from a split personality. His alter ego was a big, tough Frenchman called Pierre la Roche. It seemed that he had always secretly wanted to be a macho Frenchman. It was suggested that this reflected a suppressed homosexual element in his personality.

It was impossible to find a doctor who could confirm the split personality claim convincingly. The best medical support the doctor received came from a Dr Beaton, who said he suffered from paranoid schizophrenia (delusions of grandeur coupled with a persecution complex) as a result of his father's severities. Two chiropodists also appeared who both confirmed that the doctor had made appointments with them under the name of Pierre la Roche. Why, neither they nor anyone else could explain. Perhaps Dr Geza de Kaplany thought that having his corns cut was so infra dig that he adopted an alias for the purpose.

He was lucky that the jury was impressed by Dr Beaton's evidence. They thought the doctor guilty of murder, of course. But given his possible mental state, they recommended life imprisonment rather than the gas chamber.

Many Californians were disgusted. Geza de Kaplany was obviously one of the most horrible murderers their state had ever seen, and if he wasn't fit to die, who was? There was a lobby ready to demand his continued incarceration for the full term of his natural life when he first became eligible to apply for parole in 1973. They were deeply shocked to discover that he had been secretly released and smuggled out of the country six months earlier, before they could present their case. The parole board lamely explained that he was a special prisoner whose cardiac skills were urgently needed in Taiwan, and so he had been flown out there at the behest of the Taiwanese government. It was a major scandal, and the chairman of the board swiftly resigned 'for personal reasons'. Dr de Kaplany has been practising his skills on the innocent and unsuspecting Taiwanese ever since.

Paul Snider

Dorothy Hoogstratten was a plain, gawky adolescent, with over-large hands. That was her opinion, and it only shows how we all feel threatened by the poised and posed standards of glamour fed to us daily through the camera lens. For Dorothy was, in fact, an exceptionally beautiful girl.

Paul Snider saw this the minute he walked into the Dairy Queen in Vancouver where Dorothy was working behind the counter. He appraised her charms with professional skill and got her telephone number from another waitress.

'That girl could make me a lot of money,' he told a friend. Paul Snider was a pimp. He wasn't particularly successful. He'd been out of town for a year, fearing the vengeance of drug dealers after a burn. He'd passed some of the time in Los Angeles, hoping to break into some of the big money around Hollywood. But Paul Snider's horizons were generally too low and sleazy for him to make a killing in tinseltown. He was back in Vancouver looking for the means to start up again.

He knew at once that Dorothy had more going for her than any ordinary hooker. He probably couldn't have turned her out if he wanted to, anyway. Eighteen-year-old Dorothy was finishing high school. Her ambition was to start working with the telephone company in the autumn. She had worked during the holidays in the Dairy Queen since she was fourteen. Her Dutch immigrant mother was a divorcee who struggled to keep her family – two girls and a boy – on the limited earnings of a part-time nurse. The Hoogstrattens lived in a crowded house

beside a funfair in one of the less desirable neighbourhoods, but they were thoroughly respectable.

Snider was neither stupid nor completely insensitive.
He handled Dorothy with skill and care. He told her she
was beautiful − which was no more than the truth. He
wined her and dined her and impressed her with his street-
smart sophistication. He bought her a gown for her high
school graduation and gave her a topaz and diamond
ring. He subtly established a central place in her life.

He seduced her, of course. He was an experienced and
skilful lover, and to Dorothy, who only knew the hurried
fumblings of high school kids, he seemed Mr Wonderful.

Once he had persuaded her to trust her own good
looks, he had a professional photographer take a set of
portraits of her. They confirmed that she was strikingly
photogenic and even Dorothy was impressed. So Paul
was able to move on to the next phase. He urged her to
have a set of nude pictures taken. Dorothy was less
certain about this. But Paul told her − perfectly
truthfully − that they were essential for the successful
career as a glamour model he had in mind for her. And
when the photographer held the session, he found her
shyly eager to please.

The portfolio was an obvious success. And Paul knew
just where to send it. He dropped the 'Hoog' from
Dorothy's name, and the folder of beautiful pictures
dropped through the mail in the Playboy Mansion West.

What an extraordinary icon of our times *Playboy* is,
and what a curious cultural influence Hugh Hefner has
had! In 1953, when he had his dream of the perfect men's
magazine and assembled the dummy on his kitchen table,
he was entering unexplored and unexploited territory.
Esquire was the most obvious model. Its articles dealt
with sporting, fashionable and modestly intellectual
interests that were assumed to entertain well-bred macho
men. Its reputation for slightly 'naughty' pieces on sex
rested rather heavily on one or two over-reprinted pieces
− 'Latins Make Lousy Lovers' being the best known of

these revelations from the female erotic psyche. Its cheesecake gloat content was restricted to Vargas' cartoons of finely shaded bathing belles: mere drawings of decorously covered cuties.

Esquire's only intellectual competition was the small-format *Lilliput* in England: brilliant general journalism from the outstanding post-war *Picture Post* generation, given cheesecake support by one black-and-white nude every month, the genitals decorously airbrushed away to suggest that women are blessed with a smooth, hairless, undivided, V-shaped pad of plain flesh between the legs.

Hugh Hefner changed the market from top to bottom. Over the next fifteen years, *Playboy* and its imitative rivals cautiously tested the law with ever more revealing poses, until their superbly photographed nudes could be presented fully frontal with pubic hair intact. Hefner forced unwilling authorities to accept his upmarket girlie magazine by paying huge fees to attract major writers. The regular in-depth *Playboy Interviews* are a genuine journalistic contribution to contemporary history. And for the first few years, the '*Playboy* Philosophy' was laboriously unwound in a series of more or less turgid essays by the publisher, urging liberalism in most things, but especially sexual ethics.

Twenty years after Hefner's original pilot, his courage and enterprise had made him a millionaire. His pioneering journalism had led to quite respectable women's magazines discussing masturbation, while Scandinavian pornography offered good colour photos of quite attractive people, sometimes doing quite entertaining things. But in the process, Hugh Hefner felt he had to live the *Playboy* Philosophy. And thus, as has been said, he turned his whole life into one long fantasy.

His magazine proudly described his huge circular bed; his private jet with its own bed and sunken bath; his Playboy Mansion with its vast garden and exciting jacuzzi areas for mass skinny-dipping; his astounding parties which, readers might infer, made Roman orgies look like Sunday school picnics.

Inevitably, as the absolutely essential accessory, he was surrounded by beautiful girls. The ideal 'Playboy' might supposedly evince exquisite taste, high intelligence and classy accoutrements (though Hefner was always content to ramble through his kingdom in battered jeans with an old pipe in one hand and a can of Pepsi in the other) but the whole fantasy really depended on his having girls at his beck and call, as an educated man needs books eternally at hand.

Three girls to every man was the ratio Hefner favoured for his entourage. And the girls must be young and beautiful. His empire offered constant work for the lovelies as over-worked cocktail waitresses − dressed in ridiculous bathing-costume uniforms with fluffy tails and satin ears, teetering on foot-pinching, crippling stiletto heels − to serve customers who could ogle but not touch the 'bunnies'.

Every month the magazine printed three portfolios of nude photographs, the girl chosen for the centrefold being designated 'Playmate of the Month'. Annually, the award 'Playmate of the Year' was given to the best of the twelve. There was always the suggestion that this would lead to a glamorous career in fashion modelling or even the movies. Yet this, alas, never seemed to happen. Just as the bunnies were no more than very beautiful girls doing uncomfortable menial work under the pretext that it was glamorous, so the succession of Playmates rose in the magazine's pages, only to sink without trace when continuing careers were attempted. Acting, even in Hollywood, demands some talent for moving and speaking lines with conviction. Photogenic beauty on its own is not enough. 'The profession,' as Noël Coward told Mrs Worthington, 'is overcrowded and the going's very tough.'

The *Playboy* executives were delighted with Dorothy's portfolio. She had the classic tall, blonde, blue-eyed look Hefner preferred. She was summoned to the Playboy

Mansion West in Los Angeles for further trial pictures.

So, in 1978, Dorothy made her first aeroplane journey. Paul went with her as her manager, her support, her adviser and she was grateful to him. At nineteen she was still shy and sheltered. Paul's flashy swagger still had the air of sophistication in her eyes.

Moreover, she detected that he really cared for her. Indeed, the grubby little peddler of female flesh was coming to feel more for Dorothy than a sensible pimp feels for the merchandise. It would prove death to both of them that Paul Snider did one of the most innocent things in his squalid life: fell in love with a beautiful girl he had helped in her career.

At the Playboy Mansion the executives were all over Dorothy. Test pictures taken by their specialists were sensational and led to screen tests. And these confirmed what the stills suggested. Dorothy was the answer to a would-be intellectual, soft-core pornographer's prayer. She was the model who could definitely go further than showing off her smooth and curvy breasts and bottom in their glossy pages. She could really hope to go into the movies. Without hesitation, the executives agreed they were looking at 'the new Marilyn Monroe'.

This wasn't essentially a question of looks or even figure. Dorothy had to lean forward to make her bust look markedly full; her narrow hips and flat little bottom needed careful photography to elongate her legs instead of presenting a marked absence of the popular jutty butt. She could never emulate Marilyn's famous jiggling walk, so admired from behind.

But that wasn't the point. Even Norma-Jean Baker didn't look strikingly like the character 'Marilyn Monroe' until makeup artists and hairdressers had finished working her over, and her costumiers had literally sewn her into figure-hugging dresses. What made 'Marilyn' special was her extraordinary capacity to radiate vibrant and irresistible sexuality, overlaid with a completely plausible, naïve, dewy-eyed, little-girl unawareness of what the fuss was all about. And Dorothy Stratten had that same quality. Still photographs suggested it; moving film confirmed it.

She was welcomed into the mansion. She was made at home by Hugh Hefner. And she was groomed to be the Playmate of 1980, and launched into the spectacular career which should prove that twenty-seven years of talent spotting had finally picked a winner who could last more than a year or two.

Paul accompanied her and he loved what he found. The Playboy Mansion stank of money and self-indulgence and sex — the things Paul Snider lived for. But he was aware, too, that Dorothy was not entirely at ease with her new surroundings. Sooner or later the dark underside of Hefner's libertarian paradise would become clear. Dorothy would find that the girls had to be sexually available to at least some of the men some of the time if they wanted to stay on in the luxury surroundings. Whatever else could be the point of providing each man with the choice of at least three partners?

Paul had no prudish or selfish anxiety to keep Dorothy as his exclusive possession, but he was deeply fond of the girl who had brought him into this ambience, and he wanted her to be spared shocking or uncomfortable experiences. He advised her how to fend off unwanted advances and set her on the path to sophisticated self-controlled success.

They took a house off Santa Monica Boulevard while Dorothy prepared for her exposure as 'Playmate of the Month' in August 1979. She worked as a cocktail bunny at the Los Angeles Playboy Club. Paul kept her well away from the generally sleazy activities that earned his daily bread. He urged her not to smoke and drink. He talked of their 'lifetime bargain' together. And shortly before Dorothy's naked charms were spread across the centrefold, he married her.

Playboy was not pleased. Bunnies and Playmates were supposed to be single and available. They might have boyfriends in their private lives, but for public purposes they should just be enjoying a good time. The peculiar ethos of the Playboy world dictated that bunnies were chaperoned and could not make dates with the customers. It was a look-don't-touch scene in which real, live girls were to be reduced to masturbatory fantasy objects in men's minds, and forcibly kept out of their arms where true relationships might develop.

Paul soon found he was not wanted by the Hefner entourage. The Mansion didn't like husbands and boyfriends at the best of times. If the purpose of littering the place with lovelies was to suggest that the happy men within its walls had been admitted to a Polygamist's Paradise, the illusion would be sadly blemished should one of the beauties declare her exclusive attachment to one man. Hefner and his key aides suffered considerable angst when they occasionally found themselves in competition for a particularly desirable Playmate. All the men in the Mansion were supposed to be equally desirable to all the women.

Paul Snider was especially unwanted. He was a crude little pimp. His intellectual pretensions were nil. But he was smart enough to be unimpressed by the mere pretension to intellectual sophistication camouflaging the blatant materialism and lechery of Playboy Mansion's inmates. He didn't disguise his own sexual appetites and his own pandering to other men's lust, and he saw through the ridiculous pretence that *Playboy* purveyed a different commodity to a different appetite. He made the Hefner entourage feel phoney because they were phoney. He made them feel ashamed of being what they were because he was unashamed of being the same thing. He had to go.

His activities, away from Dorothy, seemed to justify his expulsion. Paul organized wet T-shirt competitions and male strip shows: the real grunge end of the sex market. The *Playboy* Philosophy pretended that the magazine wasn't really in that market at all.

'But he cares for me so much,' Dorothy told puzzled friends. 'I can't even imagine myself being with any other man but Paul.' And Paul certainly didn't want to be with any other woman but Dorothy. Unfortunately, his vulgar ways of showing this provided ammunition to those who whispered in her ear that he was only interested in her as a meal ticket. He decorated the house with her photographs, as though she were his prime possession. He boasted that the two of them were 'on a rocket ship to the moon'. He bought a Mercedes with vanity plates reading STAR-80 in celebration of her forthcoming Playmate of the Year title. And as he worried increasingly that she was growing away from him, he urged her ever more strongly to bind herself into contracts that would assure him of half her earnings for life.

Dorothy reached the age of 21, achieved her splashed prominence as Playmate of the Year, and felt the need to make adult decisions all much at the same time. Paul was not invited to be at her side for the star Playmate's grooming and run-up in television appearances. But from among the sophisticated men who were persona grata with Hefner and his status-conscious court, she attracted the attention of film director Peter Bogdanovich.

The maker of the sensitive and moving *The Last Picture Show* was also a man who could lose his heart totally to beautiful young women. He had become besotted with Cybill Shepherd when he starred her in the film that made them both. He was in the dismal state of playing the field after an unhappy divorce at the time when he met Dorothy. Hence his frequent presence at the Playboy Mansion. He instantly saw Dorothy's potential and he fell for her as heavily as he had done for Cybill.

He also had something to offer. He could feature her in a big film. He cast her with Audrey Hepburn and Ben Gazzara for the comedy *They All Laughed*. From a business point of view, Dorothy no longer needed Paul. She had $20,000 and a car as Playmate of the Year. She had an agent and a manager with the necessary skills to keep her career afloat in Hollywood. She had the proud support and friendship of Hugh Hefner, genuinely delighted to see one of his girls making good for herself and for his reputation. She had Bogdanovich at her side, offering everything Paul had promised, and good taste as well. She left Paul in March to go to New York where filming was to start.

In May the Sniders both took a break and met up at a hotel in their home town of Vancouver. They sensed that their union was not going to last and both cried. But Dorothy nevertheless went back to an interview with *Maclean*'s magazine in which she said of Paul, 'He's still got my heart.'

Despite this, she closed their joint bank accounts and started proceedings for a legal separation. Paul hired a private detective called Marv Goldstein to watch Dorothy and Bogdanovich. He found a seventeen-year-old called Patti who seemed to him reminiscent of Dorothy, and he started desperately trying to promote her career. He learned that Dorothy and Bogdanovich had enjoyed a holiday in London together. He see-sawed between elation and despair because although Dorothy returned to the west coast, it was to live in Bogdanovich's house. Dorothy came round to see Paul and told him she was in love and he could give her clothes to Patti.

Marv Goldstein liked Paul Snider and he was worried by the distress his client was suffering. Like Snider, Marv feared that Bogdanovich's expensive lawyers would be turned loose to prise Paul away from any share of the wealth to which his enterprise had led Dorothy. Like Snider, he believed that Dorothy was far too good-natured to want him screwed in an unjust settlement. But Goldstein was disturbed when Snider declared his fear of violent housebreakers and bought a shotgun.

They were both right about Dorothy's good nature. It was stressed by everyone who knew her. Her screen tests told an essential truth about her as well. Dorothy really was too innocent, too naïve, to comprehend the deep and intense passions her physique provoked. She really loved the men she loved as men with minds and affections. She had no idea that her overwhelming beauty could drive them to possessive lust that contaminated their own intuitive response to her lovely personality. She had lifted Paul Snider from sordid poncing on women's flesh to love for her as a human being. But by so doing she had set him on a track of jealous, possessive competition with Peter Bogdanovich that would kill the Sniders and scar Peter.

On 15 August 1980, Dorothy arranged to go and see Paul. They needed to talk about money — after all, they were tied by agreements that could not continue if Dorothy was to operate as an independent actress, or as a future Mrs Bogdanovich. She also wanted to explain to Paul her love for Peter, and try and make everything all right. She did not tell Peter where she was going. He would only have wanted to come and interfere and put her case for her. And Dorothy wanted to be quite fair to Paul for whom she still felt grateful affection.

Nobody knows what was said when she arrived. Nobody knows how the tender separation conference exploded into a horror of cruel, jealous possession. We only know that the evidence in the room showed that at some point Paul forced Dorothy into a bondage rack; raped and sodomized her brutally; shot her, and abused the corpse all over again. Finally Paul Snider blew his own brains out.

The terrible tragedy didn't end there. *Playboy* and the devastated Bogdanovich excoriated Paul Snider — the beastly little pimp who destroyed his beautiful possession as soon as she grew up and grew away from him. History is written by the survivors, so it won't be easy to win favour for the view that Paul's final ghastly cruelty was a result of his being lifted above the gutter where Dorothy found him (and he thought he found her) — a gutter where the passions of avarice and lust ruled supreme. The

Playboy crowd's indignation with Paul Snider rather transparently redirects attention from their own role in encouraging Dorothy's pursuit of 'the bitch goddess success' at the expense of her own natural loyalty.

Peter Bogdanovich came to see this clearly. He stopped filming for some time and devoted his attention to Dorothy's mother and sister. He wrote a moving book in memory of Dorothy in which his loathing and contempt for Paul Snider were understandable. He, too, came to perceive the links between *Playboy*'s perfect-mannered pornography and Snider's putrid pimping. He launched a ferocious attack on Hugh Hefner, whom he accused of seducing Dorothy in the jacuzzi on her first night in the Playboy Mansion.

But, unhappily, Bogdanovich revealed the extent to which he was equally at the mercy of external appearances. He began courting Dorothy's younger sister Louise, saying how much she reminded him of Dorothy, and in 1989 he married her − after making her undergo *plastic surgery* to make her look more like Dorothy!

Eliminating Rivals

'Wherefore hast thou despised the commandment of
the Lord, to do evil in his sight? thou hast killed
Uriah the Hittite with the sword, and hast taken his
wife to be thy wife.'

2 Samuel xii, 9

Harry Kendall Thaw

It's a cliché of masculine self-pity that young women can capitalize on rich, successful, older men's lust for them. Like all clichés, it is obviously true. The straightforward honourable man enslaved to a calculating gold-digger is a sad spectacle.

Yet there's a downside for the woman too — and it's not just having flaccid muscles and a beer belly to hug, instead of taut flesh.

Anyone under twenty-five is likely to have gained only a camouflaging veneer of sophistication. The jaw-splitting yawns of boredom that must have accompanied Christine Keeler's and Mandy Rice-Davies's attempts to stay awake through serious adult conversations about politics or business among Lord Astor's set, or Peter Rachman's associates, can all too easily be imagined.

Yet the woman may well feel that her intimate knowledge of 'great men's' uniform absurdity, when driven by desire for her, gives her power that outweighs her ignorance and inexperience. She may set out to use that power consciously, greatly extending the range of manipulative tricks that started when she wriggled on her daddy's knee as a toddler and learned a fetching winsomeness.

The really unlucky pseudo-sophisticated girl may find she has a tiger by the tail. If she heightens her sugar-daddy's passion by making him jealous, she may stir up serious trouble. If he is mentally unbalanced, she certainly will. That's what Evelyn Nesbit seems to have done.

* * *

Evelyn came from Pittsburgh, Pennsylvania. She was
born on Christmas Day 1884, the daughter of a lawyer
who fell on hard times and died when she was twelve.
Evelyn found herself forced to contribute to the family
budget. Unfortunately, the work her mother found for
her in Philadelphia was as a model.

There are two contradictory points to make about this.
The term 'model' was not, in those days, a euphemism
for prostitute. Evelyn posed as a charming young girl for
sentimental chocolate-boxy portraits. She was fully and
fluffily dressed, softly lit, softly focused, softly simper-
ing. On the other hand, the occupation of 'artist's model'
was regarded by most Victorians as entirely disreputable.
It could entail undressing in the presence of strange men.
It was the first step to ruin. In 1896, when Evelyn began
to smirk demurely at cameras, there were those who felt
she had entered an immodest profession.

When many young people discover that activities their
elders call shady don't really feel like dipping one toe into
the flames of hell, they are apt to conclude that those
virtuous elders are silly fuddy-duddies and experienced
old libertines are the really wise members of the older
generation. This seems to have happened to Evelyn.

In 1899 or 1900 she went to New York, still working as
a model. And in great big Sin City she met a very
experienced libertine who was forever widening his
acquaintance with pretty young models and chorus girls.

If you want to know what Stanford White looked like,
picture to yourself the most villainous of village squires
harbouring the basest desires you can imagine. Think of
Baron Hardup leading the broker's men to oust poor
Jack's mother in the pantomime. Give him heavy black
curling moustachios; heavy black leering eyebrows;
gleaming pomaded black hair; expensive, well-buttoned
clothes; jewelled rings and a stickpin and watchfob and
chain; all on a powerful, threatening 250 lb frame. *That's*
Stanford White.

He was forty-seven years old in 1900. He was descended from an old New York mercantile family, American since the 1630s. He was an immensely successful architect and a millionaire several times over. He had designed the Metropolitan Club and the University Club in New York University and the University of Virginia. He put the plinth under the statue of Lincoln in Washington DC. He built Mrs William K. Vanderbilt's Newport mansion, the Marble House − a piece of late-Victorianism so lavish that the proud owner placed the architect's bust in the hall, under the impression that all this Italianate gilt and onyx was high art.

He also built Madison Square Gardens on the corner of Fifth Avenue and Broadway. The complex included a restaurant, shops, an arcade, an amphitheatre for prize fights and horse shows, a tower block where White reserved a spacious apartment for his own use, and the famous roof garden, where open-air diners could watch operettas and musical comedies.

White wanted that apartment in the heart of theatre-land, among the chorus girls, because he was a dirty old man. Don't take my word for it. Hear the posthumous praise showered on him by theatre manager George Lederer: 'He was a persistent first-nighter, and liked pretty girls' . . . 'Now, Mr White was a great "rounder" . . . he was a man who always liked to talk to pretty girls and to be with them.'

Do you now believe Mr Lederer's further assertion, 'I think that throughout, his friendship [with Evelyn] . . . was entirely platonic'? Or his statement, 'I am firmly convinced that his friendship . . . grew out of sheer good-heartedness'?

And what about the staid *New York Times*, floundering with this transparent stage-door Johnny, in the words, 'Mr White was greatly interested in the stage, and was one of a group of men, young and old, who frequently were seen about the theatres where musical comedies were playing and at restaurants and other places

with actresses . . . He had befriended many young
actresses, helping them to better themselves in their
profession.'

He helped them professionally all right. He could get
them into bigger and better shows, *if* they made a
professional decision to spend a few nights in his
apartment − and sit in his red velvet swing and enjoy
being swung up to the ceiling. That way Mr Stanford
White could open his erotic entertainment by recreating
Watteau's painting, enjoying an eyeful of thighs and
knickers flashing out under their billowing skirts.

Evelyn Nesbit was probably fifteen − certainly not
more than sixteen − when she met Mr Stanford White.
She modelled for his photographs. At first she was perky
and demure, with her rich dark hair dressed carefully
upon her head; then increasingly exotic and alluring,
tumbled on bearskins in Oriental robes, or turning up
lustrous eyes between her free-falling locks and naked
shoulders.

Evelyn Nesbit was probably fifteen − not more than
sixteen − when she sat in Mr Stanford White's swing and
graduated by a natural progression into Mr Stanford
White's well-used bed. And thus she started to learn her
profession.

She wanted to be an actress, or so she told Mr White.
She was good looking and lively. He got her into the
chorus of *Floradora*, the famous musical which opened in
November 1900 and ran for a record-breaking two years.

Evelyn wanted to rise higher in her profession. In 1902
she graduated from the chorus sextette to a lead role. In
The Wild Rose, she was the eponymous Gypsy Rose.
That was a piece of *very* professional casting. Shortly
before the curtain went up on the first night, Evelyn
Nesbit's name appeared as co-respondent in a divorce
petition brought by the wife of the show's producer −
George Lederer.

While the show ran, Evelyn enjoyed an impassioned
affair with the younger brother of the leading Broadway

duo, Ethel and Lionel Barrymore. She may or may not have anticipated that their brother John, whose stage career started a year later than hers, would outshine them both for a time. But in her main career as a courtesan – looking to the bedroom to advance her socially until marriage to a rich man brought security – it was certainly worth getting almost any association with the family who dominated American theatre.

To be fair, though, Evelyn may have calculated the probable commercial and social advantages every time she joined a man in bed, but one can believe that she had a lovely time with handsome young Barrymore in the years before the bottle became his first passion.

Early in 1903, Evelyn went into a private hospital for an operation. She later swore she had her appendix removed but you can come to your own conclusions . . . In June, Evelyn and her mother went on holiday to Europe. They went to Paris, Boulogne, Paris again, and London. There Mrs Nesbit stayed, while Evelyn took a side trip via Folkestone to Amsterdam, Munich and the Austrian Tyrol. From the Tyrol she went to Switzerland and by the time she returned to London, her mamma had already sailed for New York. Evelyn followed her, and swore out an extremely sinister affidavit against the man who had invited her, accompanied her and paid for the entire trip – Harry Kendall Thaw.

Thaw was just twelve years older than Evelyn and still a very good-looking young man. Clean-shaven, powerfully built, with a smooth complexion and a boyish face, he was totally dissimilar to the raffish Stanford White – in appearance. In practice he had a record of hell-raising that made White look like a Salvation Army missioner among the chorus girls. But since he didn't actually look a dirty old man, Evelyn was favourably impressed. It would be five years before several people, including Harry Thaw, saw a distinct advantage in airing just how more-than-raffishly he had sown his vicious wild oats. And they may have exaggerated. I think it likely that

Evelyn went off with Thaw under the impression that he was a sexy young buck, like her friend John Barrymore. And with the further advantage that he had lots of money — lots and lots.

Like Evelyn, Thaw came from Pittsburgh, where his father had made an immense fortune of $40 million as a coke merchant. The elder Thaw gave his son an expensive education, but disapproved of Harry's assumption that Harvard was essentially a super-high-stakes poker school. He cut the young man's allowance to a generous $2,000 a year. Thaw's silly and doting mother quietly upped it to $8,000, and for the rest of her life, poured out millions to keep her son in the state of dissipated extravagance to which he was accustomed.

Thaw travelled to Paris and Boulogne with Evelyn and Mrs Nesbit, leaving them for a couple of weeks while he went on to London. When they joined him there, they stayed at Claridge's, while he was in the Carlton Hotel. And then, while Mrs Nesbit stayed in London, Evelyn made the rest of her continental tour in Thaw's company, the pair passing themselves off as Mr and Mrs Dellis.

Evelyn said she was ill until she and Thaw ditched Mrs Nesbit and started off on their pseudo-marital own. Presumably she was getting over her operation. Presumably that was why Mrs Nesbit's chaperonage was tolerated for so many weeks. Presumably Evelyn, the former mistress of Stanford White and lover of John Barrymore, had never doubted that some little *quid pro quo* would be demanded for this expensive European holiday. But she certainly did not expect what happened when they reached the isolated Schloss Katzenstein in the Tyrol, where Thaw had rented the entire castle and Evelyn, like the heroine of some Gothic novel, never went out and never saw anybody except three old servants.

In her own words, after breakfast on the first morning:

Thaw said he wished to tell me something, and asked me to step into my bedroom. I entered the room, when the said Thaw, without any provocation, grasped me by the throat and tore the bathrobe from my body, leaving me entirely nude except for my slippers. I saw by his face that the said Thaw was in a terrific, excited condition, and I was terrorized. His eyes were glaring, and he had in his right hand a cowhide whip. He seized hold of me and threw me on the bed. I was powerless and attempted to scream, but the said Thaw placed his fingers in my mouth and tried to choke me. He then, without any provocation and without the slightest reason, began to inflict on me several severe and violent blows with the cowhide whip. So brutally did he assault me that my skin was cut and bruised. I besought him to desist, but he refused. I was so exhausted that I shouted and cried. He stopped every minute or so to rest, and then renewed his attack upon me, which he continued for about seven minutes.

He acted like a demented man. I was absolutely in fear of my life; the servants could not hear my outcries.

In Switzerland, a very similar beating with a rattan cane took place in the Hotel Schweitzerhof. And on almost any pretext throughout the journey, Thaw would seize the opportunity to lambast his pretty companion.

Finally she learned the reason. In their hotel room she came across a hypodermic syringe and some pills. Harry Thaw was a drug-crazed cocaine addict!

Now this story sounds extraordinary, and one part of the affidavit in which it occurs is, in my opinion, false. For Evelyn claimed:

During this entire period, while I was in this condition of non-resistance, Thaw entered my bed and without my consent repeatedly wronged me. I reproved the said Thaw for his conduct, but he compelled me to submit thereto, threatening to beat and kill me if I did not do so.

That Harry Thaw was capable of violating almost anybody with a combination of threats and force is certainly true. But I cannot believe that innocent Evelyn let him take her on a long continental holiday without fully expecting to be 'wronged' over and over again. Nor can I believe in any reproof more serious than a 'Harry, you're hurting me!' if Thaw was a clumsy lover.

And most damning of all, why, if all this tale of horrible sadism is true, *why* did Evelyn Nesbit *marry* this brute two years later? Obviously we've already answered that — for his money. She was making her career on her back, and such careers climax best at the altar.

So why, then, did she put their relationship at risk by making all these accusations against him? It's difficult to be certain, because of the conflicting characters involved.

By Evelyn's account the first person she approached for help on arriving back in New York was Stanford White. And he took her to the lawyer who had her swear out the affidavit. The lawyer was the most infamous shyster ever to practise at the New York bar: an unscrupulous rogue who makes our own crooked solicitor, Arthur Newton, look as harmless as a Citizens' Advice Bureau.

Abraham Hummel was an ugly little man. In the 1860s he went to work as law clerk for an immigrant advocate named William F. Howe. Howe had begun his career in medicine in England, until he was struck off as an abortionist. In New York he shone as a golden-voiced, phoney, sentimental, rhetorical courtroom pleader. His unscrupulous concern was to win cases, regardless of injustice or his client's guilt. Abe Hummel proved such a perfect clerk that he soon rose to be Howe's partner. Hummel did not have the impressive appearance and thespian talent to move juries' hearts. But he did have a cold and astute eye for loopholes in the law. He would get prosecutors to accept guilty pleas for crimes that weren't

on the statute book; he would note when penalties were in
abeyance pending changes of the law. And he would join
Howe in making villainous clients as histrionic as their
advocate: swathing them in bandages to enact serious and
mind-confusing after-effects of concussion. He once had
a man pretend to be mute throughout his proceedings.
Howe and Hummel even published a do-it-yourself
textbook on committing crimes (they pretended it was a
warning to suckers visiting New York). It wasn't so much
that they wanted to coach criminals, rather they wanted
criminals to know their name and use their firm when in
trouble — and it worked. For a partnership in a
profession that was prohibited from advertising (let alone
to the criminal fraternity), it was a great way of reaching
their target market.

If Abe Hummel had been Evelyn's sole adviser in
swearing out this affidavit against Harry Thaw, I'd put
the whole thing down to only one motive — blackmail.
Especially as Abe Hummel made a point of contacting
Thaw's lawyer and warning him that Evelyn was under-
age and his client was in danger of being charged with
statutory rape or corrupting a minor. This wasn't true.
Evelyn was nineteen and had certainly been corrupted
some years before by Stanford White.

However, it was Stanford White who introduced her to
Abe Hummel and White certainly never dreamed of
blackmailing Harry Thaw. White was a millionaire in his
own right and a gentleman, albeit a lecherous one. He
despised Thaw as a rowdy upstart from a new-money
family, and he would have treated with contempt any
suggestion that he would rattle the skeletons in Thaw's
Tyrolean closet to extort money from him.

According to Evelyn, White promised to help her get
rid of Thaw's unwelcome advances. To that end, he took
her to see Hummel, whose office was studded with
pictures of Broadway stars whose divorces he had
negotiated.

Of course, once the affair was in that shark's hands, he

used the information to try and soak Harry Thaw in any way possible. A threat of a nasty court case should lead at worst to a handy settlement out of court. At best, silver-tongued Howe might pick up massive fees for the firm in return for a tear-stained performance portraying Evelyn's brutal treatment to a sickened jury. Only it never happened. There never was a civil suit of Nesbit v. Thaw. There never was a discreet settlement with hush-money paid over. Abe Hummel drafted the potentially lucrative blackmailing affidavit, collected his fee from Stanford White, and dropped silently out of the picture. What on earth was going on?

In the light of all that followed, I can see only one reasonable explanation of these machinations. Evelyn had been building her career under Mr White's lascivious 'protection'. But she had become street-smart enough to see that White would never marry her. He was already married, and although he normally lived apart from Mrs White, he was quite content to remain her formal legal spouse while he disported himself freely among the pretty chorus girls.

Harry Thaw, by contrast, was younger, richer and more naïve than Stanford White. Evelyn thought she could persuade him into holy wedlock if they enjoyed a sustained period of unholy bedlock in Europe. Only it turned out that Mr Thaw's tastes were unacceptably sadistic and, one suspects, he was not quite so green as he was cabbage-looking, and he did not instantly accede to the notion of spending his money on matrimony.

So Evelyn urgently needed to return to the shelter of Stanford White's sheets and the security of his velvet swing. She could best do this with a story of Thaw's forcing himself on her and maintaining his hold by brutal beatings. If it weren't for Harry Thaw's future conduct, one could really feel that Evelyn and Hummel made up the whole story between them. The infamous affidavit also contains another passage of lies which suggests that both gold-digger and lawyer were still interested in gouging Mr White, in their various ways:

> I have repeatedly been told by the said Thaw that he
> is very inimical to a married man, whom, he said, he
> wanted me to injure, and that he, Thaw, would get
> him into the penitentiary; and the said Thaw has
> begged me time and again to swear to written
> documents which he had prepared, involving this
> married man and charging him with drugging me
> and having betrayed me when I was fifteen years of
> age. This was not so; and so I told him, but because
> I refused to sign these papers, the said Thaw not
> only threatened me with bodily injury, but inflicted
> on me the great bodily injury I have herein
> described.

Now this is all a serious covert threat to Stanford White.
He was the married man who certainly had seduced
Evelyn when she was fifteen. He was therefore the
criminal who would face a stretch in the penitentiary if
the matter came to court. The drugs are probably the
melodramatic invention of Hummel and Nesbit. But
Evelyn, though dutifully denying the seduction at this
point, would no doubt have sworn it was true later if
necessary. (Indeed, she was to do just that after Stanford
White was dead.) Hummel had a useful headlock on
Stanford White with this under his belt.

Why would Evelyn Nesbit swear out something so
dangerous to White when, under his protection again,
and on his advice, she had sought legal assistance?
Obviously because she had used Harry Thaw's alleged
hostility to White as a means to enlist White's sympathy
and support. Whether Harry Thaw really cared tuppence-
ha'penny about Stanford White at this point in time we
may never know. Evelyn was such a liar that her story at
any given moment in her life was just whatever suited her
needs. In 1903, it was advantageous to crawl back to
White, sobbing, 'That horrid Mr Thaw promised me a

nice convalescent holiday in Europe and — you know what? He raped me and he beat me and he wants to damage *you*! He wanted me to charge you with assaulting a minor!'

And so White went to the most devious lawyer available to have this danger removed. The affidavit was sworn out. A copy sent to Thaw's lawyers should scare Thaw off threatening White, for fear of having his own perversions exposed. While from Evelyn and Hummel's standpoint it was a permanent warning to Stanford White that Evelyn had the goods on him, too.

Evelyn went back under Mr White's protection. She was obviously quite a charmer, worming her way into a man's affections as she needed him. Yet she was one of the most dangerous women I've ever heard of, manipulating her lovers into hostile postures from which she could control them the more easily.

Whatever Harry Thaw felt about Stanford White prior to 1903, he would certainly have feared and hated him as soon as he read the affidavit, composed with White's approval, and containing the self-serving and lying exoneration of White at its conclusion. However much Stanford White disregarded and despised Harry Thaw prior to 1903, he would have felt personal fear and loathing after learning that the younger man supposedly wanted to have him jailed for seducing a minor.

Evelyn had successfully set two dogs growling at each other over their interest in her heat. She had created jealousy, where no hostility need have existed previously.

Then, in April 1905, Evelyn ceased to be Stanford White's mistress and became Mrs Harry Thaw. The marriage was unwelcome to Thaw's upper-crust family. His sisters had married well, after the manner of American heiresses. Alice was the Countess of Yarmouth; Margaret had married millionaire philanthropist Andrew Carnegie's nephew George. Now Harry had hitched himself to a chorus girl. And one from the wrong side of his own hometown's tracks at that! It was really a very decisive move on his part. But then, Harry had always given decisive way to mad impulses.

What really were everybody's feelings at this point? Evelyn gave quite contradictory accounts at different stages of her life, each tailored to suit the temporary image she wanted to present. Thus she would claim in 1906 that she feared and disliked White, who had lured her into his apartment with the promise of marriage, disabled her with drugged champagne and raped her. By this story, Harry Thaw was the knight in shining armour who rescued her from wicked old Sir Jasper.

But in 1934 she asserted that she had felt a possessive love for the architect, writing (or having ghost-written for her), 'when I came across a birthday book in which he had recorded the birthday of every pretty girl he knew, I became violently jealous . . . Like a silly child, I wanted to make him jealous of me.'

Evelyn's multifarious accounts of her doings often serve to confuse her marriage with her trip to Europe. Many writers have insisted that she was nineteen at the time of her wedding, and the European trip was her honeymoon. But if the affidavit stated her age correctly, she was twenty-two by the time she married. And the affidavit had every reason to underestimate her age if possible, since it falsely accused Thaw of rending her under-age maidenhead.

Her reasons for wanting to mix up honeymoon travel with her actual trip are obvious. She would not appear in such a sympathetic light if she confessed to going on a long European trip with Thaw, passing herself off as Mrs Dellis, while she was still prepared to return to Stanford White. We can only make educated guesses at Evelyn's real motivation if we always ask what she stood to gain by whatever she said or did.

In marrying Harry Thaw she gained overt respectability and the security of his family wealth. She lost the advantage of a sensible man-of-the-world as her lover, however. Her husband was, as she knew, an unstable unpredictable sadist capable of mad rages.

By Evelyn's subsequent accounts, his obsession with Stanford White dominated his relations with her, and he beat her until she confessed to having been raped by the architect, whereupon his rage was turned onto White. But she tries to mix these beatings with those that had taken place in Austria and Switzerland. And Thaw had already received at least a pretty big hint of Evelyn's relations with White in the affidavit. Isn't it far more likely that she used the excuse that White had drugged and ravished her to explain her return to his protection (and Hummel's advice) after she had 'enjoyed' the sado-masochistic continental holiday? She certainly had some explaining to do before she could marry the man against whom she had sworn out that affidavit. And the easiest lie would be 'It's all Stanford's fault. He *made* me do it, like he *made* me do everything else.'

This, coupled with the affidavit, would explain Thaw's growing obsession with Stanford White. It was never disputed that Thaw made Evelyn go over and over her sufferings in the apartment with the velvet swing. It was agreed that he insisted that White should only be referred to as 'The Beast' or 'The Bastard' or 'The B' (which raises another small question about what Evelyn told her husband . . . but we'll come to that later). There is no doubt at all that Harry Kendall Thaw did develop an insane obsession with Stanford White. For on 25 June 1906, he murdered him.

That evening, the two raffish millionaires prepared to spend rather similar evenings on the town. Both went to Rector's Restaurant on Times Square before going on to the theatre. Rector's had a discreetly disreputable reputation. While great actresses patronized the place after Broadway performances, it was also a hang-out for up-market courtesans who identified themselves by wearing décolleté gowns. Rector's offered private rooms in addition to its main dining room, and as Mr and Mrs Thaw seated themselves with two friends for dinner,

Evelyn spotted Stanford White and a small party emerging from one of them. She quickly passed Harry a note reading, 'The B. is here,' as he had ordered her to do whenever she saw Stanford White.

Thaw stiffened; then relaxed, patted his wife's hand, and said, 'Yes, dear. I know he's here. I saw him. Thank you for telling me.'

White was in the middle of a more varied evening's entertainment. He had taken his son Lawrence and one of his Harvard friends to dinner at another expensive, but dubious restaurant, Martin's Café between Broadway and Fifth Avenue, where risqué illustrated Parisian magazines were stocked for the delectation of diners, and an upper foyer accommodated unaccompanied 'ladies' who hoped to be invited to impromptu 'parties' in the private rooms. The three had not sampled the upstairs wares after eating, but went on to the New Amsterdam Aerial Roof Garden, where Lawrence and his friend wanted to see the George M. Cohan play *The Governor's Son*. White declined to join them, and history does not relate exactly who accompanied him to the private room in Rector's and what went on behind its closed doors, nor where he went while the Thaws finished their meal.

It was not until 10.55 p.m. that Stanford White arrived at the Madison Square Roof Garden, where the new musical *Mam'zelle Champagne* was opening. The Thaws had been there throughout the performance. Harry had seated himself beside Stanford White's brother-in-law, James Clinch Smith, and engaged in animated conversation on the stock market, the companionship of pretty girls, ocean liner travel, and the play they were supposed to be watching. Throughout the chatter, he kept turning to a prominent table in front of the stage which was reserved for Stanford White who, as the building's designer and occupant of the best apartment in its tower, had his own place as and when he wanted it.

White wanted it this evening to cultivate the acquaintance of a new young lady in the chorus who was to be introduced to him at the show's end. But his interest in her did not extend to making him watch the play. He appeared toward the end of the final act.

Thaw rose from his place, and drew the attention of several diners by pacing, ashen-faced, up and down the aisles. Every so often he glanced at White. Once he went into the lobby where the elevators were, shepherding away Evelyn and her party, she having indicated that she did not want to stay after White's arrival. Then, muttering to himself so that several people thought he was drunk, Thaw made his way back to White and stood over him.

'Yes, Thaw? What is it?' asked Stanford White.

In answer, Thaw shot him three times. Two bullets entered his shoulder. The third penetrated his head and killed him. Stanford White slumped onto his table, knocking a glass over, before his body fell to the floor and lay there in the steadily growing pool of his blood.

Thaw looked at him, and said with a curse, 'You'll never go out with that woman again.'

The singer on stage froze in the middle of his song, 'I Could Love a Million Girls'. The audience froze, some thinking that this was a new instance of putting actors in the auditorium for novelty effect. Then Harry Thaw slowly lifted up his pistol and let it droop in the air, as if to show that he intended no harm to anyone else, before walking firmly to the elevator lobby.

Women screamed and demanded that their escorts take them away. A rush for the doors started. The manager leapt onto a table and demanded that the show go on and the chorus be brought in. The band attempted to keep their tune going raggedly. And the frightened chorus girls went half-heartedly through their paces, peering anxiously into the audience to see what new threat awaited them.

Out in the lobby, a fireman quietly took Thaw's pistol away. The murderer made no resistance. A policeman who had been on duty at the main door rushed in and arrested Thaw. Constable Debes had carefully asked the management whether there was any shooting in the play, as only the previous week he had caused an accidental disturbance at another theatre when he rushed in to investigate pistol shots, only to find that they were ordinary blanks fired on the stage as part of the performance. This time he was right to think he was wanted.

Thaw came quietly, making a remark to the policeman which Debes did not catch perfectly. Probably he said, 'He deserved it. I can prove it. He ruined my wife and then deserted the girl.' Only Debes wasn't sure that he hadn't said 'life' rather than wife.

Before the officer and his charge reached the lift, Evelyn hurried forward, pale and shocked. She kissed her husband, saying, 'My God, Harry, what have you done?' Thaw suggested that he had probably saved her life, to which she responded, 'I never thought you'd do it this way'.

At the police station Thaw gave his name as John Smith, occupation, student. He chain-smoked cigarettes. He asked for a leading lawyer, though stipulating that the man need not be called till the morning and shouldn't be woken up. He refused to explain his actions. He had no comment to offer when his visiting cards in the name Harry K. Thaw were found in his pocket.

Harry Thaw's mother announced that she would spend a million dollars to secure her son's freedom. And in the first instance she engaged Californian lawyer Delphin Delmas, whose record included nineteen murder defences with nineteen murder acquittals. Delmas advised Mrs Thaw that her son had obviously murdered a defenceless man in full view of the public. It was therefore unlikely that he could secure complete acquittal. But he antici- pated escaping the death sentence.

On the other side, aggressive District Attorney William Travers Jerome made the usual aggressive noises to the press about securing a conviction and not letting anyone's money stand in the way of the people of New York securing justice against a murderer. But in private Jerome was known to doubt Thaw's sanity, and to feel very unhappy about seeking the capital penalty for a man he suspected might not be fit to stand trial. He had no alternative, however. Mrs William Thaw would not let her son plea-bargain an insanity and manslaughter compromise.

The newspapers had a field day. Delmas hired press agent Ben Atwell to create sympathy for Thaw by blackening White's character before the case came to trial. Sensational stories of the goings-on in the Madison Gardens Tower apartment appeared in the tabloids.

It seemed Mr White liked his girls young. Susan Johnson was another who had visited him when she was only fifteen, had found herself plied with champagne and seduced. Then, having had his wicked way with her, the cruel bounder twirled his moustaches and abandoned her to drag her shame through the gutters, penniless and deserted.

And if Susan Johnson supported Evelyn's stories of the quality of White's love-making, name after name was cited to build up the quantity. Sometimes it seemed that half the female population of New York had dressed itself in childish clothes, swung on the velvet swing and let wicked Mr White enjoy a lustful peep at its knickers!

But the prosecution was not to be outdone. Jerome discovered that one Ethel Thomas had tried to bring charges against Thaw in 1902. Ethel said that Thaw had plied her with flowers, jewels, clothes and tender expressions of affection and respect. Lulled by this gentlemanly wooing, she agreed to meet him and go to his apartment, and wondered why he stopped on the way to buy a dog whip.

'What's that for?' she asked, innocently.

'That's for you, dear,' was Thaw's laughing reply.

But it was no joke when they entered his rooms and Thaw seized the whip and beat her so savagely that his blows stripped her clothes from her in tatters. It's unsurprising that Ethel reported 'a wild expression' in his eyes.

The case came to court in January 1907. Evelyn was standing by her husband. With Delmas's enthusiastic approval she was dressed very simply in a plain navy suit and shirt-waister blouse. Had her skirt been calf- rather than ankle-length, she would have been a schoolgirl in appearance. Her hat was plain black velvet, trimmed with violets, and the wonderful contrast between her demurely innocent appearance and the raunchy experiences she related with timid bashfulness made her appearance instant fashion. Every black hat trimmed with violets in New York was sold before the trial was out.

Evelyn gave the fullest account of the wickedness of Stanford White — velvet swing, drugged champagne and all. She did it so well, and Mr Delmas built it up so luridly in his final speech, that almost everybody overlooked the prosecution's expert witness who testified that any known drug capable of rendering Evelyn helpless with the speed she claimed would have killed her!

It also suited the defence tactics that Evelyn should make the most of her husband's ferocious rages; the brutality of his treatment of her until she had fully confessed; his uncontrollable anger against the 'Beast', the 'Bastard', the 'B'. Indeed, at times Mr Jerome's cross-examination invited answers so deeply embarrassing to her that she was permitted to whisper her replies to the prosecutor under cover of her modestly gloved hand. Jerome in turn passed them on in an undertone to the court stenographer, who quickly had typed copies made up for the judge and jury.

It is so extraordinary a procedure that it leads me to wonder whether Evelyn was confessing that in calling Mr White the 'B', Harry Thaw was angrily drawing attention to an alleged appetite for anal intercourse on the great seducer's part. It would at least represent a practice that was not included in Thaw's own extensive repertoire, and the abbreviation of 'Bugger' was certainly common in educated British Edwardian circles.

My only doubt is that the word bugger (a corruption of 'Bulgar' after Bulgaria became infiltrated by the Cattar heresy, whose Catholic enemies, with the dirty-mindedness of orthodox anti-heretics, accused them of emulating the Cities of the Plain) has lost all its sodomitical force in most parts of America and just means 'fellow' or 'boy'.

But in any case, we can all enjoy a good shiver at the fact that Evelyn Thaw revealed things *so dreadful* at her husband's first murder trial that they were never allowed into the cold light of day, and we can all protest that justice has not been seen to be done, because we haven't all learned the full, exquisitely dirty details.

Mr Delmas was perfectly happy for all this to come out. He was trying a most extraordinary defence, mixing a hint of insanity with a daring hint of 'the unwritten law'. New York does not rest upon the Code Napoleon, and so *crime passionel* is not recognized. Still, there can be few juries anywhere that would not feel some smidgin of sympathy for an unsuspecting husband who, arriving home unexpectedly to find his wife in bed with a stranger, kills one or both of them on the spot. And by extension shouldn't you be allowed to kill the adulterous profaner of your bed a little later? Or such an outrageous bounder as Stanford White at any time at all? There were certainly those who believed that Thaw had rendered the city a great service after they read Ben Atwell's lurid account of the procession of ladies defiled in Madison Square Gardens' tower.

Of course, Mr Delmas couldn't openly argue that the unwritten law allowed Thaw to go round shooting cads like they were squirrels. The judge wouldn't accept that. Nor could Delmas plead his client not guilty by reason of insanity. Mrs William Thaw wouldn't allow that. So he invented a new species of insanity: *dementia Americana* – that uncontrollable rage which possesses every American male who learns that his marital bed has been violated. It was rather a holy madness, according to Mr Delmas. It 'makes every home sacred.' It 'makes a man believe that his wife is sacred.' And it meant that, 'Whoever stains the virtue of his wife has forfeited the protection of human laws and must look to the eternal justice and mercy of God.'

And, of course, it had the incalculable advantage that it was of very short duration. Once sated by the death of the beast, the dementia subsided and the patient was calm and rational again − fit to take his place in society once more. There was no need for Harry Thaw to be locked up in an insane asylum.

Mr Delmas saved his best efforts for his powerful and rhetorical summing up. He had this difficult and irrational concept of the imaginary ailment to put over, allowing the jury to find his client guilty but insane at the time of the killing, or even − if they accepted the undertone of unwritten law − not guilty of anything any decent man wouldn't do.

He also had to dispose of the embarrassing Hummel affidavit which the prosecution had dredged up. More intense emotional pleading was called for to explain this away: to confuse it with Mr Thaw's justified wrath as his suspicions of Stanford White grew; to remark that Evelyn denied the whole thing, saying it was just something the brutal White had forced her to sign as part of his dreadful schemes to incriminate Mr Thaw.

Actually, Delmas could have spared his breath to cool his porridge over the affidavit. The jury afterwards acknowledged that they didn't pay any attention to it whatsoever. Quite fortuitously, Hummel's partner, Howe, died that year and the unsavoury law firm's jiggery-pokery was given an airing in the press. In fact, attention fastened onto Hummel so securely that he was caught handing out bribes in a divorce action the following year, disbarred and imprisoned. So as soon as the jury in the Thaw case heard Hummel's name, they simply disregarded all the testimony in any way connected with him. And I think they were very wise.

After two uncomfortable nights kipping down on the hard chairs and tables of the jury room, the twelve good men and true were compelled to admit they could not reach a verdict. Seven were strong for conviction; four for acquittal on the grounds of insanity; one would have accepted a compromise verdict of manslaughter with some clemency reference to insanity.

Thaw was very disappointed that he would have to return to prison and await a further trial. He had taken to issuing public statements and he now pronounced that all the intelligent jurors had found him innocent, and the only hold-out was a man whose wife had died in the course of the trial. He was wrong.

His mother, more sensibly, realized it had been a close-run thing. She changed lawyers and changed tactics for the retrial in 1908. Martin W. Littleton ran the insanity defence as hard as he could, without attempting melodramatic appeals to the 'unwritten law' or positing the new and widespread affliction of *dementia Americana*. He called witnesses from London, Montreal and Toronto to testify to Thaw's mad outbreaks. The 'alienists' (as psychologists were then termed) agreed that these were symptomatic of manic depression. In his manic moods, Thaw threw outrageous tantrums and put other people's property, life and limb at risk. In the depressive phases, he was dangerously suicidal.

Still, a picture of a most unpleasant young man emerged, whose frantic misconduct might be seen as that of a spoiled brat. He had been blackballed from New York's best gentlemen's clubs and responded by hiring a horse which he attempted to ride into them. Porters and doormen had been knocked over by his charger, and his mother had paid his fines when he was arrested and convicted for these assaults.

He played one of the longest poker games on record with a group of New York sharpers. His final losses were $40,000. His mother paid up without a murmur.

He rented an apartment in Susan Merrill's ritzy Manhattan brothel. There he lured young women with the promise of getting them Broadway careers. Unlike Stanford White, however, he never carried out his promises. Also unlike Stanford White, he didn't play games with little-girl costumes and velvet swings. He raped his lovers. He tied them up and whipped them till they screamed.

Susan Merrill, retired by the time of the trial, testified that she had been so appalled by the cries coming from his rooms that she finally forced her way in. 'He had tied the girl to the bed, naked,' she stated, 'and was whipping her. She was covered with welts. Thaw's eyes protruded and he looked mad.'

The Madam feared he would kill someone sooner or later, so she summoned the police to have him ejected. Thaw protested strongly that he had paid a year's rent in advance. Madam Merrill was happy to repay the money and see the back of him.

Soon after this, Thaw gathered together a bevy of Broadway streetwalkers and ushered his giggling group into one of Fifth Avenue's best shops to be fitted for gowns. The manager indignantly refused to serve them, whereupon, he testified, Thaw had 'a sort of fit. His eyes bulged and rolled, and he screamed like a child having a tantrum.'

Thaw was gently escorted off the premises by police. The ladies were taken less gently to the cells. That should have been the end of the incident, but no. Back came Thaw the following day in a rented car which he drove through the plate-glass display window, attempting to run down the offending manager. Once again, his doting mother paid the fines and sent him out to amuse himself further.

In Paris, Thaw rented one whole floor of the Hotel George V and threw a party for some of the city's most prominent prostitutes that lasted several days and cost $50,000. In the end he was asked to leave the hotel, which could not accept his practice of whipping naked women along the corridors.

With all this exotic smut going for him, Evelyn's story of the continental tour fell simply into place as part of the pattern. She had an easier time in the witness box as Mr Jerome had decided to accept her story of Stanford White's improbable rape. The fact that the prosecution didn't dispute the incident spared her the distasteful duty of whispering the horrid details into the District Attorney's unsympathetic ear. And, of course, it prevented the jury from seeing that sympathy arousing performance.

The new defence strategy was successful. Thaw was found not guilty by reason of insanity, and he confidently expected that it was all over now and he could go home. The insane episodes had all been in the past, hadn't they? He suffered a rude awakening. The court agreed that he was mad, bad and dangerous to know, and committed him to Matteawan Asylum for life.

Hitherto, Harry's incarceration on remand had been as luxurious as mother's millions could make it. He had worn his own clothes; had access to his own writing materials; enjoyed slap-up meals specially brought in from Delmonico's with white linen napery and silver cutlery to accompany them.

All that changed. He went into a bare dormitory in the first instance, with only the possibility of a room to himself after he had been carefully examined and diagnosed. He ate the same food as other inmates. He could no longer have the endless supply of expensive cigarettes and cigars that satisfied his tobacco craving. (One witness had described him as a 'cigarette fiend'. This was meant to show that he was permanently demented by his debauched drug abuse.) His freedom to summon the press and issue silly statements was ended.

Evelyn's self-interest also asserted itself strongly. It seems likely she had been paid off by Mother Thaw during the trials, to make sure she stayed in line and gave whatever testimony suited the defence attorney's tactics.

Now the young woman made an unsuccessful attempt to gain administration of her certified husband's estate. When this was blocked, she turned against him and withdrew her support from Mrs William Thaw's attempts to win her son's release.

A new battery of lawyers swung into action with Habeas Corpus suits. On Thaw's behalf, they appealed right up to the US Supreme Court for a new jury trial to determine Thaw's sanity. They were refused.

In 1909 they started again. This time, Evelyn and Susan Merrill testified against Thaw, both asserting that they believed him to be congenitally mad. Thaw offered rebutting evidence, claiming that he had only lodged in Susan's brothel in the hope of securing evidence against Stanford White! Thaw lost his case again, and would have divorced Evelyn had not his official state of insanity precluded him from starting proceedings.

Nonetheless, she announced the following year that her newborn baby son was Harry's. She had, she claimed, enjoyed intimate moments with Thaw on her visits to Matteawan and Harry Russell Thaw was the outcome. It was an astute move. Now she could claim that all her legal efforts to secure a large share of the Thaw millions were sheer maternal concern that her child should not be robbed of his patrimony. As for the alleged father, she told the press, 'Harry Thaw has turned out to be a degenerate scoundrel. He hid behind my skirts through two dirty trials and I won't stand for it again.'

In the meantime she was travelling across Europe with a newspaper man whom she had engaged as her manager, and was preparing for a new career in vaudeville with an initial offer of $3,500 a week to appear as 'The Girl on the Velvet Swing'. She would sing the song that had been echoing round Madison Square Roof Garden as Stanford White was shot, changing one word to make it, 'I Could Love a Million Men'. Likely enough, if they all had money.

Mrs Thaw was indefatigable. Habeas Corpus proceed-

ings were started for the third time and another plot came
to light. A lawyer was disbarred and the asylum
superintendent fired when a grand jury heard that the
former had solicited $120,000 from Harry, offering to
give $20,000 to the superintendent in return for his good
intent to declare before the courts that Harry Thaw was
now cured and sane.

In 1913, the admirers of Harry Thaw tried a different
tack to secure his freedom. Instead of hiring lawyers and
bribing administrators, they hired hoods and bribed
gatekeepers. On Sunday 17 August, Harry Thaw walked
calmly through the gates of Matteawan as they opened to
admit the daily milk supply. A waiting car whisked him
north to a change of vehicles. The second car rushed at
70 mph to a railway station, where Harry's minders
packed him onto a train to be carried almost to the
Canadian border. There another car hurried him out of
the jurisdiction of Uncle Sam and Harry became a
temporary resident of the village of St Hermengilde de
Garford.

When the news broke, Evelyn did her best to secure
publicity for herself. 'Harry has threatened to kill me,'
she told the press. 'And I believe my presence in New
York prompted him to escape.' And onto this extremely
unlikely tale she hung a new and self-serving explanation
of the murder, designed, perhaps, to distract attention
from her own history.

'He's terribly revengeful,' she declared of her husband.
'He was that way before he killed Stanford White. In
fact, Harry's trouble with Stanford White started over
another girl long before he met me.' Possible, I suppose,
especially if Stanford White's enthusiastic skirt-lifting
brought him face to face with weals left by Harry's whips
and he justly reprimanded the younger man for disfigur-
ing the merchandise.

Two days after his escape, Harry Thaw was arrested by
the Mounties and taken to Sherbrooke. There the
Quebecoises shouted 'Laisse-le tranquille!' (let him go),

and Anglo-Canadians supported them competitively with cries of 'Hip hip hurrah! for British justice!' The one-time mad sadist graciously accepted this public acclamation as no more than his due.

District Attorney Jerome travelled up to Canada to negotiate Harry's extradition. In September, the Mounties took their man over the border and dumped him in New Hampshire, where the state authorities engaged New York in yet another round of extradition proceedings. And finally, in 1915, Harry Thaw faced a New York jury for the third time. Now he was trying to prove his recovered sanity and obtain his release.

The story of Evelyn's seduction by lecherous Stanford White, her beatings in the Austrian Schloss and Swiss hotel at Harry's manic hands, and Harry's subsequent trials and tribulations, all got another good going over. And at the end of it all, Harry was declared sane and set free at last.

He celebrated at once by divorcing Evelyn, citing her pressman companion as co-respondent. Evelyn sniffed that she was too busy to comment, as she was improving her ballroom dancing with a new partner, Harry Clifford. Her bedroom dancing too, perhaps, as she was to marry and divorce Clifford in short order.

But this isn't the end of this shocking affair. In 1917 Harry Thaw was arrested and charged with abducting and whipping nineteen-year-old Frederick B. Gump of Kansas City. It appeared that the gender of Harry's preferred partners might have changed, but his idea of a rollicking good time was still the same.

It transpired that one of Harry's minders was carrying a lot of letters in which youths responded to Harry's advertisements offering jobs with the Highland Iron Works of Pittsburgh — a company which acknowledged his family connections by making him non-executive director.

The New York District Attorney's office rubbed its hands together as it saw the chance of extraditing this flagellomaniac and having another crack at getting him behind bars. Mrs Thaw saw the danger and promptly collapsed the scrum under New York. She announced that she was 'unable to resist the facts' demonstrating her son's insanity and had him committed to the mental ward of the Pennsylvania State Hospital. The law was snookered.

The Gump family weren't finished, however. They brought a civil suit against Harry demanding $650,000 damages for the kidnapping, beating and sexual assault of young Frederick. In the end, the Gumps were Harry's salvation. Mrs Thaw's lawyers strung out negotiations with them until 1926 and then published a settlement out of court for $25,000. It remains highly likely that the family received the remaining $625,000 under the table. In return they agreed to drop all proceedings against Harry Thaw, and the way was clear for a fresh hearing to declare him sane again.

It was opposed by Evelyn, who wanted him declared mad so that she could get her hands on his estate — for their son, of course.

It was also opposed by Pennsylvania State Hospital staff, who thought the practice of throwing pet rabbits in the air and biting them represented something less desirable than lovable eccentricity on Harry's part. But twelve good men and true found Harry sane and fit to enter society again. Evelyn was probably right in her suspicion that Mrs Thaw's money had been paid out to the charities or bank accounts of the jurors' choice as an encouragement.

The rest was a slow downhill descent along the lines on which these two rather undesirable people had set their lives. Evelyn's night-club career faded and she attempted suicide by drinking disinfectant. In 1927 she opened a speakeasy on Fifty-second Street. Harry turned up one night, ignored her, and made a rumpus when the bill was brought.

In 1928, Chez Evelyn closed when she could no longer

meet the huge bribes demanded by the police. She sang in night-clubs around the country and at a brothel in Panama City.

Harry was dragged through the courts in a succession of suits brought by a waitress who claimed he had beaten her up. As he probably had.

His mother died, and Harry attended the funeral with those sisters whose marriages to European and American aristocracy had been so much better than his. Harry didn't make many more waves. He just went on buying his way through life, dying as a nasty, wizened little man in rented lodgings at the age of seventy-six in 1947.

Evelyn lived on to the swinging sixties, ending her life in a Californian nursing home with her attention divided between theosophy, painting and potting. But she didn't enjoy her old age. Her last remark on the murder she had provoked by inflaming a maniac's jealousy was selfishly rueful: 'Stanny was lucky. He died. I lived.'

Thomas Ley

There was nothing in his appearance to suggest he was a man consumed by passionate jealousy. Thomas Ley was sixty-six years old in 1947. Fat, self-important and domineering. Rich, rude and retired. He was a man of pretty fixed and boring habits; well past his prime. A man whose love-life was pretty much confined to playing repetitive games of gin-rummy and eating dull and uninspiring meals with the attractive widow who had been his mistress for twenty years. They lived apart, slept apart, met daily, and were as improbable an Othello and Desdemona as a pair of chintz-covered, well-stuffed armchairs. Yet Thomas Ley seethed internally, consumed with the delusory belief that nice Maggie Brook, a woman of his own age, spent all her time bounding into bed with younger, more attractive men whenever she was out of his sight.

Ley had a distinguished public career behind him. But it was a career with its murky corners. He was born in England and emigrated to Australia with his parents while he was still a child. He grew up to become a solicitor, and quickly applied his abilities to making deals and promoting enterprises. With growing contacts and associates in the business world, he soon turned his talents to politics. He became effective as a diplomatic mediator and go-between. He was elected to the New South Wales Assembly, and became respectively the State's Minister of Education, Minister of Labour and Minister of Justice. He held this last, appropriate appointment for three years, before crowning his career with election to the Federal Australian Parliament. Still, he liked to be remembered as the former Minister of Justice, even if it was only in the restricted arena of the State of New South Wales.

When Ley retired at the age of forty-eight, he was a very rich man. Self-made, too, for his origins had been quite humble. But his prosperity was no source of pride. Australians knew that his wealth far exceeded anything he could have earned by the fair practice of law and the reasonable remunerations of public office. He was notorious as a corrupt and sleazy fixer.

No wonder, perhaps, that he decided to retire to England. His title as the ex-Minister of Justice would be recognized in the Mother Country. His reputation as a man grown fat from taking bribes need not accompany him. Some Australians believed that he had to leave their shores before investigations into the sources of his prosperity caught up with him. It was pretty certain that a charge of accepting bribes would be proved against him if he stayed around. Worse still, two of his business associates had disappeared in suspicious circumstances. And their disappearance seemed very much to Ley's advantage . . . But it was not for a rational murder motivated by clear business ends that he would ultimately find himself in the dock.

Thomas Ley settled in London in 1929 and proceeded to live off his investments. Ley did not bring his wife with him to London, though he remained legally married to her and visited her whenever she came 'home' on holiday. Instead he settled in England in the company of somebody else's wife.

In the early 1920s, Mrs Evelyn 'Maggie' Brook was married to a magistrate in Perth. During Ley's period as Minister of Justice, he made an official visit to Western Australia and was formally introduced to Mr Brook. Ley had eyes only for his fellow lawyer's attractive wife.

Everyone liked Maggie Brook. She was friendly and considerate: 'nice' was the word universally applied to her. Even women, it seems, forgave her flirtatious manner with their husbands. Maggie just seemed to like everybody, and responded to them in a manner fitting the way they approached her. So if men came on flirtatiously with Maggie Brook, Maggie charmingly flirted back. It was all quite harmless. Until Thomas Ley from New South Wales writhed his ophidian way into the Eden of Perth. Very soon, he and Mrs Brook were enjoying a covert illicit liaison.

Maggie came quite openly with him to London. They lived together in flats and in hotels until, in the late 1930s, they ended their sexual union. But not their general interdependence. They still met daily, passing their time together playing endless games of gin-rummy, until Ley would go back to whatever flat or hotel he was sleeping in and Maggie returned to her lonely bed at home in the Cromwell Road.

But during the war years, the green-eyed monster began to cast its shadow over Thomas Ley. The solitary man in his solitary bed at night began to wonder whether Maggie was equally solitary. He began to torture himself with the idea that she was not, began to persuade himself that he had spotted her making sheep's eyes at virile young men: waiters, hall porters, chauffeurs, labourers.

Nor could Ley bottle up these suspicions and keep them to himself. He started making small scenes in public, like accusing Maggie in stormy undertones of plotting to inveigle hotel staff into her bed as the couple ate their customary dinner at the Cumberland Grill. He took to rushing her out of public places and back to the endless gin-rummy in the Cromwell Road, so as to remove her from the temptation of anything young and in trousers.

Maggie simply put up with this treatment. Why? We don't really know. Possibly she was so financially dependent on Ley, so much a stranger in a strange land that she had no alternative. But those who knew her, and admired her unfailing niceness, believed that the answer had to be love. Love as mysterious as Ley's jealousy.

To all objective appearances, Thomas Ley was a

completely unlovable man. His personality was abrasive; his appearance was unerotic; his manners were repellant. But Maggie was habituated to loving him and still seemed to see him as that slimmer, younger man, who had risen so quickly to political power by his gifts of diplomacy. She still felt the glamour of the big politician from the more cosmopolitan state, who had overshadowed her own husband when he made his condescending rounds in Perth.

Anyway, whatever the reason, Maggie Brook was undoubtedly attached to Thomas Ley, and nobody who knew her thought that attachment was a gold-digger's lust for his ill-gotten bank balance.

Ley's paranoid suspicions spilled out when he started besmirching other people in 1946. Maggie's married daughter lived in Wimbledon, where she was taken ill and went into hospital. Ley, who could still remember normal human consideration in his rational moments, suggested to Maggie that she should go down to Wimbledon and keep house for her son-in-law while he was on his own. No one has ever heard of Maggie questioning Ley's suggestions. She went to Wimbledon.

No sooner had she done what Ley asked, than he began to imagine that she had made the move of her own volition and for her own ulterior motive. A sexual motive, of course. Here was Maggie living in a large house divided into small flats and in some of those flats lived men — single men. Ley became convinced that Maggie was using her freedom to sleep with one of them.

He settled first on a respectable businessman who used his Wimbledon flat as a *pied-à-terre* during the working week and returned every weekend to his family. Ley sent the man an invitation to tea at 5 Beaufort Gardens, Knightsbridge. The businessman, fortunately for him, had neither the time nor the inclination to accept a pointless social invitation from someone he did not know. He politely declined, and Ley was left to think again. An extraordinary feature of his growing jealous paranoia was that it changed object swiftly for no obvious, let alone sensible, reason.

The next villanous seducer Ley's sick mind hit upon was Maggie's son-in-law. At least the young man knew exactly who Ley and Mrs Brook were — which is more than can be said for certain of any of Ley's other suspects! He, too, received an invitation to tea. He asked Maggie why Ley wanted to see him and found, to his surprise, that she knew nothing about it. If it were not really a family affair then he, too, had no time to spend trotting up to Knightsbridge for scones and Earl Grey. Mr Ley received another polite refusal. And again, instead of intensifying his overheated suspicion, this served only to change its direction.

John McMain Mudie was a thirty-five-year-old barman who roomed in the same house as Maggie Brook's daughter and son-in-law. He worked at the Dog and Duck in Wimbledon where he was very popular, then shifted to the Reigate Hotel when that institution offered slightly better pay and prospects. If he knew Mrs Brook by sight during the time she stayed in his lodging house, it was as much as he did know. He certainly never went into the flat she was staying in and she certainly never went into his rooms. And by the time Ley focused the spotlight of his dotty suspicions on Mudie, Mrs Brook had gone back to the Cromwell Road.

This time, Ley set a trap to prove the validity of his horrid imaginings. He sent two cheques to Mudie, drawn on a company he and Mrs Brook co-directed and requiring her second signature. He asked Mudie to pass them on to Mrs Brook for completion. Mudie simply sent the cheques back to Ley, saying that he had no idea where Mrs Brook was now she had left Wimbledon.

So Mudie had passed the test. He was not in secret communication with Ley's mistress. He should have been cleared of all suspicion, and Ley's mind should have devised an alternative fevered fantasy. But rationality had no place in the hurricane of Ley's emotions. If his two previous suspects had proved their innocence by blandly disregarding and sidestepping Ley's attempts to ensnare them, Mudie had apparently proved his guilt by behaving in the most innocent manner imaginable as a response to Ley's trap!

On 30 November 1947, a man walking home from work discovered Mudie's body in an old chalk pit near Woldingham. There were two heavy ropes and a piece of rag around his neck. He had been strangled with the ropes. Marks on the body showed that he had been beaten before he died.

His clothes were smeared with the muddy clay which surrounded the chalk pit, yet his shoes and their soles were unmarked. Evidently he had been carried to his last resting place, probably by two men, one of whom held his feet off the ground until he was finally dropped.

Mudie carried a visiting card in his pocket, so his identity was quickly established. Inquiries at the Reigate Hotel showed that he had not been seen at work for two days: not since he went out with a private commission to serve drinks at a cocktail party on 28 November.

A few days prior to that, a wealthy lady had come into the Reigate Hotel and bought a dry Martini for herself and a light ale for her uniformed chauffeur. Apparently well satisfied with Mudie's service, she asked him if he ever hired himself out for private parties and booked him to serve cocktails for her in her house near Brompton Oratory. On 28 November she and the chauffeur had arrived at Reigate and taken Mudie with them. He was not seen again until his body was found at Woldingham.

Detective work around the chalk pit threw up some useful clues. The ropes that had strangled Mudie were traced back to the West End shop that had sold them on 28 November to a man who said he wanted them as washing lines. The piece of rag wrapped in the ropes smelled strongly of French polishers' varnish.

A man had been seen driving around the vicinity of the

chalk pit on 29 November, apparently reconnoitring the
site. The car was either an Austin or a Ford and its
registration included the numbers 101.

A car hire firm in Knightsbridge had rented a Ford
Eight, registration number FGP 101, to a carpenter
named John Lawrence Smith on 27 November. He
returned it on 30 November. Smith could offer no good
explanation why he, an ordinary London working man
living in Dulwich, went to the extraordinary expense of
hiring a car for three days.

Smith was currently working on the conversion of 5
Beaufort Gardens, Knightsbridge, into self-contained
flats. Some of the work entailed French polishing. The
owner of 5 Beaufort Gardens, who had commissioned the
work, was Thomas Ley.

Earlier in the month, Thomas Ley had approached the
head waiter at the Royal Hotel in Woburn Place and
asked if he knew a taxi-driver or car hirer who could keep
his mouth shut about a highly paid job. After receiving
assurance that the job would be perfectly legal, Minden,
the head waiter, introduced Ley to a dodgy Dunkirk
deserter named John Buckingham, who now ran a car
hire business. Ley and Buckingham had a furtive private
meeting in the Royal Hotel.

When the trail led to Buckingham, the police had
found the conspirator who cracked. Buckingham, with
his charge for army desertion hanging over his head,
wanted no more flight from the law. He turned King's
Evidence and told the police what had happened — or his
version of what had happened. Nobody doubted that his
story was as self-serving as he could make it, and all the
lawyers at the trial — defence, prosecution and judge
alike — agreed that his evidence was tainted. But it gave
an outline of events, much of which was confirmed by
Smith.

Ley had told Buckingham that he was a solicitor, acting
for two women who were being blackmailed by a seducer.
He said that he wanted the blackmailer brought to his

house in London to 'be dealt with'. He offered a fee of £200 and arranged for Buckingham to meet with Smith to discuss the method of inveigling the villain up to town.

Smith had come into Ley's conspiratorial orbit when the ex-Minister discovered that the chippy wanted to emigrate to South Africa and was quite interested in little fiddles on the side. These ambitions gave considerable leverage to an influential ex-politician from the colonies with a lot of money. Smith willingly went to discuss with Buckingham how John Mudie might be kidnapped in Reigate and brought to Beaufort Gardens.

Buckingham's first suggestion was that he would go to the hotel and pretend to get drunk. At the end of the evening, he would ask the barman to help him back to his car, and in the darkness of the car park Buckingham's son would slosh Mudie and bundle him into a car. Ley turned that scheme down pointblank when Smith reported it back to him. It ran the risk of Mudie's attracting attention with a yell for help.

The next scheme was better. A well-dressed lady with a chauffeur and a glossy car was to show up at the Reigate Hotel. After expressing herself pleased with Mudie's service, she was to offer him a private commission to serve cocktails to a party of famous actors, politicians and other celebrities at her Knightsbridge residence. That plan was accepted.

Buckingham knew just the girl for the 'rich lady': a bus driver's wife called Lillian Bruce. And it was, indeed, Lil Bruce who had turned up at the Reigate Hotel and booked Mudie's services for 28 November. Her chauffeur was Buckingham's son.

On the night of the kidnapping, Ley, Buckingham and Smith had gone down to Reigate in one car and watched as the unsuspecting Mudie came out to the chauffeured limousine in which young Buckingham drove him and Lil Bruce up to town. When the two cars reached Knightsbridge, Ley, Buckingham and Smith drove up to the front door of 5 Beaufort Gardens and let themselves in. Young

Buckingham and Lil Bruce drove to the back door, which Mrs Bruce opened with a key Ley had given her. Then she invited Mudie to step inside, while she had a word with her chauffeur.

Mudie stepped into the dark passage where Smith and Buckingham grabbed him and threw a blanket over his head. Young Buckingham and Mrs Bruce drove quickly away and out of the story. Mudie was frog-marched into the basement where he was tied to a chair. Then Buckingham was paid his £200 and he left. He went to the nearby Crown and Sceptre pub, where he and Smith had previously arranged to have a drink together after the delivery of Mudie. In the event, Smith said he could not join his fellow kidnapper as Ley was expecting friends and he would have to stay with Mudie awaiting their arrival. So Buckingham only spent two or three minutes at the pub before driving himself home.

In the end, the most surprising thing about this story is that Smith confirmed it all, except for adding that he produced the varnish rag with which Buckingham gagged Mudie – something Buckingham resolutely denied. (One suspects that Buckingham feared a pathologist might come forward and argue that Mudie had choked on his gag, in which case, like Donovan and Wade in 1905 or O'Brien, Noonan and Wilkinson in 1974, he could have been charged with murder. Unintentionally causing the death of a victim while perpetrating a felony is still recognized in law as murder rather than accident or manslaughter.)

Smith's other additions to Buckingham's tale, when he reached the dock, were simple. He had stayed with Ley and the helpless Mudie for about ten minutes. Then footsteps approached the front door and Ley told him he could go. He received his payment, left through the back door, and seeing that Buckingham's car was not outside the Crown and Sceptre, took himself home to Dulwich where he went to bed.

Both Smith and Buckingham agreed that they helped

abduct Mudie and render him helpless in Beaufort Gardens. Both agreed that they did him no physical harm beyond restraining him – Smith, alone, adding that he was gagged. Both agreed that Buckingham left before Smith, and Mudie was alive and well at that time. There was only Smith's word for it that the barman was still alive and well ten minutes later when he left.

It could not, of course, escape anybody's consideration that Smith couldn't easily say so if Mudie had been dead before Buckingham left. That would mean that he confessed, at the very least, to standing by and watching murder take place – something which, at the very least, the prosecution insisted he had done. Though, dependent as they were on Buckingham's King's Evidence, the prosecutors had to let the Dunkirk deserter go free and satisfy themselves with the implication that Ley was the principal or commanding assassin, with Smith as his sole sidekick at the death.

And Ley? What was his account of the night's events? It was a bland denial. He knew nothing about Smith's and Buckingham's outrageous caper in the basement of his house. He had gone for tea with Mrs Brook in the Cromwell Road, as was his wont. He had left her in the early evening to go and see a man (whose name he had forgotten) in the National Liberal Club where he often conducted business. He had proceeded to eat dinner at the Cumberland Grill, as was his wont, forgetting that he had made no arrangement with Mrs Brook to meet her there. And after dinner he had gone back to the Cromwell Road and played – yet again – gin-rummy, until it was time for bed.

Mrs Brook confirmed the parts of his story which took place at her house and nobody doubted her. But that alone did not give Ley an alibi. It left plenty of time for him to motor down to Reigate and back to Knightsbridge and supervise the beating and murder of John Mudie, before strolling casually down to join the woman on whose imagined account this savage punishment had been inflicted. Not a soul could vouch for Ley's movements during the vital hours when Smith and Buckingham concurred that the abduction and securing of Mudie had taken place.

Ley produced one utterly implausible witness to try and account for Mudie's strange death, given that for some unknown reason, Buckingham and Smith had decided to leave a man they did not know tied up in the Beaufort Gardens basement. An ex-convict named Robert Cruikshank came forward to make the extraordinary claim that he had visited England from Berne on 18 November, carrying a package of contraband goods in a private plane that made an illegal landing somewhere near London – he didn't know where. Before he made contact with a man whose name he didn't know in Sloane Square that night, to have himself ferried back to the continent, he decided to call on Ley in Beaufort Gardens. He had never met him, but another man whose name he did not know had told him Ley was 'a big pot' who could wangle immigration papers to Australia for him.

When he came to 5 Beaufort Gardens, the house was dark and apparently empty. So Cruikshank decided to burgle it and cautiously made his way into the basement through the back door. There he found a man who was definitely alive (for he made inarticulate sounds) tied up in a chair. Cruikshank pulled nervously at his ropes, but did not untie him. Then he heard a noise – he couldn't remember exactly what – and scuttled quickly away outside.

Cruikshank didn't actually say he had killed the man in the chair. But he did say that his anxious tug at the ropes might have strangled the unfortunate man. All accidentally and unwittingly, of course. Even Cruikshank acknowledged that his story looked very like one he had been bribed to tell. And not even Ley's counsel, Sir Walter Monckton, tried to persuade the jury that it represented one iota of truth.

In the end, the problem that Smith's counsel, as well as

the prosecution, hammered home, was the basic question of motive. Neither Smith, the Buckinghams nor Mrs Bruce had ever heard of Mudie until the conspiracy. Ley was the only link to Mudie. Ley, by his own admission, had encountered the barman when he was trying to find Mrs Brook to countersign the company cheques. Ley's house, 5 Beaufort Gardens, was the only link between Mudie and Smith. And the only reason anyone could offer for Ley's wanting to kill a man he hardly knew was the extreme paranoid jealousy which had already shown itself when he threatened other tenants in Mudie's Wimbledon home.

Ley did not plead insanity. The law in 1947 would not have recognised a plea of 'diminished responsibility' had he been willing to make it. Ley and Smith were both found guilty and condemned to death.

But imprisonment awaiting execution stripped off Ley's mask. It became apparent to all who observed him that this man really was mad: he really did have a paranoid schizophrenic detachment from reality. He was transferred to Broadmoor, where he died shortly afterwards.

And Smith benefited from the humane and sensible convention, that was so wickedly and foolishly broken in Derek Bentley's case, whereby a secondary participant in a capital offence would not be hanged if the primary participant was, for one reason or another, spared. Smith's sentence was commuted to life imprisonment.

Thomas John Ley could truly be called madly jealous. Indeed, unusually among the jealous madmen, it might be remarked of him that his unrealistic jealousy was the entirety of his madness. His self-interested, sane criminality had been demonstrated pretty clearly in his political career, and the strong suspicion hung over him that he had somehow engineered the disappearance of two inconvenient business associates long before the body of a man he barely knew was found in the Woldingham chalk pit.

Frederick Emmett-Dunne

In 1947, a young German girl went to a dance at the British Army barracks in her home town of Mulheim. Maria Weiniger had worked in a shop and had some ambitions as a night-club singer. But most notably, the petite, fine-boned, dark-haired fräulein exuded a quiet sultriness that attracted men and outraged women. She wasn't brazen; she wasn't suggestive or teasing; she just seemed, without making any effort, to possess an innate sexiness that irradiated her slender good looks.

She danced with a young English corporal. He was a tiny man, just 5 feet 1 inch tall, with a shock of fair wavy hair. He managed, by combing it straight back, to retain an impressive mane, even after the army barbers had run the clippers around his ears for a regulation short back and sides. He was lively, outgoing and hilarious. Maria liked him and accepted a date later in the week.

After they had been walking out three times a week for three months, she took Corporal Reg Watters home to meet her parents. After Reg had taken her to get the formal documentation required by the British Army – a police certificate that she was of good character with no criminal record, and a doctor's certificate that she suffered from no communicable disease – the two arranged to marry in the local Protestant church on 15 May 1947. Reg saved his profits from the sale of black market coffee to buy her wedding dress.

A year later Reg was demobbed and the couple returned to England. Civvy street was not like the army. In Germany, they'd had their own married accommodation together. In England, Mia (as everyone called

Maria) had to live with Reg's sister in Leeds, while he
went down to the Midlands to look for a job. After six
months, Reg Watters was fed up with the independent life
and he signed on again for the regular army.

He was swiftly made up to Sergeant and posted to
Blandford, where his Company Sergeant Major realized
he was a little rusty on the regulations after six months
out of uniform. So he amiably took 'Tich' Watters in
hand and the two became great friends.

Company Sergeant Major Frederick Emmett-Dunne's
double-barrelled surname was no inheritance from a
socially pretentious family. Quite the reverse. He was a
workhouse child from Dublin, and once the authorities
knew that his unmarried parents were abandoning him to
be brought up by the city, they just tacked his mother's
surname onto his father's to give him a name. I don't
know where 'Frederick' came from, but it wasn't a name
he used much once he was in the British Army. There, as
an Irishman, he was nicknamed 'Mick'. And this became
the forename all his friends, male and female, used from
then on.

CSM Emmett-Dunne had only one relative: his half-
brother, Ronald Emmett. The two were fond of each
other and Ronald had followed Mick into the army,
where big brother kept an unobtrusively watchful eye on
the welfare of his mother's other son.

Mick Emmett-Dunne and Reg Watters were an odd
couple in the sergeants' mess. One dark, the other fair,
they were the long and the short of it. Lively, tiny,
thickset, gregarious Tich Watters, with his open beaming
face, was at the centre of drinking and partying. Mick
Emmett-Dunne, standing 6 feet 2 inches tall, with a
splendid, broad-shouldered physique, had a face whose
dignified grandeur reminded some people of a Roman
emperor. Though he could join in horseplay – once he
was photographed lifting little Reg off the floor with one
hand, and mock-threatening him with a bar stool in the
other – he was more commonly grave.

At Blandford he had fallen in love for the first time in his life with a local girl from nearby Ringwood. It was important to him. There had not been a lot of affection in the workhouse boy's life. And the army reinforced his tendency to cover strong emotions under a mask of stoicism. Emmett-Dunne was to love and be loved deeply. Yet it was never easy for him to drop the rather wooden exterior of the proudly correct NCO.

In fact, the army probably gave Emmett-Dunne the first real emotional security and respect he knew. He was a good soldier. He did his duty steadfastly throughout the Second World War, as a row of campaign medals showed. He was injured escaping as a PoW, but otherwise no particular heroics or special honours distinguished him.

Reg Watters was not a highly decorated soldier. And his hail-fellow-well-met merriment contrasted strongly with his friend's gravity. When Reg heard that he was to be transferred to Germany he was thrilled. He had loved it there, and he knew Mia would be pleased to go home. He was given leave to go to Leeds to tell her, and his broadly smiling satisfaction was mirrored in her delight.

When the pair arrived at Duisburg, they were stationed in married quarters about a mile away from the Glamorgan Barracks. Reg cheerfully poured out his pay on nylon stockings and pretty frocks and fetching lingerie for Mia. But she noticed that he showed small signs of suspicion and resentment if other men admired her wearing them. A fear that her husband was irrationally jealous made her start to hold back in their relationship. And Reg Watters' response to the slight cooling-off in his devoted marriage was to take his pleasures in the sergeants' mess − to prop up the bar all night, laughing and chaffing and drinking with mates who were content with good humour and friendliness. The Watters' marriage, no better and no worse than many, was in no shape to withstand a serious challenge.

* * *

Back in England, Mick Emmett-Dunne was confronting emotional challenges for which he was ill-prepared. One of his colleagues' wives fancied him and she let him know it.

The sergeant was perturbed. Nothing like this had happened during the war years, when soldiers left their wives at home and led bachelor lives in barracks and at the front. Sexual intrigue in the mess was a peacetime experience and Emmett-Dunne wanted no part of it. He didn't want to threaten his own career, his comrade's marriage, or his love for the girl from Ringwood. His abrupt and decisive action managed to damage two of the three.

He applied immediately for a transfer. Then he told his girlfriend. She was annoyed. It seemed clear he did not love her if he was simply having himself taken out of the district without warning her or consulting her. Mick's worst fear was realized as a consequence of the very action he had taken to avoid it: the girl he loved broke off with him.

He took it very hard. The pain was still with him three years later, when the big, handsome, newly married thirty-two-year-old's understanding of women was still so limited that he thought his wife, on their honeymoon, would want to meet the Ringwood girl who had once meant so much to him. But in 1952 he kept his suffering to himself under a mask of stoicism. Indeed, the girl from Ringwood would later comment that he had always been so distant and reserved that she and her mother never felt they really got to know him closely. She certainly did not realize the pain she was causing by breaking off. She only ever wanted the man as a friend, since he seemed unable to open up. And, probably rightly, she put this emotional stiffness down to Emmett-Dunne's lack of a mother.

When Reg Watters learned that Emmett-Dunne was to be posted to Duisburg he was overjoyed. He rated the big CSM the best friend he had made since rejoining the army, and Mia was looking forward to meeting him for the first time.

So Mick Emmett-Dunne joined the Watters' companionable table in the sergeants' mess at Duisburg in 1952. There was usually an empty seat beside Mia, since Reg habitually made for the bar after seating his wife and seeing her comfortable.

Mick and Mia were strikingly attractive people. Mick had learned that this could lead to unwelcome advances from a colleague's wife. His background left him peculiarly insensitive to other people's emotional reactions. But he said of his time at Duisburg that he flirted with everyone, and several German women who drank there agreed that there was an atmosphere of general flirtation in the sergeants' mess.

What about Mia? Was she the innocent young army wife she later tried to suggest, faintly disapproving of the 'immoral' women who came in trying to pick up boyfriends? Or did she recall finding her own husband in an occupying army mess? Did she know full well that she had a magnetic appeal for men, and enjoyed the freedom to take her pick? Picking, with little hesitation, the handsome CSM who came and sat beside her night after night?

I have little doubt that Emmett-Dunne and Mrs Watters consciously and deliberately played with fire. By their own account, they spent a great deal of time dancing together. They could hardly deny this: everybody saw them. But their explanation was hardly plausible. Mia wanted to dance because she was a good dancer and enjoyed it, and Reg was always too busy drinking. Mick wanted to dance because he was a very bad dancer and he hoped Mia would teach him to dance better. Unfortunately that just doesn't ring true! Good dancers who love dancing seek good dancers to partner. Bad dancers who want to improve don't want to be made to look clumsy by adept partners. Mick and Mia's dancing has to be the excuse for two attractive people gravitating to each other.

And whatever their subsequent denials, there can be little doubt that they fell in love. In November 1952, Mick was at an engagement party where his brooding melancholy provoked questions from a young woman. Mick blurted out that he was unhappy because he was in love with a married woman. Later that evening, the same young woman suggested that she might come round to Mick's flat. She was firmly turned down.

Mick was obviously ready to fall in love after his disappointment with the Ringwood girl. Mia, too, felt unhappy and neglected in her marriage. NCOs are notoriously hard drinkers. But, by her own account, Mia loathed drunkenness and Reg was coming home drunk night after night. Even Mick drank more than she liked but she didn't have to live with him and watch his nightly stupor and morning hangover.

What went on between Mick and Mia was just obvious enough to attract a little attention: not obvious enough to create a real scandal. They sat together, talked together and danced together in the mess. Mia walked her dogs in the afternoons, often meeting Mick on the way and walking with him. Once she told a friend she was going to walk a certain route in order to meet Mick.

When the troops went off on Exercise Grand Repulse in September 1953, Mick was not involved. He was given leave which he proposed to take in the American zone. He departed for his holiday, but returned later in the day with the absurd excuse that he had forgotten his cigarettes. For the rest of the exercise period he remained in Duisburg — so did Mia. While Reg was away on Grand Repulse, Mia and Mick went driving together and he was often at her flat.

Mia's neighbour had a telephone and Emmett-Dunne started ringing her, three or four times a week, to speak to Mia. Mrs Bannerman couldn't overhear the conversations but she was acutely aware of them. And another neighbour's maid received letters from Mick to pass on to Mia.

What did Reg feel about all this? His personality was mercurial — he could be happy as Larry one minute; sourly suspicious the next. He certainly mentioned his doubts about the relationship between his wife and his friend to colleagues. But since he had no proof of any misconduct, only vague suspicions, they were inclined to put it down to his personal obsession. A few people thought he was concerned that Mick and Mia might have been sleeping together while he was away on Exercise Grand Repulse. But Mia's fear that Reg was prone to jealousy reflects something other people noticed in him, too.

The strongest concern about Reg was voiced by Mick, in a rather obscure way. He mentioned to another sergeant that there was one man at the barracks who was likely to commit suicide if his wife didn't behave herself. He didn't name the couple. But later . . . well, you might think Mick was perceptive or you might think he was laying cover for a murderous plan.

We shouldn't imagine that the whole of Sergeant Emmett-Dunne's being was taken up with his love-life. He was still concerned about Ronald. He heard on the grapevine that his little brother had been drafted to Germany and was unhappy. So Mick applied to have him transferred to his own unit where he could keep an eye on him. And Ronald's happiness improved.

Mick was also in a spot of trouble. He was less skilful on the fiddle than Reg had been in black marketeering. He had done a crooked deal with a supplies firm, getting at least a woollen sweater out of participating in or conniving at fraud. This was catching up with him and he was afraid that he was facing court martial.

Later, he and Mia would claim that this was why he telephoned and wrote to her under cover of her neighbours. He was trying to buy deutschmarks to skip the country if things turned out badly, and they knew Reg would not approve.

At 10 p.m. on Sunday 29 November, Mick came to the

Watters' flat with a message for Reg. A major from Hilden had turned up at the barracks expressing interest in a second-hand car Reg was selling. (Casual dealing in used cars was a hobby of Reg's.) The major had left after spending the evening in the sergeants' mess, but would be back next day at 7 p.m.

At 6.30 p.m. on Monday 30 November, Reg Watters took a bath in his flat and merrily carolled, 'You are my heart's delight'. Shortly before 7 p.m. he left on foot, shouting something to Mia she did not catch.

At 7 p.m. Sergeant Major Emmett-Dunne took a telephone call in the mess and left saying he had to meet someone. He checked out of the barracks in his car at 7.05 p.m. He checked back in not long after. But we don't know exactly when because somebody got hold of the book and made a crude erasure of the entry time, replacing it with '19.40'. It's quite certain that Emmett-Dunne came back earlier than 7.40 p.m.

Later, he said that the telephone call had come from Sergeant Watters, who asked him for a lift into camp from a hotel in Duisburg. He had dropped Reg just outside the barrack gate around 7.30 p.m.

When Sergeant Watters was not home at midnight, Mia telephoned the barracks. QSM Fry, the duty sergeant, found Emmett-Dunne in the mess, and after Mick had told Mia about bringing Reg to the camp at 7.30 p.m., the two sergeants went on a thorough search.

At 3 a.m. they found Reg Watters in the entry to a little used block. He was hanging from a wash line strung across three bannisters on the stairway. His feet were six inches off the ground. One shoe and a bucket on its side lay below him, showing how he had committed suicide. This was what the inquiry concluded he had done. The pathologist reported that Reg had died of shock caused by hanging himself. Sergeant Watters was buried with full military honours and Mia collected her widow's pension and left Germany.

She went back to England to stay with Reg's sister, Mrs

de Clifford, at her pub, the Ingram Arms in Leeds. Imagine her surprise when Mrs de Clifford came up to her room one evening in the spring of 1954 to say there was someone in the bar who knew her from Germany! Imagine her astonishment to find it was Mick! Imagine his complete amazement to discover Mia, actually staying in a little pub he had only wandered into by chance because he had heard singing from it while visiting the city to order a suit on his weekend leave from Catterick Camp where he was now stationed! Considering the Ingram Arms is well outside Leeds city centre in Harewood it seems an amazing coincidence!

Nor was this the last coincidence to strike this happy pair. Three weeks later, Mia was in the queue outside the Odeon Cinema in the Headrow, when, unexpectedly, who should address her but Mick! They went in together and arranged to meet in the cinema café three weeks later on his next weekend leave. And at that meeting, to Mia's complete surprise, Mick proposed to her. It was a most unusual proposal. He said he felt responsible for her and she needed a roof over her head. He said he didn't expect her to love him. He promised that he would never make any sexual demands on her whatsoever!

Mia well might say, sixteen months later, 'That must be the strangest proposal any girl ever had.' And, having heard the full tale of the meetings and proposal in Leeds, with the corollary that Mia accepted the proposal on the terms offered, Judge-Advocate Charles Cahn might well remark, 'It is indeed by any account a remarkable story.'

But Mia might have been forgiven for postponing the consummation of her marriage till after the honeymoon. For Mick took her to Ringwood and told her how much the place meant to him as the home of a girl he had loved two years previously! And after spoiling their wedding night in the hotel with that information, he capped his thoughtlessness by hunting out his old girlfriend to introduce the two women who meant so much to him. Neither was overjoyed!

Still, it strains belief that this couple, whose sexual appeal to others was so strong, felt none for each other until their marriage was a couple of months old and Mick had been transferred to Taunton! The marriage itself was enough to set off alarm bells in two men's minds.

Ronald Emmett was appalled. But he said nothing.

Metropolitan Police Sergeant Frank Walters felt his suspicions were confirmed and he signalled the Rhine Army Special Investigation Branch. Sergeant Walters had been a BAOR Special Investigator himself at the time of Sergeant Watters' death. He had not been satisfied by the verdict of suicide. He had traced the rumours of Mick's and Mia's liaison. He did not believe that the man who was singing in his bath early one evening had proceeded to hang himself a few hours later. He did not believe that the alteration of Emmett-Dunne's time of return to barracks with Watters was unconnected with Watters' violent end. He found a sergeant whom Watters had told that he thought the story of the major from Hilden wanting to buy his car was a pack of bloody lies. Walters thought so, too. Nor did Walters believe the telephone call Emmett-Dunne received in the mess came from Watters appealing for a lift. He believed it was a signal from someone else that Watters was on his way to the camp. He did not believe it was any accident that the last person to see Sergeant Watters alive should marry his widow six months later.

Investigations into the death of Sergeant Watters were reopened, and Scotland Yard was invited to assist. When that news appeared in the papers, Ronald Emmett panicked completely and went straight to the police in Cheshire, where he was living by then.

At about 7.35 p.m. on 30 November 1953, Emmett had gone to bed early in barracks. A private came to his hut with the message that his brother wanted him, so Emmett put a track suit over his pyjamas and went to the sergeants' mess where Mick was waiting outside by his car. In a quick undertone, Mick told Ronald he had accidentally killed a man by striking him during an argument.

After they had mooched around together in obvious places, which Emmett-Dunne hoped would establish an alibi, the two had gone to the block where Watters' body was later found hanging. Reg was crouched there, dead, his body covered by a gas cape. Ronald helped Mick stage the suicide, getting a bad scare when a party from the shooting range came by.

He was fond of his brother and completely believed his story of the accidental lethal blow struck during an argument. But on learning of his wedding to Watters' widow, he suffered severe doubts. On learning that Scotland Yard was involved, he feared that he might be accessory after the fact of murder.

Professor Francis Camps, the Home Office pathologist, was sent out to undertake a new examination of Watters' exhumed body. He discovered that the young pathologist, Dr Womack, who had diagnosed suicide, had made an extremely thorough and accurate examination of the body. But he had not had the experience to interpret both what he saw and what he did not see. Some of his observations were of features entirely new to forensic medicine, anyway.

Dr Womack's first and most important oversight was the absence of minute subcutaneous haemorrhages around the eyes and in the face, which should definitely have been present if Sergeant Watters had blocked his own breathing by hanging himself. And he had failed to pay proper attention to the discoloration he observed around the upper back and shoulders, which showed the body had lain in a crouching position, bent forward immediately after death, for blood to drain to those points and leave markings on the skin. Had Watters died on the rope, all his blood would have drained to his legs.

But Womack could not have been expected to understand the tears in the carotid artery – such injuries had never been observed before. It took some macabre experimentation on corpses to prove that these were caused by a karate chop to the Adam's apple: a lethal blow taught in an unarmed combat training programme Emmett-Dunne had attended during the war.

Sergeant Major Emmett-Dunne was arrested and charged with murder. He had to be tried by court martial in Germany as he was an Irish citizen and the British courts had no jurisdiction over him for an offence committed outside the United Kingdom.

Emmett-Dunne could not deny Ronald's story. He admitted he had killed Reg Watters, but he claimed it was in self-defence. As Watters sat in the passenger seat of his car, he had accused Emmett-Dunne of sleeping with Mia during the exercise period in September. Watters dismissed Mick's denials and said he was going to put a stop to it. With this, he pulled a pistol from his pocket. Emmett-Dunne could see that it was loaded, and a charged chamber was just starting to turn in the cylinder as he lashed out with his left arm, defending himself, but killing Watters. He and Mia both denied that there had ever been an affair between them, and put forward the astonishing story of their chance meeting in Leeds and initially celibate marriage.

Professor Camps drily pointed out that the sequence of events Emmett-Dunne described was impossible. The injuries were not compatible with the angle from which he would have struck the blow if he was in the car. An army unarmed combat instructor declared that the karate strike would be the last method of self-defence a trained man would use if threatened by a gun. He would know he must go for the gun itself. The court found Emmett-Dunne guilty of murder and sentenced him to death.

However, the sentence could not be carried out. West Germany had abolished capital punishment after the war and it was a condition of the army bases in the British zone that they would never operate laws that conflicted with local law.

So Emmett-Dunne returned to Norwich prison to serve

a life sentence. I feel rather sorry for him. He was not a man who had much opportunity to learn about the love of women, and he easily found himself behaving badly without meaning to. He certainly would not have wanted to put his brother in the intolerable situation of having to give evidence against him, and both of them seem to have regretted deeply the tragic events which led to their rift.

Mia, on the other hand, loudly protested her love for both Reg and Mick, and declared that she would wait for Emmett-Dunne until he was eligible for parole (by which time she would be forty-two and he forty-four). A year later she changed her mind and her name, and let Mick divorce her for her adultery in a Gloucester Road flat.

Sheila Garvie and
Brian Tevendale

Here's a moral tale for our times. A forceful warning against letting free-wheeling sexual experimentation assume that making love doesn't, as the words suggest, generate attachment. A reminder that attachment may engender possessiveness and jealousy.

In May 1968, Mrs Hilda Kerr went to the police. Her brother, Maxwell Garvie, had disappeared from his home at Fordoun, Kincardineshire, between the Grampians and the sea, in the neighbourhood of the ruined Kincardine Castle where Malcolm graciously accepted Macbeth's severed head. Mr Garvie's blue Ford Cortina was parked on the runway of Fordoun Flying Club. There was no other trace of him.

Mrs Sheila Garvie, Maxwell's wife, was unperturbed. Though her husband had apparently left her bed during the night of 15 May, so that she woke up to find him gone, she was sure he would return soon. There was an important meeting of the Flying Club coming up and Max would certainly be back for that. He had, after all, founded the club. When he didn't show up for the meeting, Mrs Garvie conceded that something was wrong.

The neighbours expressed no surprise that Mr Garvie had disappeared. They nicknamed his luxurious farmhouse at West Cairnbeg 'Kinky Cottage'. They believed the Garvies to be orgiasts, and never knew how many people would be staying overnight nor who would be sleeping with whom. Such a man might easily have run off with another woman. Or man. Or women. Or men.

Maxwell Garvie was a prosperous farmer. When he

married Sheila Watson in 1955 he was only twenty-two.
But already he was rich, self-supporting and a keen pilot.
Sheila, about two years younger, was delighted by her
good-looking, wealthy admirer. She herself had quite
humble origins. Her father was a stone mason, and
though he was employed on the royal property at
Balmoral for three years during Sheila's teens, the
Watson family were definitely hired help and not gentry.
After leaving school, Sheila Watson worked briefly as a
maid at Balmoral. She and her colleagues were given tea
by the Queen once, after presenting her with an
embroidered teacloth. But the job was not one with
prospects.

When the Watson family moved to Stonehaven on the
coast near Aberdeen, Sheila went with them, and took a
clerical job with a local bus company. She was just
eighteen when she met Maxwell Garvie at a village hop.
She married him a year later.

They were a handsome and provincially glamorous
young couple. They looked idyllically happy. They had
three children. And with their shared pleasure in the
Flying Club, there seemed no reason to predict any
serious rough passages for the future.

But Maxwell Garvie's smooth passage through life had
not prepared him for the challenges of the 1960s. Seven
years into his marriage, he began to feel the itch of
discontent. At the time when he first married, this might
just have led to a brief infatuation with a passing
stranger, as in the Tom Ewell and Marilyn Monroe film.
But by 1962 the sixties were starting to swing. Stephen
Ward and his friends were enjoying their orgies in
London. Anthony Asquith was establishing his mysterious underground reputation as the masochistic 'man in
the mask' – an identity so shrouded in secrecy that
rumour would attach it wrongly to various cabinet
ministers. Raunchier and raunchier imitations of *Playboy*
magazine were sweeping the old nudie mags like *Spick*
and *Span* out of existence. The pornography which the

Olympia Press had always sold to travellers in Paris was beginning to emerge in the backs of Soho shops. *Lady Chatterley's Lover* came out of the closet and was recognized as literature by Penguin Books and the law of the land. Maxwell Garvie felt a social pressure to indulge his growing randiness.

But he was a man who had grown to maturity in the 1950s. He kicked off his swinging with the rather old-fashioned delight of attending nudist clubs. The 'nudist' magazine *Health and Efficiency* and the ludicrous 'nudist' films of the period flirtatiously combined sun-loving sportiness with the exposure of bosoms and decorously airbrushed or discreetly concealed genitals. A non-partisan nudist might be someone who simply prefers working and sleeping with no clothes on in total privacy when the weather is warm enough. Suspect suburban nudists may be harmless groups like the 'witches' who meet friends formally for quite respectable rituals where everyone is 'skyclad'. But nudist clubs can also attract voyeurs.

Maxwell Garvie was a voyeur. He took Sheila to nudist clubs on the continent. He decided he wanted to enjoy the same freedom at home and involve their daughters. He could afford to indulge his fancy: he had, after all, founded the Fordoun Flying Club with his own money. Now he bought some land at Alford, planted a thousand trees and opened a nudist colony.

Sheila Garvie, too, had reached maturity before the sexual revolution. She had three children and a comfortable, prosperous life. A decent upbringing in the environs of royalty had in no way prepared her for the notion of sex as sport. She disliked Maxwell's increasing obsession, and no one warned her that her own blonde good looks, in the intimacy of matrimony, would keep him perpetually aroused. No counsellor advised that her best hope of keeping him faithful would be to enter enthusiastically into his erotic games. Sheila unwillingly accepted her husband's constant attentions and regretfully let him take revealing photos of her.

She was, I feel, absolutely justified in being furious when he showed them around to friends without her knowledge or consent. It was humiliating to have a man she'd never met leer at her at a party and say, 'I've seen more of you than you think!' Maxwell's conduct cannot be exonerated. Sexual freedom must, as the absolute minimum, be conducted with good manners and consideration.

But I think his next move shows that at this stage what Maxwell still wanted, more than anything else, was for his wife to share his new-found drive to erotic experimentation. He didn't follow the bad old pattern of sleeping around behind her back. Oddly enough, it might have been better had he done so. Sheila could have felt contemptuous superiority had he shown himself a conventional liar and deceiver. But she couldn't cope with being asked to involve herself in something she found dirty. She probably wanted sex to be undemanding and romantic, and might have found it tolerable, if distasteful, had Maxwell worked off the hard edge of his ever-increasing randiness somewhere else. Instead, he tried to get her to perform vicariously for him. For it was becoming clear to Maxwell that he had bisexual tendencies. He became hugely attracted to a young barman called Brian Tevendale.

Garvie and Tevendale were both members of the Scottish Nationalist Party. Garvie was a party official and Tevendale, whose late father had been a war hero, was a useful member. There was nothing particularly surprising about Maxwell's inviting fellow Scot Nat Brian to come and spend weekends at his farm.

But it was surprising that he persistently ensured that Brian and Sheila were left alone together, with plenty to drink. Sheila was disgusted that her husband would then excitedly ask her 'What happened?' in such a way that it was clear he hoped *something* had happened. Indeed, his questions were openly, avidly, repulsively urgent and sexual. Sheila was revolted. Nor was it reassuring when Maxwell started to hint that he found Brian more attractive than her.

In September 1967, when Tevendale was staying and all three had had quite a bit to drink, Maxwell shoved his wife into Brian's bedroom and left her there. She stayed all night. In the morning, an enthusiastic Maxwell pounced on her and she was disgusted to realize that he got an extra kick out of having sex with her immediately after Tevendale had done so. His probing questions, too, were more revolting than ever.

According to Tevendale, Garvie now started making direct passes at him – passes which he rejected. He also introduced him to an unpleasant aerobatic game, 'shooting up' motorists. This meant flying low and threateningly at an approaching car on a lonely road until the driver stopped or pulled off to the side. It was while excited by this petty sadism that Garvie confided to Tevendale that he intended to sodomize Sheila. It was something he had apparently never done, and which it was extremely likely she would resist and detest given her distaste for such adventurous sex as they had tried. She thought it all kinky and nasty.

Tevendale may have been protecting his own virtue when he introduced Maxwell to his sister, Mrs Trudi Birse. He may have felt that his sister was bored with her marriage to an Aberdeen policeman. Or he may just have naïvely failed to realize that he was introducing potassium to water. Whatever his expectations, Maxwell and Trudi ignited instantly. They became lovers, and soon Maxwell was telling Sheila that he had enjoyed more fun with Trudi in two weeks than he had experienced in twelve years of marriage.

Sheila, by contrast, desperately retained the moral outlook of 1955. She begged Max not to keep a date with Trudi. May as well beg the magnet to leave the iron filings alone! Maxwell imperiously told her it was 1968 and people did this sort of thing nowadays. (They always had, of course. The real difference was that formerly they had been secretive and furtive. Now the values of openness and integrity were becoming realized. But Maxwell was really proving an exemplary case of the problems crude heartlessness and downright bad manners caused in 'the new morality'.)

Max insisted on going out with Brian and Trudi, and he insisted on involving Sheila. He started taking her and Brian and Trudi on foursome weekends in country hotels. Brian would sleep with Sheila. Maxie would sleep with Trudi. And sometimes Maxie would send Trudi to fetch Sheila for another change of beds, so that he could sleep with Sheila after she had slept with Brian. And what did PC Fred Birse think of his wife's violent immersion in the swinging sixties? He may have accepted it and dipped a toe in the water himself. At any rate, Maxwell threw one small party at West Cairnbeg where he laid on a girl specially for Fred.

For what it's worth, foursomes, whether simple regular wife-swapping, or all piling into one bed, seem to be among the riskiest sexual practices. Simple habitual swapping with one other couple usually leads to a transfer of affections on the part of two and jealous distress for the others. As novelist John Irving quoted bleakly from Ford Madox Ford when he wrote about four people in just such an unhappy tangle, 'All things considered, and in the sight of God, they might as well have stuck knives into one another. For these were *good* people.'

There's no evidence that Maxwell Garvie was an especially good person. But there doesn't seem to have been anything notably bad about Brian and Sheila before they were bundled into one another's beds. The consequence was they fell in love.

Max was horrified. He broke up with Trudi and demanded that Sheila give up Brian. She refused. He hired thugs to beat up Brian. A stranger slashed Brian's face, saying this was 'a present from the Skipper' (Maxwell's nickname in the Flying Club). When Brian

complained to Max, his former friend said threateningly,
'You won't get a chance to run next time'.

Sheila left Max. He threatened to kill Brian and the
children. Sheila came back. It didn't work and she left
again. Max repeated his sinister threat and she came back
again. It was a relief to everyone when Maxwell Garvie
disappeared in May.

The police shared the neighbours' view that his
disappearance was a spin-off from his swinging lifestyle.
The *Scottish Police Gazette*, circulating a notice of his
disappearance, mentioned his openhandedness, his heavy
drinking and his homosexual tendencies, coupled with a
delight in young female company. He took pep pills and
tranquillizers, which mixed dangerously with his alcoholic intake. He dealt in pornography and he frequented
nudist camps. The police probably didn't expect to hear
anything more of Maxwell Garvie unless he emerged as
king of a sex commune in California. He looked quite
capable of flipping off to a new life as a rich, thirtyish
hippy.

The other three of the erstwhile foursome kept up
contact, meanwhile. Brian Tevendale stayed at Trudi
Birse's home in Aberdeen. Sheila divided her time
between looking after the children back at the farm and
staying with Brian in Aberdeen. On 14 August she
decided to take the children and go to start a new life with
Brian.

Sheila's mother, Mrs Watson, had never approved of
Brian Tevendale. She had been pleased when Maxwell
quarrelled with him, and supportive when her son-in-law
asked her to take care of the children if anything
happened to him, making particularly sure they were kept
away from Brian. Since Sheila was apparently determined
to take the kids under Tevendale's roof, Mrs Watson
went to the police – with quite a story. Apparently,
Sheila had told her, soon after Max's disappearance, that
he had actually been murdered by Brian Tevendale and a
friend of his called Alan Peters.

The police didn't need telling twice. This was, in their eyes, a rats' nest of the new morality, and no doubt these people were quite capable of killing each other. Sheila and Brian and twenty-year-old Alan Peters were all arrested. Sheila and Brian were allowed a few minutes together at Stonehaven Police Station and Brian thought they had agreed their story at that point. He assumed he was only wanted as a witness and Sheila was being arrested for murder. He told the police that on the night of 14 May, a hysterical Sheila had telephoned him to say she had just killed Max. Her husband had insisted on sodomizing her again and threatened her with a rifle when she refused. There had been a struggle . . . the gun went off . . . and Max was dead. Tevendale offered to remove the body, and he and Peters drove it to an underground culvert running from Lauriston Castle, near St Cyrus, where Tevendale had played as a child. They left Max's car at the Flying Club to suggest his voluntary departure.

But immediately after Max's death, Brian had told his sister a very different story. Then he claimed that he and Alan Peters had gone together to West Cairnbeg. There they quarrelled with Max and Peters hit the older man over the head with an iron bar. Brian was sure this had killed him, but nonetheless shot their victim in the head before the body was dumped.

Alan Peters' story was different again. Brian had wanted to go to West Cairnbeg to face Max Garvie over the continued threats and beatings. Alan agreed to go along and support him. When they reached the farm-house, Sheila welcomed them enthusiastically. Brian took a rifle off the wall as he came into the house and loaded it. He had brought the ammunition in his pocket. Sheila gave the young men drinks and took them to an empty room upstairs. After forty-five minutes she came in and, saying, 'He's asleep now', led them to the master bedroom. Garvie was sleeping face down in bed. Brian battered his head with the gunstock, then threw a pillow over it and shot him through the pillow. Alan helped

Brian drag the body out to his own old Ford Zephyr, after which Brian drove Max's Cortina out to the Flying Club, where he transferred to the Zephyr and navigated Alan to the culvert at Lauriston Castle.

One part of Alan's story was supported by an independent witness. On the way back, he said, the car got stuck in a rut. They roused a local farmer who lent them his tractor to drag it out. Mr Kevin Thompson, the farmer, confirmed this story, adding that he had recognized Tevendale, though he had not mentioned it at the time.

Peters claimed to have kept quiet because he was afraid of Tevendale. (Perhaps he admired him a little, too. When he married, shortly after the murder, Brian Tevendale was his best man and Sheila Garvie was his wife's matron of honour.)

Sheila had nothing to offer about the journeys to the Flying Club and the castle. She did, however, put forward a fourth version of the murder. She had fallen asleep in bed with Max after one of their usual quarrels over love-making. She was woken by someone pulling her arm. She recognized Tevendale's voice as he told her to go into the bathroom and wait inside. Dopey from her sleeping pills, she did as she was told. There were savage bumps and thumps from the bedroom. Then Tevendale told her to go and hold the children's door closed. She did so, while he and another man dragged Max's sheet-enshrouded body downstairs.

It fell to the jury to decide which of these tales they believed, and how they apportioned responsibility.

They found Alan Peters not proven guilty of murder. With only the conflicting tales of accomplices standing against him, he was certainly not proven guilty or not guilty of conspiring to kill Max Garvie. He might well be seen as accessory after the fact — but he hadn't been charged with this. And he didn't seem to be the only one. Trudi Birse had heard her brother's confession and helped Sheila wash bloodstained sheets. Fred Birse had told Sheila how to wipe fingerprints off a rifle, using an oiled rag. And he had burned the blood-soaked mattress for her in a rubbish dump.

Sheila and Brian were both found guilty. She spent ten and her lover nine years in prison. They did not reunite on their release.

Local gossip was very severe on them and the Birses. The vicar said he had heard that Max asked a friend to seduce his wife, and Sheila had complained to him of Maxwell's perverse and homosexual tendencies. But the vicar, better versed, no doubt, in comparative scriptural studies than the vagaries of human conduct, simply didn't believe her! So she did not get what Shakespeare would have called 'ghostly comfort' in her affliction.

The shocked local innocents weren't all quite as innocent as they pretended, however. Somebody broke into the guest house of the Alford nudist colony and ripped out several pages from the visitors' book. Somebody had something to conceal. Not complicity in murder, of course. Just the sort of furtive pleasure in sex for which the Birses were now being criticized. Just a willingness to join in the sort of fun and games which Maxwell Garvie had unsuccessfully pioneered. Just a case of good old-fashioned hypocrisy.

But maybe they were prudent to destroy all evidence of a possible cause for deadly jealousy.

Susan Christie

In 1982, Lt Duncan McAllister of the Royal Signals
Corps went to a party in the officers' mess at Lippstadt,
Germany. There he ran into a close friend who had the
most beautiful girl he'd ever seen on his arm.

'Oh, Duncan, meet Penny. Penny, meet Duncan,' said
his friend. Duncan, a rather callow twenty-one-year-old,
felt distinctly put down that he had no such striking
partner; felt, rightly or wrongly, that his friend was
showing off the trophy won by his manly charms.

'Oh, yeah, not bad,' said Duncan, and he walked
away.

But he was not really such a nasty young man as that
comment suggests. He realized at once that, whatever his
friend might or might not have intended, his conduct was
insufferably rude to the girl. It nagged at him and about
an hour later he went over and asked her to dance with
him to make amends. They danced together for the rest of
the evening.

'What do you do?' he asked her.

'I'm at school.'

'Well, what do you teach?'

'No,' said the girl, a little embarrassed. 'I'm doing my
O' levels.'

Duncan was staggered. He couldn't believe that this
stunning creature was only sixteen. In makeup and party
clothes she looked far closer to his own age. But she was
really something special. He asked her out to dinner with
him the following night. She apologized, saying she was
already busy. Duncan took it he'd been firmly brushed
off, and accepted that it probably served him right for

treating her as just an appendage to his best friend's arm.

Still, he couldn't get the lovely girl out of his mind. She'd told him that her name was Penny Squire and her father was deputy head of the Lippstadt English primary school. Three months later he was sitting around the officers' mess at Soest with nothing to do for the weekend, so he decided to drive over to Lippstadt and look her up again.

Mrs Squire answered the door, and the smart young lieutenant explained that she didn't know him and he'd only met Penny the once, a few months before. But he would like to take her out for the evening.

'You're Duncan,' said Mrs Squire. And he knew that, against all the odds, he had clicked with beautiful Penny.

By Christmas, he knew he was deeply in love with the girl. He had to go to Norway with the regimental skiing team and before he went he made his position quite clear. He told Penny that if she didn't feel she was with him, and no one else, he wanted to break it all off before he went away. He couldn't stand uncertainty. He couldn't sit around in Norway humming 'I wonder who's seeing her now?' He could put her out of his mind and try to forget her, or he could accept commitment. Penny opted for commitment.

The following year the Squires found a room to billet Duncan in their house. He and Penny had a wonderful summer. Both sporty, outdoors people, they enjoyed picnics and wind-surfing. Penny had spent all her life around army bases, so she fully understood the nuances of service social life. (Always look first at a man's shoulders, an old army daughter once told me, to see whether he outranks your father or not!)

When Duncan was posted back to England in 1983, it was tears all round. When he and Penny found they missed each other desperately and letters and telephone calls were no substitute, he asked her how she liked the idea of his asking her father for permission to marry her. She liked it very much.

Des Squire didn't say yes or no over the telephone. He asked Duncan to call him back again in four hours after they'd talked it over with Penny. There was serious talking to be done. The proposal meant breaking into her education. She was just seventeen. She was preparing for her A' levels and it had always been assumed that she would go on to university. Did she really want to abandon all that? Give up the different options for life that were available to her? Commit herself to nothing but the old-fashioned lifestyle of a wife and mother?

Penny did. She was sure Duncan was right for her. She believed the conventional conservative ethos of the army would support her through the trials of post-feminist life as a housewife and hostess. The Squires decided that she really did know her own mind; that Duncan was a nice boy with a promising army career ahead of him, and they might never encounter a better. So they gave their consent.

Penny Squire married Duncan McAllister at Ashton Keynes church in Wiltshire. It was a picture-book wedding. Penny looked entrancing, her veil held in place by a small white coif, her hands clasping a bouquet of white roses relieved by little blue flowers. The couple flew off to a wonderful honeymoon in Tunisia. It was the first of many holidays on the sunnier seashores of the world over the next decade, as Duncan's career progressed steadily; the army saw him through an engineering degree; and the boyish lieutenant became a handsome captain.

Captain McAllister was posted to Northern Ireland in June 1989. It's just about the most unpopular posting a British soldier can get. But Duncan McAllister didn't sit and grouch about the lousy tour of duty. He got on with improving the situation with the best recreational comfort he knew – sport. In January 1989, Duncan started a scuba-diving club.

The members were, naturally, drawn from forces personnel. For three months, Duncan didn't notice twenty-one-year-old Ulster Defence Regiment Private Susan Christie as anything but another diving club member. He had a very beautiful wife, and Susan (in his ungracious words) is not 'classically sexy'. Who or what is? Sexual tastes alter so much from generation to generation that I don't think the words mean anything. I shouldn't, myself, call Nefertiti sexy or Nell Gwyn classic. The captain's lack of gallantry is confirmed by his description of Susan as short and squat and unsophisticated. But by the time he said all that she'd destroyed his wife, his reputation and his career with a few savage strokes of a butcher's knife.

Susan caught his attention soon after making her first open-water dive. She completed it satisfactorily, but later injured her eardrums in a swimming pool. The officer who drove her to hospital asked her out for dinner. She refused, and in refusing talked so much about Duncan that the officer realized she had a definite crush on her diving instructor. And he told Duncan.

Duncan was flattered. He kept an eye open to see if there was any truth in the suggestion and he decided there was. Susan always tried to sit close to him in the diving boat. She made a point of sitting behind him when the club travelled by van. So Duncan spoke to her about it.

Now what did he say? We have two completely contradictory stories about the development of their affair which the two put forward at Susan's trial. No doubt, in part, they reflect the different temperaments of the two and the different ways in which they interpreted each other's remarks. But Duncan tells a story of a cautious, ordered move toward sexual intimacy, planned with all the care of a military route-march and the considerate good manners of an officer and a gentleman. Susan tells of a passionate man who urged her into his bed and utterly overwhelmed her maiden modesty.

Duncan says he put it to Susan that she seemed to be paying a lot of attention to him and she had better stop it unless she intended it to mean something. Then, after giving her a few days to ingest this first feeler, he again raised the subject, asking whether she really wanted to see him away from the club and have an affair with him. When she said she did, he gave her a lecture on the dangers of a liaison with a married man who was not going to leave his wife. But he still left the possibility open to her and gave her another three days to consider it.

When she came back, still saying yes, he asked her why she had seemed hesitant previously (which does rather contradict his claim that he spent all his time putting the cons before her without any pros or pressure!) and she told him she was still a virgin. The information excited Duncan, who was immensely flattered at being offered a hymen to rupture. But he still confined himself to long walks and earnest Victorian talks until one day, beside the lake, they found they were making love.

Susan's story is quite different. She says she was a virgin and she wanted to retain her virginity. But Duncan pressed and badgered her, took her to his house and finally led her upstairs and seduced her against her deepest inclinations. She says they met in the house repeatedly and that was where most of their love-making took place.

Duncan says they hardly ever went to the house, and whenever they did he was always scrupulous about making love in the spare bedroom and never defiling the matrimonial bed.

Well, they're both alive and capable of telling their own stories. No doubt Susan will enlarge on her version when she comes out of prison and some keen crime historian approaches her. In the meantime, I don't intend to try and choose between them.

What nobody denies is that they had an affair. And nobody ever forgets that its zenith was the time they made love under water, and Duncan gave Susan two gold stars. It happened off Ascension Island. The scuba-diving club went there in October and Susan remarked that she wanted to do something Duncan had never done with

Penny. Making love at a depth of 20 metres fitted the bill, and when they came up they had, as a matter of course, to log accounts of their partners' dives.

Duncan commemorated the occasion by giving Susan two gold stars on her report. He says he only did this because she had done a very good technical dive the previous day and he had given her a well-deserved single star. So he had to improve on that when Susan asked him whether it wasn't better with sex. In fact, he says, the sex was pretty much a failure.

Maybe he's right. He says partners had to report on each other's dives and there's no record of Susan giving *him* any stars for his performance! But Susan herself was cock-a-hoop at getting this secret thumbs-up signal in the diving log from her lover.

The affair dragged on over Christmas. By Duncan's account he was tiring of it, but whenever he tried to break off Susan threw a hysterical fit, and he felt he could not say no to a lady. He complains that she sent him a Christmas card on which she listed, among other things, sexual variations to which he had introduced her.

Certainly for him, as for Susan, spring arrived with a need to ensure that Penny remained ignorant of the affair. Susan had difficulty in concealing her distaste for Duncan's wife. The middle-class English woman, who had nearly gone to university and whose grace and beauty were coming to perfect fruition as she approached thirty, might have aroused the little working-class Ulster girl's envy even had she not been married to her lover.

Duncan surely didn't help by dropping large hints that Susan was not sufficiently ladylike to make officer material. He knew she was ambitious for promotion. But ex-public schoolboy Duncan is of the old stiff-upper-lip brigade. Officers, in his opinion, just don't show their emotions. So a passionate little Irish girl who screamed her adoration and jealousy at him was just showing her lack of class.

The poor man seems to have little idea that this advice

came over as a toffee-nosed putdown. And since Susan
was in love with him, she transferred the blame to his
wife: pretentious Penny, whose cool stylishness was such
an obvious contrast to her own warm emotions.

On 27 March something a little disturbing happened.
Susan arranged with Penny that the two should go
walking the McAllisters' red setters through Drumkeer-
agh Forest in the late morning. It was Susan's idea and
Duncan hated it − naturally. No man likes the idea of his
wife and his mistress getting together alone. Especially if
there's a hint of suspicion or tension between the two.
They might compare notes. They might come to blows.
But whether they agree unanimously that he's a horrible
cad, or each accuse the other of unmentionable things,
he's sure to be the whipping-boy for both, whether they
attack him jointly or separately. If, that is, they talk
frankly about the thing that's on all their minds.

But it didn't come to that. At 2.30 p.m., Duncan's CO
came personally to see him with some very bad news. He
put it kindly, sympathetically and directly. Penny was
dead.

Part of the hell of a soldier's lot in Northern Ireland is
that this message might be brought to anyone at any time.
The terrorists are not so efficient that they always strike
the right targets. Duncan assumed Penny and Susan had
been the victims of an IRA outrage.

But, no. The story was different. A lone man had
attacked the two women. They had separated a short
distance, following the dogs, when Susan heard a cry and
saw a man with a knife standing over Penny. She rushed
to her aid and tried to pull him off, whereupon he slashed
savagely at her, cutting her abdomen and stabbing her
thighs. With admirable presence of mind, she called,
'Daddy, Daddy! Come quickly!' and while the assailant
was distracted, looking for the help she was apparently
summoning, she raced away from him in the direction of
some cottages.

Susan was now in hospital, suffering from cuts,

bruising and shock. But Penny's throat had been cut.

These were army women. In no time, helicopters were scouring the forest, looking for the evil molester to make a break from cover. As soon as Susan was fit to talk, army interrogators were asking her to give precise details of where the man had come from and which direction he had moved away.

Duncan questioned her, too. He asked her whether she had anything to do with it and then apologised at once, dismissing the idea as ridiculous. But it came back to him when he listened to Susan's story a couple of times and noted that she just wasn't describing the terrain consistently. And the same point struck her professional interviewers. Susan telephoned Duncan in tears saying two of her questioners were absolute beasts and kept trying to trip her up.

Gradually it dawned on Duncan that the investigation into his wife's murder could not possibly be complete unless he told the investigators that her companion on her last walk had also been his mistress. As he drove with a heavy heart to make this confession, which he knew would blast his career, he allowed himself to recognize that he now suspected Susan.

So did the investigators. With the motive supplied, they quickly moved to the clues pointing to her involvement. The previous Sunday she had reconnoitred the area where she and Penny took the dogs. She had access to a butcher's knife like the one that killed Penny. She had the combat training to know how to seize her victim from behind and cut her throat while she was surprised and over-powered. She wore gloves like the ones she said the murdering man had worn. She would have the courage and determination to cut herself: the skill to make the injuries striking, but not serious.

By the time she came to trial the following year, Susan had as good as confessed. Her only defence was that she couldn't remember actually doing the killing.

Duncan and the Squires were appalled that she was

convicted of manslaughter and given a mere five-year sentence, which meant she could be back on the streets in a year. A sympathetic Irish judge seemed to them to have let Susan play the poor little 'colleen bawn' seduced by the big bad English captain, whose heartlessness showed in the wooden way he gave his evidence. But Parliament had recently decided that prosecutors might appeal against sentences that seemed too low, just as defendants could always appeal against too much punishment. Susan's jail sentence was increased to nine years by the appeal court.

She'll still be out before she's thirty, if she behaves herself.

Carolyn Warmus

Carolyn Warmus seems to have fuelled her private life on possessive jealousy. It couldn't be stated at her trials, but all the lawyers knew that her adult emotions were dominated by affairs and relationships in which, typically, Carolyn would claim a far greater attachment than her partner felt. Carolyn used her glamorous blonde good looks and busty body to attract and seduce men. She was an imaginative and uninhibited lover who expected to hook the men she had once seduced. If a man wanted to break things off, Carolyn would bully and badger him. If the man had a prior commitment to another woman, Carolyn used threats and lies to try and push her out of his life.

Carolyn gives us, perhaps, our purest example of the sheer egocentricity of jealousy: the jealous person's uncontrollable subjective need which prevents them from imagining other people's feelings — an inability which ultimately cripples their relations with the object of their adoration. She also demonstrates to us the tragic lack of self-confidence and self-esteem which leads the jealous person to place unrealistic value on the imagined prop of another's love.

The eldest child of Thomas and Elizabeth Warmus, Carolyn was born in the posh Detroit suburb of St Clair Shores in 1964. Her father was an ambitious insurance man. He became chief executive of Michigan Benefit Plans, Inc; then founded his own chain of companies under the umbrella of American Way Insurance. Thirty years after his 1961 marriage, Thomas Aloysius Warmus was a millionaire, with a fleet of private planes; a collection of vintage cars; a holiday estate in Florida as well as town house and country mansion in his native Michigan. Along the way he lost Carolyn's mother.

There were two younger Warmus children: Tracey and Thomas Jr. After the latter's birth in 1968, Elizabeth Warmus knew she could not cope with her husband's persistent workaholism and absence from home. She took refuge in the bottle.

In 1972 she divorced Tom. She was granted custody of the children, and this led to irresponsible spats and squabbles in their presence, including the terrifying abduction of Tom Jr by his father on one occasion.

All three children took the break very hard — especially Carolyn. When Tom married his secretary, Nancy Dailey, Carolyn made no bones about loathing her new stepmother. Nancy loved fast cars, fur coats, skintight dresses. Carolyn used this appetite for the glitzy end of consumerism to portray her stepmother as a greedy bimbo — a hussy dolling herself up to take advantage of men. So it was not good news for Carolyn when Elizabeth decided to remarry and move to New York, leaving the children in the care and control of Tom and Nancy.

Carolyn's deep insecurity showed up in high school. Her younger sister Tracey was very beautiful and very popular. Carolyn was good-looking, but evidently feared she could not compete. So she used her father's money in the hopeless attempt to buy friends. She would invite other kids to freeload on ridiculously expensive jaunts to New York or Florida with her. She bribed them with big presents to come to her parties. Saddest of all is the tale that she once gave her best friend $100 to set her up with a date. What a tragic misconception of friendship that reveals, and what utter desperation for adolescent sexual recognition!

Carolyn was not a very nice person once she grew up, so let's take our last opportunity to off-load some guilt and responsibility from her. It looks as though Thomas

Warmus unconsciously trained his daughter to mis-understand love. He saw his loving duty to his family as being a provider — to excess. He was always willing to pick up the tab. Carolyn as a child was extraordinarily free to enjoy Daddy's money. His wives, too, were expected to be grateful recipients of Big Daddy's largesse rather than constant companions of his leisure hours. It didn't hold Elizabeth but did win Nancy's devotion.

Carolyn evidently wanted the true reassurance that could only come from her father's attention and conver-sation. His presents would never substitute for his presence. She deeply resented Nancy, who was perfectly satisfied that gifts of conventional goodies proved her to be loved. Yet, not having experienced close parental friendship, Carolyn did not herself know any way of expressing affection other than by buying love. Ultima-tely sex would substitute for money in her emotional commerce.

How desperately and unrealistically she needed someone to tell her they loved her became apparent when she went to college. The University of Michigan at Ann Arbor is one of the world's finest academies. Carolyn was a good student, consistently achieving B+ and A grades in her courses as she majored in psychology and education. But the proximity to her wealthy home and the campus's reputation for partying mattered more to her.

In 1983, her third year as an undergraduate, she became a public problem. She fell for a graduate teaching assistant named Paul Laven. She forced herself on his attention and started dating him in June. For Carolyn this was Love, Devotion, Heart's Desire. For Paul it was some dates with a nice-looking girl.

For Carolyn, Paul's wish must be her command. And if he wouldn't express a wish, she would bore all their friends asking whether they thought Paul would like this pair of shoes, that outfit, the other hair style.

For Paul, this was a slightly embarrassing conquest, which (since he was a decent man) would have to be dealt with gently, firmly and openly if and when he became certain that their Match was not Made in Heaven. Which came to pass in November. Paul met a girl named Wendy Siegel, and realized that he felt serious about a future with her.

His conduct was irreproachable. He took Carolyn to dinner to explain amiably and frankly that he had met someone else and their relationship would now have to end. A lot of young men and women just don't have the courage to do that when, inevitably, they move on from early experimental relationships.

But Carolyn could neither appreciate his decency nor accept the truth he put before her. She kept watch on his apartment to see who had supplanted her. When Paul and Wendy announced their engagement she lost all control of herself and filled Paul's answerphone with jealous hate-filled messages, until he disconnected it. She wrote him a stream of impassioned, imploring letters. She tracked down Wendy's unlisted phone number and subjected her to harassing calls. She became a perfect nuisance.

Then she suddenly exhibited the sad child's response to wanting affection. She stole from her parents. She stole $7,000 worth of jewellery from Nancy: a diamond necklace, diamond ear-rings and a diamond brooch spelling 'Love'. She pawned the lot for $3,000 and was horribly surprised when the pawnbroker contacted the police, doubting the girl's story that her mother had asked her to hock all that jewellery on her behalf. Thomas Warmus angrily repaid the pawnbroker and reclaimed the jewels. But he did not allow charges to be brought against Carolyn.

Paul and Wendy knew nothing about this. They did know that Carolyn stepped up her campaign of harassment, culminating in an outburst on 10 April 1984, when she went to their house and made such a scene beating on the door and screaming that they had to call the police to take her away.

Carolyn took a brief holiday in Florida. From there she wrote to Wendy asserting that Paul was more devoted to her than ever and Wendy was being deceived. When that didn't work, she claimed to be pregnant, naming Paul as the father.

Paul and Wendy had finally had enough. Fearing that Carolyn would turn up and disrupt their wedding in July, they went to a lawyer. Threatened with an invasion of privacy suit, Carolyn signed an order enjoining her against harassing them and forbidding her to go near their wedding. And at last they were free of the jealous co-ed.

There was just one odd consequence of this tangle. Carolyn told anyone who would listen that the reason Paul dropped her was because she wasn't Jewish. She proceeded to take instruction and leave her Catholic background for conversion to the Jewish faith.

In the summer of 1986 she graduated with a BA in psychology. Before going on to New York, where she was to take her Master's at Columbia University's Teachers' College, she worked for the holiday as a waitress in Michigan. This job brought her two new doses of ill-repute. A student called Buddy Fetter enjoyed a fling with her, and then didn't enjoy it when she became emotionally demanding and clogged his answering machine with messages. He got rid of her by introducing her to a married friend who fancied her. But Buddy felt he was well shot of Carolyn Warmus.

Worse was her firing by the Jukebox Bar where she worked. They found that one of their waitresses was practising an ingenious scam by double-entering customers' credit card payments, and using the duplicate vouchers subsequently to make up the bar's accounts for cash payments which she pocketed. All the evidence pointed to Carolyn, and though she denied it vehemently, she didn't argue when she was sacked on the spot.

She was lucky not to face charges. Credit card fraud is a Federal offence and the Secret Service was informed of the malpractice. Only the lack of sufficient evidence to bring a case to court kept Carolyn out of serious trouble. And it left her name on Federal crime suspect records.

Early in 1987, graduate student Carolyn met a good-looking waiter from New Jersey called Matthew Nicolosi. He was married, but that didn't stop them from enjoying each other in bed. And it didn't stop Carolyn from her habit of monopolizing her lover's telephone line as many hours of the day and night as she could manage. Nicolosi feared that his wife would find out and tried to break the affair off.

But resistance always seems to have excited Carolyn. She lured Nicolosi back with her sensational bedroom versatility. And she spied on him to find out who his wife was and exactly where they lived.

Then, in June 1987, she ran through the Yellow Pages looking for a private detective and hit on Vincent Parco. Rich, elegant, successful Vinnie Parco was delighted when the shapely, sun-tanned blonde came into his expensively furnished office wearing a tennis outfit that showed off her long slender legs to perfection. This was a touch of the glamour Mr Parco felt appertained to being a private eye.

Carolyn's request wasn't really unusual in his business. She wanted him to find out whether Nicolosi was dating any other women on the side; find out whether he would ever be likely to marry Carolyn; and perhaps help her prepare a little scandalous evidence that would persuade Mrs Nicolosi to divorce Matthew.

Parco handed the more mundane side of the business over to an associate called Jimmy Russo. Jimmy joined Carolyn in staking out Nicolosi's work-place and his home and taking photographs of them. She also wanted pictures of Nicolosi taken unobtrusively.

His work with her came to an end after he carried out the final assignment of taking a lot of pictures of Carolyn at her place. He was startled when she appeared in a pink wig and filmy nightwear for the photo session: more startled still when she changed into different sets of underwear – some completely see-through – for further photographs.

At the end of the session Carolyn asked him to go to bed with her. Mr Russo was a smart guy. He would later admit in court that when investigating a prostitution racket he had happily 'penetrated the organization' in ways that gave him the utmost satisfaction. But he did *not* want to end up in bed with Carolyn. He politely declined her offer.

Carolyn was very annoyed at being turned down. She brought her knee sharply and painfully into his groin, saying, 'Maybe this will help you get it up'. Mr Russo left in a hurry.

His next encounter with Carolyn was vicarious. He was in Vinnie Parco's office and saw a lot of cut-up photographs on his desk. They were photographs of Matthew Nicolosi mixed with the suggestive pink-wigged Carolyn pictures Jimmy had taken. The two were being superimposed on each other to suggest that the couple had been snapped in some compromising situation. Mr Russo concluded that the intention was to send faked pictures to Mrs Nicolosi. He also thought he had never seen such unconvincing looking fakery in his life. And there is no evidence that the superimpositions were ever finally photographed or used.

Her mixed experiences with the private eyes added new excitement to Carolyn's life, however. She became a private eye groupie. She hung around Vinnie Parco's offices and accepted dinner dates with him. He admittedly fancied her rotten, but has said under oath they they never actually got it together. Since, by his own account, the main reason was that the times when it was possible for her were never quite convenient for him, this may well be true. But the woman he was later to call, 'a real ditzy blonde, and somewhat schizophrenic' would prove an embarrassing client.

Carolyn's sex-life moved off in a new direction in

September. Newly appointed as elementary computer instructor at Greenville School in the Edgemont district, New York, she met forty-one-year-old Paul Solomon — another teacher.

The twenty-three-year-old fluffy blonde Carolyn, with huge doe-like eyes, proved a most exciting mid-life crisis for Paul. He flirted with her; started having secret dinner dates with her; started enjoying absolutely wi-i-i-i-ld sex with her in motel rooms. And as Paul's occasional affairs during his nineteen years of marriage had sometimes been handicapped by his sporadic impotence, it was great for him to have an exciting young lover whose lips and tongue would ensure that he *always* made it.

But like Matthew Nicolosi, Paul had no intention of leaving his marriage for Carolyn. Although his wife, Betty Jeanne, had enjoyed an affair of her own with another manager at the bank where she worked, the Solomons had no intention of disrupting their seventeen-year-old daughter Kristan's life by divorcing. Nor did they wish to give up the excellent address in Scarsdale Apartments which their joint salaries afforded them.

Unfortunately, the wise and mature Paul, old enough to be Carolyn's father, gave her the most encouraging come-ons in what purported to be letters warning her off! He would tell her — perfectly truthfully — that he didn't intend leaving Betty Jeanne and it was always the mistress who got hurt in these situations. But then he would add that she might want to take the wild gamble on their finding some way to spend their lives together . . . !

Betty Jeanne seems to have been aware that there was something between her husband and his colleague and she didn't much like having Carolyn in the house. But she raised no objection when it was suggested that Carolyn might take Kristan on a skiing holiday. (It gave her a chance to enjoy a little time with her own lover.)

All these twists and permutations of marital bed-hopping have been used to suggest that Paul and Betty Jeanne were a pretty depraved pair. But there probably wasn't anything really new about such a suburban lifestyle, even when John Updike had his great 1960s success describing it in *Couples*. I think the really deplorable aspect of it all was the framework of lies and half-hearted deception in which it was carried out.

In June 1988, Carolyn changed jobs, moving into the classy Pleasantville school system. But she and Paul went on seeing each other. He grew a beard which she felt made him look even more handsome. And she told all her friends how much in love they were and how sure she was he would leave his wife for her.

During her dinners with Vinnie Parco, she suddenly introduced a new topic of conversation: her anxiety about her own safety; her fears that she might be a victim of one of the burglaries occurring in her neighbourhood; her distinct fear that a dark-haired woman from New York was posing a threat to her family. This woman, she claimed, had deliberately caused a serious car accident her sister Tracey had just suffered in Washington DC. And one of Tom Warmus's planes had crashed mysteriously. The dark-haired woman had been seen lurking around its hangar before it took off. Surely Carolyn, the Warmus family member living nearest her, must be under the greatest threat . . . from Betty Jeanne Solomon?

Ditzy Carolyn might be, but Vinny had no reason to suspect she was making up these accusations off the top of her head. When it transpired that she wanted a gun for self-protection − well, he had just the job! The tiny Beretta ·25 automatic was a perfect ladies' gun which fitted in a handbag. It had been given to him by an associate who opened a franchise for him in Florida, and Parco had never registered it. He would be happy to sell it to Carolyn.

Which of them first talked about a silencer? According to Parco, Carolyn worried about disturbing people when she practised with the weapon, and 'somehow' the topic of a silencer came up between them. Silencing a firearm is a Federal offence. In the eyes of law-enforcement, the *only* reason for silencing a weapon is to conceal a crime. In the eyes of the police, a woman approaching a private detective for a silenced pistol intends to kill someone. Everyone knew that.

But that's not Vinny Parco's story. In December 1988 he called to mind his friend George Peters, an engineer who knew the techniques and had access to a workshop to manufacture a silencer. Carolyn was willing to pay the $2,500 Vinny asked. In the first week of January, 1989, he delivered the silenced Beretta to his client with a box containing a few bullets.

On Sunday 15 January, Paul and Betty Jeanne were enjoying a lazy day at home, watching the television. At 1.40 p.m. the telephone in the den rang and Paul found Carolyn on the line. He closed the door and chatted happily to her for over fifty minutes. He mentioned during the call that Kristan was away for the weekend. And, knowing Carolyn was a little sore that he'd gone to a friend's son's bar-mitzvah the previous night, he offered to meet her that evening at their favourite bar, the Treetops in Ramada Inn. Carolyn was delighted. Paul explained that he would tell Betty Jeanne he was going bowling with colleagues.

At 3 p.m., somebody used Carolyn Warmus's telephone to call Ray's Sport Shop in Plainfield, New Jersey. Nobody at the shop could later remember the caller or the subject of the call.

Some time during the afternoon, a woman came into Ray's and identified herself with a driving licence as telephonist Liisa Kattai. It was essential that she produce such identification as she purchased fifty rounds of Winchester Western ·25 cartridges, and such a sale had, by law, to be verified and recorded.

At 5.30 p.m., Paul called a friend, Marshall Tilden, and arranged to go to a basketball match with him and his sons and Kristan the following day. Then he pressed his clothes for the evening and left for the bowling alley at 6.30 p.m. He took Betty Jeanne's car, because his own flat battery was linked up to a trickle-charger.

At 6.50 p.m., Betty Jeanne was disturbed by the telephone. Marshall Tilden's wife Josette called to say her elder son was too poorly to go to the match the following night, and they hoped Paul and Kristan wouldn't mind if someone else went instead. At about the same time, Paul arrived at Yonkers Bowling Alley and told his friends there he wouldn't be playing that night – just watching a bit. He chatted to acquaintances and watched the bowls.

At 7.10 p.m., Josette Tilden called Betty Jeanne again to say the Tildens had arranged for another boy of Kristan's age to go to the basketball.

At 7.15 p.m., the emergency services operator in Peekskill took a call from Betty Jeanne's number. A woman was screaming either 'he' or 'she' – the operator could never recall which – 'is trying to kill me!' Then the line went dead.

The operator advised the police, who sent a patrol car round to the address the exchange identified. Alas, it was the wrong one. The Solomons had only been allocated that number a week previously and the police went to the empty flat of some people called Berman who were away for the weekend.

At about that time, Paul left the Bowling Alley and drove to the Ramada Inn, arriving at 7.25 p.m. Carolyn hadn't arrived yet, so he bought himself a vodka collins and sat down to wait for her.

She breezed in at 7.45 p.m. and accepted champagne. They had a couple more drinks before going to eat. Paul had oysters. Carolyn had hamburger and chips, washed down with champagne.

At 10.30 p.m. the pair went outside and Carolyn led Paul over to her red Hyundai, parked just beyond the fluorescent lighting illuminating the car park. She turned on the engine and the heater, and the pair necked and petted for forty-five minutes.

At 11.15 p.m., Carolyn whispered urgently, 'Please, Paul. Can I? Will you let me?' Paul nodded, and she unzipped his fly, pulled his trousers and underpants down his thighs and fastened her mouth over his organ. Both of them derived an extra thrill from the oral sex in an almost public place.

When Paul was satisfied, he buttoned his clothes; they kissed goodbye; and he went back to Betty Jeanne's Dodge Colt, driving home to arrive at the flat at 11.40 p.m. He was surprised to hear the television going full blast. By this hour he hoped and expected to find his wife in bed and asleep. He was less surprised to see her lying on the floor. At forty-one she suffered occasional back trouble and he'd come home before to find her sleeping on the hard surface.

He went over to her, saying, 'Honey, wake up!' But as he turned her over, he realized she would never wake up again.

Somebody had pumped eight or nine ·25 bullets into Betty Jeanne Solomon while her husband was out behind her back on an illicit date, culminating in fellatio in a car park.

The police suspected Paul as soon as they arrived at the scene of the crime. Not only was he the deceased's husband, and so statistically the most probable killer, he was evidently holding something back. Not till they had interviewed Carolyn and heard her cheerful and shameless account of the evening did Paul come clean about his extra-marital oral sex.

Still he could not lift the cloud of police suspicion. There had been no forced entry, so either Betty Jeanne had confidently admitted somebody she knew, or else someone who lived in the house had committed the crime. Was there time for Paul to have done this before turning up at Yonkers Bowling Alley to be seen by his friends? Preliminary medical reports suggested there could have been, with Betty Jeanne's time of death estimated at 6 p.m.

Luckily for Paul, Josette Tilden's second telephone call made it crystal clear that Mrs Solomon was alive at

Duncan and Penny McAllister on holiday *(Syndication International)*

Susan Christie eliminated her rival by cutting her throat *(Daily Mail/Solo)*

Sheila Garvie and Brian Tevendale,
unwilling swingers who became lovers
(Popperfoto)

Maxwell Garvie, the founder and
'skipper' of Fordoun Flying Club
(Syndication International)

G-AVKR

'Kinky Cottage' where Maxwell Garvie directed the fun and games
(Syndication International)

Carolyn Warmus, a sensational lover who killed to get her man
(Popperfoto)

Yvonne Sleightholme on her way to court, rendered blind by her arrest and trial *(Rex)*

William and Jayne Smith on their wedding day *(The Press Agency [Yorkshire] Ltd)*

The yard at Broat's Farm where Jayne Smith's body was found *(The Press Agency [Yorkshire] Ltd)*

Nicholas Hall with Thelma before she regressed to drugs and promiscuity *(Devon News Agency Ltd)*

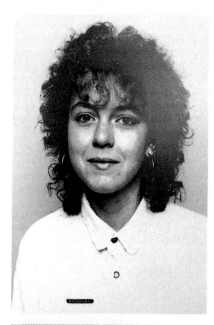

Rachel McLean, the Oxford undergraduate who was strangled by her jealous lover, John Tanner *(Sun/Rex)*

John Tanner poses with a policewoman standing in for Rachel McLean in a televised reconstruction of his story of her disappearance *(Syndication International)*

Pame and Gregg Smart on their wedding day *(Rex/Sipa)*

Billy Flynn, Vance 'JR' Lattime and Pete Randall, the schoolfriends who killed at Pame Smart's instigation *(Rex/Sipa)*

Margi Dunbar – jealousy led her to recruit the heavies who murdered her lesbian lover, Christie Offord *(Topham)*

Barry Parsons *(left)* and Robert Casaubon-Vincent *(right)* who were jailed for life after being found guilty of the murder of Christie Offord, whose trussed body was found in her bath *(Topham)*

7.10 p.m., and beyond a doubt was the frenzied emergency caller who screamed that someone was trying to kill her five minutes later.

Could Paul, nonetheless, have hired a hit-man to do the job? On the floor of his car in the garage, just in front of the driving seat, lay a key. It was the key to his front door. The cable running to the trickle-charger clearly identified Paul's car to anyone who had been given the clue.

Unfortunately, the key yielded no fingerprints – and this could be blamed on the police officers who incautiously picked it up and tried it in the lock as soon as they found it.

The scene-of-crime evidence was peculiarly unhelpful. There was nothing unusual to be seen in the flat. There was a black glove under the body that Paul didn't recognise, but it yielded no signs of blood to on-the-spot testing. A feather just outside the door might have meant anything. No stranger's fingerprints. Nothing, even, from Betty Jeanne's fingernail scrapings that could be linked to any of Paul's clothes or to those of other suspects.

But experienced detectives could make a few deductions about the murder. It was definitely not a robbery. Television, video, state-of-the-art stereo equipment and a pile of dollar bills all lay untouched in full view. Nothing was missing.

It was not a sex crime. Though there was semen in Betty Jeanne's vagina it had been there some hours before her death, indicating to disgusted detectives (who took a very high moral line over the Solomons) that Paul had made love to his wife a few hours before going off for an assignation with Carolyn Warmus. In other respects her clothing was not disordered.

It was not one of the professional rub-outs one would expect from a mob killer. A cartridge by the door suggested that the murderer had fired one first shot that had not taken effect. Mafia hit-men clasp their victim, if possible, and fire a first lethal bullet straight into the head.

Betty Jeanne had been clumsily clubbed over the back of the head; she was given time to run to the kitchen telephone and dial emergency before the cord was pulled out of the wall; she had been shot in the leg as she ran, and finally despatched with four bullets in the back as she lay on the floor. This was amateurish work.

And, to the astonishment of the police detectives, ballistics reported that the bullets had been fired through a silenced weapon. This was something extremely unusual which, again, suggested it was not the work of a professional hit-man. Professionals never want the extra bulk a silencer creates, and they always have a pre-planned getaway to obviate the need for such secrecy.

Paul Solomon remained the chief suspect for some time. Detectives were shocked that he and Kristan continued to live in the apartment, only changing the bloodstained carpet. They were shocked anew when they learned that he had another girlfriend. Even though Kristan and his friends had urged that he must start a new life without letting grief and guilt drag him into depression, the homicide squad thought it might be more seemly if he kept his zipper up for more than a few months after his wife had been brutally murdered.

As informants were starting to bring information about Carolyn Warmus's strange purchase of a silenced pistol, it began to look possible that the pair had colluded to eliminate Betty Jeanne. Detectives had virtually reached the point that they would believe *anything* of Paul Solomon, and felt it was hardly surprising that he should then ditch Carolyn and take up with a new love.

It was Carolyn's reaction to Barbara Ballor, and Paul's manifest terror over that little adventure, that changed the direction of the inquiry.

Barbara was another teacher at Paul's school. When Carolyn saw a strange car in Paul's parking space, she used skills learned from Vinny Parco to run a check on the licence plates. When she learned this was the vehicle of an attractive young teacher, she went into such rage that her lawyer telephoned her father, and Tom Warmus had Tom Jr and Tracey fly to New York to see that their sister was all right.

Far from being all right, Carolyn threw such a violent tantrum that her frightened siblings had her committed to a hospital's mental ward immediately. She calmed down enough to have herself discharged. And then set about a scheme to break up Paul Solomon and Barbara Ballor.

Pretending to be another colleague of Barbara's, she rang up the teacher's room-mate and discovered from her that Paul and Barbara had gone to Puerto Rico for a break. She learned which hotel, but not which room. And she made several suspicious calls under assumed names which filled Barbara's room-mate with alarm.

Carolyn, never short of money, flew to Puerto Rico and, from another hotel, set about trying to learn which room Paul was in. She telephoned the Condado so often trying to leave messages for her lover and discover his whereabouts that the desk staff handed her calls over to the hotel detective.

But Carolyn wasn't stopped by a firm brush-off from a security man. She used an elaborate little confidence trick, pretending to be the sister of a messenger service agent to deliver her 'personal' message to Mr Paul Solomon. She sat in the foyer of the Condado waiting to see Paul come down and collect her hotel room key from the desk, with a message inviting him to join her there wrapped round it.

She did not realize that Paul had been terrified by her succession of calls and devious ploys to get him to appear. He was starting to have his own serious suspicions about Betty Jeanne's death, and he was so frightened that he persuaded the Condado hotel security and the Puerto Rico police to give him an armed escort to the airport. He and Barbara simply fled from Carolyn Warmus, and Barbara prepared to take herself instantly out of the life of this hysterical character she'd mistakenly shacked up with for a quiet holiday in the Caribbean.

Not that Carolyn was finished with her yet. She left a warm and welcoming message on Paul's answerphone, pretending it responded to an invitation from him that she should join him in Puerto Rico. She rightly thought this would be the first thing Barbara would hear as she came to recover from the flight.

Then, posing as a detective, she telephoned a warning to Barbara's mother that her daughter was in the company of a man suspected of having shot his wife eight or nine times. And with that she gave herself away. The police had never released that information to the public. Paul himself believed Betty Jeanne had been shot four or five times. When Paul's lawyer and best friend revealed that he personally knew the true number of wounds, he immediately came under suspicion until he explained that his brother owned the funeral parlour where Betty Jeanne was embalmed. (Moreover, he had the perfect alibi for the murder time: he had been on a kidney machine undergoing dialysis.)

After the Puerto Rico episode, the police and District Attorney's office alike turned all their attention to Carolyn. Her dealings with Parco and his associates were exposed, and the dodgy private detectives were forced to testify to their own illegal activities. In Parco's case this cost the authorities a grant of immunity for his outrageous crime of supplying an illegally silenced and unlicensed gun to a woman he himself called 'ditzy'.

Carolyn's telephone records were impounded. They revealed that she had called Parco again the day after the murder. He admitted that this had been with a request that he take and hide the gun for her: a request he claimed she later withdrew, telling him she had thrown it away.

The telephone records also revealed that call from Carolyn's number to Ray's Sporting Goods on the afternoon of the murder: a call to the shop where a woman bought ·25 cartridges that day, identifying herself as Liisa Kattai. But the woman certainly wasn't Liisa. Liisa had lost her driving licence the previous August.

At that time Carolyn had been working as Liisa's temporary colleague during the school holidays. The two had lunched and socialized together frequently and Carolyn would have had endless opportunities to steal the licence from Liisa's handbag.

But had she done so? Had she done anything that definitely and tangibly linked her to the murder? The whole case against her was tenuous and circumstantial. She was shown to have a jealous personality. She was capable of violent rage. She was a cunning manipulator with a bag of tricks honed in the sleazy world of private eyes. She owned a silenced gun of the right calibre.

But – and a very big but – she appeared to have broken that first law of forensic science, that every perpetrator of a violent crime leaves something of him or herself at the scene. Absolutely nothing could be positively linked to Carolyn. Even the scrapings from under Betty Jeanne's nails showed no similarity to any clothes or possessions of Carolyn Warmus.

She was lucky. George Lewis, a brilliant lawyer with the misleading appearance of a kindly bearded teddy bear, fought furiously for her, pulling out every trick of the trade to delay and bemuse the prosecution. He was aided by a sympathetic, if eccentric judge, whose concern for the rights of defendants led him to accede to some pretty outrageous defence submissions. As a result, Carolyn came away from her first trial for the murder of Betty Jeanne Solomon with a hung jury.

The ditzy blonde promptly blew it. Her jealousy included frenzied over-rating of her main squeeze of the moment. When she started an affair with the private detective hired as Lewis's researcher and her minder during the trial, she lost her temper with Lewis for not treating her Vic with the respect she felt he deserved. Lewis declined to act for her in a second trial. Carolyn hung on to Vic at the expense of the one lawyer who *might* have saved her. Might, but probably couldn't have because the missing direct evidence turned up opportunely at the second trial.

Lewis had made great play with police mistakes at the first hearing, treating the unfortunate homicide squad as a bunch of Keystone Kops whose clownish ineptitude made it all too probable they had arrested the wrong person.

One of his best lines of attack had been the glove Paul Solomon saw under Betty Jeanne's body. After the on-the-spot test for blood proved negative, everybody forgot about this piece of tangible evidence. Nobody bagged it and tagged it and sent it along to be held with the other scene of the crime items. Paul, who thought it was a man's glove, was sure it was not his. It was visible in one of the scene of the crime photographs, and although it didn't look much like a man's glove, if it could be found and proved to be the property of a male intruder, Carolyn would walk free.

Before the second trial the glove was recovered. It had become snared in one of Paul's motor-cycling gauntlets and tossed into a box with it.

It was a woman's glove. A laboratory test with more sensitive equipment showed that a blood-covered hand had grabbed it at the wrist, apparently trying to force it away defensively. Its fabric matched the scrapings from Betty Jeanne Solomon's fingernails.

It was also a glove of a kind that had definitely been owned by Carolyn Warmus, though she claimed hers had been a different colour. Who, by this time, would believe her? Not the jury. The sensational murder case that the press had compared with the popular film *Fatal Attraction* ended with the once-sympathetic judge John Carey looking coldly at a defendant who raved claims of innocence at him, before declaring contemptuously, 'I can't hear you!' He sentenced her to twenty-five years to life for the second degree murder proved against her.

Jilted and Jealous

'Heaven has no rage like love to hatred turned,
Nor Hell a fury, like a woman scorned.'
                    Congreve *The Mourning Bride*

Ruby McCollum

At first glance it wasn't a jealousy case at all. Open and shut murder – yes, of course. But not jealousy.

Mrs Ruby McCollum went to Dr LeRoy Adams' office on Sunday 3 August 1952. It was church time, but there were a few patients in the doctor's office. Ruby waited while the white patients were attended to (for this was Live Oak, Florida, more than a decade before Lyndon Johnson said to Congress, 'We shall overcome!' and changed the face of the South).

Then, as the most socially prominent black patient present, Mrs McCollum went into the consulting room, and after a short conversation she fired two shots from a handgun. There was a pause: apparently the doctor stirred after nearly a minute, for she fired again. There was another pause and a minute later she delivered the final coup de grâce.

'Why didja do it, Ruby?' asked the Live Oak police chief as he drove her to the station under arrest. (Everybody knew everybody in Live Oak.)

'Why didja do it, Ruby?' asked State's Attorney Keith Black, an old friend of Doc Adams and someone else who knew Ruby well.

She didn't say.

The answer seemed to lie in the conversation the waiting black patients had overheard. Something about $100 or $117. Ruby said, real sharp, she was tired of paying money she didn't owe. The doctor said, 'By God, I'm going to get what's coming to me, even if I have to go to the judge.'

'Yeah, you're going to get what's coming to you,' was

Ruby's ominous response. But with that she meekly opened her purse, took out a $100 bill and asked for a receipt.

Was this a ruse to make him turn his back? He did so anyway, saying, 'I don't write no receipts. Woman, I'm goddam tired of you!'

Then she shot him. After which she went quietly home, changed her dress and warmed some milk for her baby. A really simple case. Just a black family that couldn't pay its doctor's bill. A woman who couldn't take the pressure of being harried for cash she owed. A doctor who was too easy-going about letting people run up debts to him and never imagined anybody would gun him down if he insisted he must be paid. Nothing to do with jealousy there at all.

That was how it was presented to the courts and how Circuit Judge Hal W. Adams heard it. That's how Ruby was convicted and sentenced to death, and that's where it should have ended − a silly squabble over money in a little town in the South.

But the trial was attended by the up-and-coming young black journalist Zora Neale Hurston. It was not because she expected anything sensational. She just wanted to see how a case was conducted in the court of one of the state's highly respected local jurists. Like everyone else around, Zora had heard that Judge Hal Adams (no connection to the doctor) was a good and honest lawyer; that he never allowed bias or prejudice to outweigh justice in his courtroom; and that he was a fine corrective to the legendary stereotype of the corrupt, racist, cigar-chomping southern white functionary.

So Zora was shocked when she saw something horribly familiar in Judge Adams' courtroom. She saw a black woman being railroaded. She didn't know why. She didn't know what it was all about. But she sure as hell knew when she was watching the painful and all-too-common experience of a lot of white men making sure a black woman's story didn't get a hearing.

Every time Ruby McCollum or her lawyer tried to raise

the issue of her relations with Dr Adams — relations that in some way went beyond those of doctor-patient or debtor-creditor — State's Attorney Keith Black objected that the question was irrelevant. And every time Judge Adams upheld the objection.

Something was being kept out of the court, out of the hearing of the jury, out of the eye of the public. Zora Neale Hurston was a journalist. She wanted to find out what was going on and she wanted to make it public.

But she was the wrong person to break the story and she knew it. Although she was starting to collect prizes for her work, she was still black and a woman in a culture that marginalized both groups. The former were written off as 'nigras'. The latter were confined to constricting pedestals as gracious ladies.

Zora needed a man. A white man. A Southerner. A man who could not be instantly written off as a Dam' Yankee Communistic Liberal. And she knew just the man. Pulitzer prize-winning journalist William Bradford Huie came from Mississippi and was proud of it. He wasn't offended if you called him a good ol' boy. He was of the South, he loved the South and he enjoyed the unbuttoned leisurely hospitality and easy courtesy of his region.

He *was* offended if someone called him a 'nigger-lover'. He came from the South, and for him the term meant someone who came from somewhere else and didn't know any black people personally. It was someone who turned off all moral discrimination in any dispute between black and white people, someone who assumed that blacks are *always* in the right.

Yet Huie was decisively more liberal than the culture around him and sometimes his fellow-Dixielanders did call him nigger-lover. His response to Zora Neale Hurston's invitation to check out the peculiar injustice going on in Live Oak led to his being roundly damned as a nigger-lovin' traitor to Southern standards. But he puzzled out what had happened, published it and thereby suffered a heavy fine for contempt of court.

Dr LeRoy Adams was one of the most deeply loved citizens of Live Oak. He was the doctor who treated the poor for free; the doctor who never charged what patients couldn't afford; the one doctor in town who treated black patients without quibble. And if they couldn't pay, he treated them for free.

Together with Florida's Senator Claude Pepper, he had been instrumental in getting a hospital built in town. He built himself a home on the premises, so that poor patients who couldn't afford any medical bills got some treatment from him if they couldn't get it from the hospital. He nearly always fixed it so that they could, however. He helped them understand the rules and fill out the Blue Cross and Blue Shield forms to get the free welfare insurance medication to which they were entitled. The poor and the black adored him.

His cronies in the police helped him with treating the poor. Jeff Jennings Elliott, the Governor's Special Investigator attached to Clearwater Police Force, and highway patrolman Frank Milliken would signal the doc at once in the event of an accident, so he could get out and help. Business for the doctor, of course, but good for the injured, too, to know there was one medic who would always drop everything and come running, even if they were raggedly dressed drivers of clapped-out jalopies. Milliken let Doc Adams use the police radio to keep in touch with possible assistance when he went to treat people too poor to have a phone.

Dr Adams was a Southerner and so a Democrat, of course. But while nobody could imagine a Republican winning votes in Live Oak, the Democratic Party machine was happy to run candidates as popular as Dr LeRoy Adams. It was pretty widely known that in the November elections of 1952, Dr Adams would be on the ballot running for State Senator. It was absolutely certain that he would win. Who wouldn't want a man who did so much good for the poor locally to go up to the Statehouse and bring the benefits of his benevolence to the whole of Florida?

It wasn't really surprising that the doctor had such empathy with the indigent. Although he came of distinguished Floridian lineage and stiff portraits of ancestral office-holding Adamses lined the corridors of the State Capitol, LeRoy was not a rich and successful white plantocrat. Born in 1908 and married just as the Great Slump struck, he was instantly unemployed as a young man and only struggled to hold himself together through President Roosevelt's New Deal WPA — a programme of public works to soak up some of the jobless.

In 1937, LeRoy Adams took a free course in pharmacy and held a couple of jobs as a chemist's salesman. He proved extremely good at facing the public and promoting medications his employers wanted sold. And with his enthusiasm for a serious career fired, Adams went to Arkansas (where academic standards were not too demanding) and worked his way through Little Rock Junior College before going to the University of Arkansas Medical School.

He was a mature student — over thirty when he really got his medical training under way. And while this made him hard-working and reliable, he also had some difficulty with actual studying. It was a long slow process acquiring the grades and credits that added up to the medical degree and Adams bravely weathered repeated failures and retakes before, at the age of forty, he was at last able to put his shingle up on a little office back in Live Oak, and prove that a poor kid who'd struggled his way up by sheer hard work didn't have to kick away the ladder and forget the disadvantaged once he was there.

Prove it he did and not just by being generous over fees. He knew what it was like to feel in trouble with the bigshots and the authorities, and he would help people when the law didn't understand the complicated realities of life at the bottom of the heap. Take La Vergne Blue, whose name in itself screams of semi-educated Southern parents trying to dignify their offspring above the level of 'po' white trash'. Like the doctor, La Vergne had lifted himself out of the gutter and was running a successful hotel-restaurant, the Blue Lodge. But his prosperity was seriously threatened when a customer slipped and fell, and started proceedings against him. According to the customer, he had broken his pelvis and he wanted massive damages for this heavy injury.

The doctor came to La Vergne's assistance. He examined the plaintiff. Then, as an expert witness, he went and told the court just how much exaggeration was involved in this attempt to steal Mr Blue's livelihood. There was no broken pelvis. There were just abrasions.

After winning his case hands-down, La Vergne Blue, as you may well imagine, became a lifelong friend of his star witness. But it wasn't just people of his own race and self-made class who benefited from Adams's willingness to make the courts do justice for the poor. Eddie Redden was a poor black man. And sadly like an awful lot of poor people, black and white, living in domestic tension and over-crowded conditions, Eddie would beat up his wife when he got drunk or the quarrels became too fierce. When Eddie beat up his wife harder than usual and the poor woman was taken to hospital, Eddie was arrested on a charge of assault with intent to murder. In hospital Mrs Redden died, and now Eddie was charged with murder in a state which would send him to the electric chair without a qualm. Eddie turned to Adams for help.

It was an inspired move. Doc Adams knew the lives of the poor and black with an intimacy denied to most law enforcement officers. He knew their medical records and their medical habits. He went to the court and he told them about Mrs Redden. Apparently she'd contracted a vaginal infection and didn't think a white man practising white medicine was going to do any good. So she went to the backstreets and found a little old black magic woman and took her medicine. And that's what killed her.

Certainly, Eddie shouldn't have beaten her, but for sure the beating didn't kill her, and Eddie oughtn't to be charged with murder.

The doctor's homespun knowledge of shantytown life and his medical diagnosis saved Eddie Redden from Old Sparky, and no doubt the whole experience served as a traumatic warning to Eddie never to beat up women again.

With such a record of service to the community, doesn't it leave you, too, asking, 'Why didja do it, Ruby?' If this man was such a friend of black people; if this doctor was to some extent disliked by his own profession because of his habit of treating the poor for nothing, how on earth came he to be killed for pestering a black woman for payment? Perhaps the answer lay in Ruby McCollum.

The McCollums were not poor blacks. Ruby was the wife of the richest black man in town. As far as sheer money in the bank went, Sam McCollum could pretty certainly lay his hands on far more of it at a moment's notice than Dr LeRoy Adams and his wife Florrie Lee. Ruby stuck for a $100 medicine bill? It hardly made sense when thousands of dollars in cash were usually to be found lying around in drawers in the McCollum house for immediate needs.

The McCollums came to Live Oak in 1937 when Ruby was twenty-two and Sam a few years older. They brought with them $700 and an old car – not a fortune, but a good deal more than LeRoy and Florrie Lee Adams had when they came to town ten years later. By that time Sam and Ruby were settled in and prosperous.

In the little upstate New York town of Zuber, near Ocala, where they met, pretty young Ruby Jackson boasted many dates, and she was choosy. She only liked 'big men': not husky weightlifters, not well-endowed sexual athletes, what she wanted was men with power or wealth or obvious prospects.

Ruby could choose easily in the black community

(inter-racial dating, even in northern states, didn't happen in the 1930s) because she had visible ethnic class. She was relatively light-skinned and this counted for something. As Jamaican novelist Andrew Salkey remarked a decade later, the black diaspora wasn't so much colour-conscious as 'tint-conscious'. The lighter your tint the better. So Ruby was a catch for an ambitious man, and she knew it.

Sam McCollum was obviously going places when Ruby started going out with him. He was darker than she and he was less intelligent, but he had drive and determination and not a lot of scruples. He was going to be rich and Ruby hitched her wagon to his star.

They lived in Nyack at first and then they moved south to Florida. Even in the bad old Jim Crow days quite a lot of black people preferred living in the South. If you weren't interested in political rights and you didn't mind segregated public facilities, there were advantages to be gained from living in neighbourhoods where the majority shared your race, and where the dominant minority was actually used to you. Provided you followed the formal obsequiousness they demanded, you could be more or less accepted and prosper in your little niche in society. You were less likely to confront people to whom, indeed, all black people look alike. White Southerners with black servants and labourers learned automatically how to identify faces by size and shape and tint and disposition of features, instead of relying heavily on hair colour and length.

But it may well be that Sam was directed to move south to get into the black suburban communities of Florida and carry on his bosses' business there. For by the time the Adamses came to Live Oak, Sam McCollum was widely known as 'Bolita' Sam, king of the local numbers racket.

'Numbers' or 'policy' is the highly lucrative gambling scam by which organized crime drains the money of the poor and, especially, the black into its own well-tailored pockets. During the day, touts go round the streets and houses, collecting bets and issuing tickets which, with their counterfoils, bear whatever number between 1 and 999 the punter has picked. At the end of the day, the organizers declare a different three digits as the winning number. If anybody was lucky enough to pick the right number, the tout comes back and pays out the winnings.

Assuming the chosen number to be completely random, the odds against any number you choose winning are 998 to 1. Put it another way, the organizers can be sure of averaging 998 suckers for every winner to whom they have to pay out. So they can offer temptingly high odds of 600 to 1, and still make an enormous killing. The high odds surely do tempt the suckers and the suckers, like all suckers on the paying-out end of any vice racket, lose badly.

In New York, the numbers racket is based on curious permutations of the numbers of winning horses at the day's racetrack meetings. That system allowed a mathematical genius called Abbadabba Berman to help gangster Dutch Schultz cheat the suckers even more, by working out quickly, as the results came in, which declared 'winning' number was bound to pay out least.

Bolita Sam's racket was, by comparison, reasonably honest. His winning digits were picked at random from a cage full of spinning numbered balls, much like a bingo caller's. The game, though, was still sufficiently stacked that Sam became a rich citizen, with solid investments in tobacco allotments and a directorship for Central Life Insurance, as well as the permanent Bolita racket — named after the Mexican gambling game which supplied the cage and balls. He drove a blue two-tone Chrysler, and the wealthy white citizens respected his wealth.

I said Sam might have been sent to Florida. The policy scam was, of course, controlled by the all-powerful white syndicate. But you can't imagine the likes of Lucky Luciano and Bugsy Siegel knocking on doors in Harlem and asking black housewives (in their tens of thousands) to put their fifty cents on their chosen number of the day! Black touts were needed, and black intermediaries to collect from the touts. Sam was a very senior middleman, with white controllers. He behaved respectfully to white men and they accepted him as a rich black man.

The policy racket does honestly pay out when, once in a thousand times, somebody comes up with the lucky number. Otherwise the suckers would stop 'investing'. Sam often had as much as $10,000 lying around the house in used notes ready to meet any immediate pay-off.

All that was public knowledge by the time William Bradford Huie came to Live Oak to bring his brilliant investigative reporter's talent to the problem of Ruby McCollum's apparently biased trial and conviction. Yet all that also left obvious questions.

Apart from wondering why a very rich woman should shoot a doctor who usually gave free treatment over a measly $117 bill, Huie wondered how LeRoy Adams made his own living in the first place? If his patients were almost always poor and he almost never charged them, how come a man who reached town owning nothing was a prosperous citizen when he died, five years later?

With those questions the legend started to come apart, and Huie started to grow very unpopular with the white establishment of Live Oak.

A simple matter first: LeRoy's house. It was built on the same site as the hospital he had campaigned for – not a bad way of trying to get his own building done free. Furthermore, it turned out the builder had a lot of difficulty getting payment from the doctor, and still felt he was owed money in 1952. But credit-juggling couldn't explain the security and financial esteem in which Adams was cushioned. Huie dug further.

LeRoy Adams, the people's friend against the wicked shyster lawyers, was quickly shown to have feet of clay. Eddie Redden, the black man who escaped the murder charge because of LeRoy's testimony that Mrs Redden died from backstreet medical treatment, was not so poor a black that he didn't have something to give the doctor in exchange for his testimony. He had two houses, valued at $2,500, and the doctor made him sign them over to him before promising to get him off. After that, he insured one and sold the other. The insured house burned down in the small hours of one morning and the doctor collected. He successfully made $3,250 on Redden's estimated $2,500 worth of property. All for telling a plausible little story to a jury; a story whose truth looked increasingly doubtful.

La Vergne Blue, whom the doctor saved from bank-ruptcy at the hands of his litigious customer with the broken pelvis, was white. He couldn't be robbed quite so openly. In his case, Dr Adams was content that the whole town should know how grateful Blue was: so grateful that the doctor and his cronies were welcome to free meals at the Blue Lodge whenever they went there. He must have expected that this public gratitude would explain the extraordinary will that turned up in the Adams's house after his murder. It was a will in which Dr Adams was left the whole of La Vergne Blue's property. La Vergne's son was formally disinherited and the doctor scooped the lot.

It was a forgery — perpetrated by Dr Adams himself, according to handwriting analysts. La Vergne Blue was absolutely furious, and understandably bad-mouthed his deceased friend as soon as he learned about it. Only he wouldn't quite help William Bradford Huie with the further information he needed about the doctor's con-nection with the McCollums.

Before that came out, Huie found something else that was a matter of public record. The National Veterans' Administration had brought charges against the doctor for fraud. He had billed them for treatment given to patients who were never ill and never received any treatment. Two patients on his panel had confessed this: they had signed faked Blue Cross forms at the doctor's request, knowing that in return they would be treated free if ever they needed it. And, the NVA indicated, this was only the tip of the iceberg. The doctor made his living by claiming against the national medical insurance schemes for fictitious and expensive treatments, while actually giving free cheap treatment to the poor who agreed to let him use their names and signatures for the scam.

Since Adams was an inferior doctor (he had only passed his exams with the greatest difficulty) the poor were being taken for a ride as usual. They were getting second-rate treatment, which might have come very cheaply, at the cost of forgoing the free first-rate treatment they might need in the event of serious illness. Adams's medical practice was in effect professionally sustained by his nurse, Edith Sharp. She was competent – but she wasn't a doctor.

So why wasn't Adams convicted and struck off when two blue-collar workers had come forward and sworn to helping him by falsely signing declarations that they had been ill and received treatment from him? Because the court was swamped with character witnesses who poured in to say that it was impossible. It was not just the poor, who happily came forward to talk about their free treatment. The respectable establishment came along, too, confirming that this fine upstanding Democratic Party member, this associate of Senator Claude Pepper in campaigning for proper hospital facilities, this true Southern gentleman couldn't possibly be defrauding Uncle Sam. State's Attorney Keith Black turned out at their head to assure the court that this was a case he could never have prosecuted; it was so obviously unreasonable. The doctor went free. The Federal government went on paying his fraudulent claims.

Huie soon established that the doctor's whole career had been built on theft and fraud. He had lost his early jobs with the chemists and druggists because the excellence of his sales record didn't compensate for his habitual thefts from their tills. He got into college using forged testimonials in which he promoted a humble co-worker to 'manager' of their store – without the man's knowledge. Only he was unable to cheat his way through college and so he took ten years to complete his training, managing only with difficulty.

All of which made Edith Sharp vital to him. He had to keep her happy; he had to keep a competent nurse working in his practice to cover for his possible mistakes. How did he do this? Here Huie uncovered something very sinister.

Dr Adams showed Edith the forged will making over La Vergne Blue's property to him. She believed it was genuine. He promised her that as soon as he owned it she would be set up as independent manageress, and she accepted all this as legally valid and likely. Why Mr Blue might be expected to die suddenly is not immediately apparent. Perhaps it's a good thing no sudden minor illness brought him under Dr Adams's tender loving care . . .

Miss Sharp knew more about Adams than most people. She knew that, like La Vergne, he was a member of the Ku Klux Klan and said openly that he hated dogs, blacks and Yankees. Well, that could help to explain the rush of character witnesses and his acquittal from fraud. But she also knew that he hated everyone, including the constituents he glad-handed and jollied into supporting his campaign for State Senatorship. He would drive out of his way to run down a dog on the road. She went along with his hypocrisy because of the promise of the Blue Lodge.

But even she didn't know it was also promised to someone else! The doctor had a girlfriend on the side – Evelyn Anderson. He had given her a house and a car (or so she thought, until he died, when she learned that with typical crooked duplicity he had retained legal title to them). But when that didn't seem enough to attach her to his bloated and greedy sixteen-stone body, he promised her she would have the Blue Lodge on La Vergne's death.

Yet that still isn't the end of the Blue Lodge's potential inheritors. Before Evelyn Anderson appeared on the scene the doctor had promised it to . . . Ruby McCollum.

When the Adamses arrived in Live Oak, the McCollum marriage was under strain. Sam's wealth had enabled him to afford a girlfriend. She was younger than Ruby and lighter skinned. A schoolteacher, this was a woman with more education and more class. Ruby couldn't compete.

And then the doctor, always needful of the readies whatever their source might be, came into the numbers racket in a slot above Sam (the doctor was white, after all). It wasn't a permanent position. Huie concluded that half the respectable upper-crust of the town were circulating shares in this racket among themselves. But when Adams came into close contact with Sam, he also saw Ruby and he fancied what he saw. He probably virtually raped her when they found themselves alone. He was a vile man who heard a younger colleague say, 'I'm gonna fuck a nigger woman and change my luck,' and he responded, 'That's the best fuck in the world. I've got me one over in Live Oak: Ruby McCollum.'

Ruby couldn't complain to anyone. In those days, they wouldn't have listened. They'd probably have laughed. Sam couldn't have done anything. He'd have been run out of town if he tried: tarred and feathered, probably, if he kicked up too much fuss. He might have been assassinated by the KKK if he looked like getting anywhere.

Unlike many of her black sisters, however, Ruby could find some compensation in the situation. Dr LeRoy Adams fulfilled her main criterion in a man. He was a 'big man' − socially powerful. She could profit by the relationship.

She was a sexy lady. And much as the contemptible Dr Adams boasted of having got himself a sample of 'the best fuck in the world' over in Live Oak − as though making love to a woman were equivalent to eating a biscuit − it's likely that she got her hooks pretty deeply into his self-indulgent lustfulness, and he didn't really want to let her go for some time. Why else would he promise her the Blue Lodge? The Lodge would also give her independence from Sam — something she rather wanted.

This was because Dr Adams had another nasty habit. He wouldn't practise any birth control with his women. He took a macho pride in begetting children he had no intention of supporting. Ruby's baby Loretta turned out far too light to be Sam's. Sam beat her. The doctor wouldn't do anything about it. He wouldn't check Sam. He wouldn't rescue Ruby. Neither would he stop sleeping with her or, as she constantly pleaded, fit her with a diaphragm. He did one thing: he prescribed her drugs to take her mind off her troubles. Like Dr Herman Tarnower, shot by Jean Harris, he used his pharmacopoeia to keep his women peppy, not having the personality to keep them happy.

Ruby suffered from steadily increasing depression. She was hospitalized several times for this, and each time the responsible medical attendants were shocked by the 'medication' Dr Adams was pumping into her.

Each time she discharged herself and went for new prescriptions when his dangerous happy pills ran out. Until there came the last straw. LeRoy took up with Evelyn Anderson. He began spending more and more time with her, openly. He gave her a house and a car and made it clear to Ruby that she was in second place.

It came to a head on 31 July 1952. Ruby was pregnant again and she asked LeRoy for an abortion. He was furious and beat her. How dare a black woman try to reject his sacred seed! Yet while forcing her to bear his child, he was making it clear, too, that he wanted her out of his life before the autumn election campaigning started. Ruby bought a heavy handgun firing shotgun cartridges: a murderous weapon.

On Friday 1 August, Sam McCollum got a note from the doc. It read: 'Sam, you keep this goddam woman out of my office from now on. She's gone crazy as a bat.' Sam did his best. He shut her in all Saturday and Ruby couldn't get to LeRoy's office. She still made forty operator-connected attempts to call the doctor, who refused steadfastly to come to the telephone.

The next day, while Sam took the children to church, Ruby killed her horrible, cheating, fraudulent lover.

The rest is easily and sadly told. Having uncovered this massive can of worms, William Bradford Huie couldn't get very far with it. He concluded that effectively the whole law-enforcement establishment of the neighbourhood was in cahoots to cover up their leading members' involvement with the numbers racket, the Ku Klux Klan and black women. And the politicians didn't want it to be seen how low they would stoop to back a winning glad-handing candidate. They'd railroaded Ruby once, and though Huie and her local lawyer, Frank Cannon, got enough details to take to Appeal and win a retrial, it was certain she'd be railroaded again if she were tried in Live Oak. Huie and Cannon were Southerners and they resolutely resisted the National Council for Civil Liberties and National Council for the Advancement of Colored People's offers of eminent northern lawyers to take the case. Those Yankees would only have lost Ruby to the electric chair in a blaze of sensational publicity.

Instead, her white Southern defenders used the tactic of psychiatric examination to save her life. Ruby's depression had understandably grown worse through her ordeals and she was almost catatonic by the time she was due to stand trial again. She was sent to the State Secure Mental Hospital and subsequently released into the custody of her daughter.

Yvonne Sleightholme

It's very difficult to tell a lover when you know it's time to finish and you know there's no future in the relationship. Even if things have never seemed perfect, the jilted party may take it very hard. It takes courage to face a lover's misery — let alone stimulate it without malice — and there are no etiquette books explaining how it should best be done; no moral philosophers to examine the rights and the wrongs of balancing truthfulness against hurtfulness or short-term pain against long-term unhappiness.

But the young man who makes the effort to explain, honestly and fully, why he can't go through with a wedding he knows will only lead to a futile marriage of continuing deception and pretence deserves better fortune than came to William Smith.

While he was very young — just out of school — William captured the affections of a schoolgirl called Jayne Wilmore. He was seven years older than she, but as many of us can sadly recall, adolescent girls are often attracted by more sophisticated older men, leaving frustrated adolescent boys with a lot of unrequited love to endure.

William and Jayne went out together for several years. Then, when she had left school and was well into her training as a nurse, they gradually drifted apart. There were no fierce recriminations. Jayne was an attractive and pleasant girl and she had other boyfriends. William thought she had outgrown a schoolgirl crush on him. Nobody felt any exaggerated guilt or distress over the situation. So William was ill-prepared for the alternative behaviour of a hysterically possessive woman.

William Smith got on with his life as a farmer in the Yorkshire Dales. Broat's Farm needed a good deal of attention. His social life was largely sporting. Every week he played five-a-side football and he went to rugby club functions.

In 1979 he met Yvonne Sleightholme at a rugby club disco. She was a few years older than he: a farmer's daughter, living at home with her parents and working as a doctor's receptionist. She was instantly attracted to the gentle young farmer with the light beard, and hoped her years of single blessedness might be coming to an end.

Yvonne was a competent and managing woman. She had little difficulty in making the running and started to organize William's life efficiently. And she began to manipulate him into thinking that he might some day marry her . . . Eighteen months after their first meeting, Yvonne had moved into Broat's Farm and was ready to make definite suggestions about marriage.

They cleared William's mind wonderfully. He thought it over carefully and realized that, while he was happy to live with Yvonne for the time being and let her bring her own forms of household management into his domestic life, he did not really see this as a basis for lifelong commitment. With admirable sense, courage and honesty, he told her so. He told her, too, that if she was starting to look so much further than their relationship justified, then it was better for all concerned that it should come quickly and cleanly to an end.

Yvonne was flabbergasted. Part of William's suitability as a husband, she felt, was the ease with which she could control him. The last thing on earth she had expected was for the gentle farmer to turn round and politely kick her out of his house.

A few weeks later she demanded another meeting. William agreed, and was confronted with a tirade of bitter reproaches and accusations. She had got leukemia, she told him, and it was all his fault. Her health was perfectly under control until he jilted her. Then it gave way and his emotional cruelty was killing her.

This was staggering news. William had never imagined that an honest sorting out of their relationship could lead to a fatal disease for Yvonne. But, being himself a fundamentally straightforward person, he never doubted her claim that breaking the informal 'engagement' had precipitated her lethal psychosomatic disorder. Being an essentially kind person, he wanted to do what he could to help. It seemed the best thing he could offer was a return to Broat's Farm. Yvonne moved her things back in and the 'leukemia' disappeared as if by magic.

The obvious conclusion would be that Yvonne invented it to manipulate William. And there were those who confirmed that this was, indeed, what happened. But subsequent events show that Yvonne is definitely prone to unhappy and disabling hysterical disorders and she probably became very ill when William broke off with her; she may very well have believed she had leukemia.

Whatever William thought about her miraculous recovery, the passage of several years' cohabitation prompted Yvonne to reopen the question of matrimony. It seemed the natural and inevitable outcome of an ongoing live-in lovers' relationship. Yvonne was a regular church-goer. She wanted the satisfaction of a white church wedding with flowers and bridesmaids and all the trimmings. And she wanted the status of being 'Mrs Smith, the farmer's wife,' not just, 'yon' Miss Sleightholme as lives wi' yoong William.'

Yvonne wanted everything at the wedding perfectly organized. The church, the organist, the wedding dress, the reception, the honeymoon — all these things had to be elaborately pre-planned to run smoothly. She gave herself six months to devote to her wedding preparations, while William got on with the farm and quietly arranged to have a morning suit fitted.

It was in the town of Salton that William ran into Jayne Wilmore again. It was quite by chance but Jayne was pleased. She had heard about William's engagement — Yvonne's formalities would surely have included a town-crier going all over Yorkshire, bellowing, 'I publish the banns of marriage . . .' had such a thing been traditional. She wanted to congratulate her old flame. But more than that, if it seemed appropriate, she wanted a little private talk with him.

William's manner on meeting her did seem fully appropriate so Jayne, amiably but directly, broached what was on her mind. She knew William very well. Although she'd been very young when they first kissed and held hands behind the bicycle shed, their juvenile courtship had lasted a goodly time. And she knew women. She had no doubt that William's honest and trusting nature was being abused by an older female who was lying and scheming and conniving her way into wedlock. She thought William deserved better than that.

Her suspicions struck a chord. William himself had quietly wondered about the suddenly flowering, suddenly fading leukemia. It couldn't really escape him that Yvonne's briskness, managerial competence and regular church-going were not the same thing as his placid, decent frankness. He felt Jayne was right and he was grateful to her for speaking out with an honest candour which matched his own. And he said so.

This led Jayne to confess that she hadn't really outgrown him; she didn't think of their past friendship as just a schoolgirl crush; in the back of her mind she had always wondered whether she shouldn't have held on and married William.

Now all this caused William to think furiously, until it was clear that he needed to reopen the subject of the forthcoming wedding with Yvonne and voice his doubts and reservations. But every time he tried to do so, she cut him off with bright and bubbling chatter about her formal arrangements. In the end he went back to talk to Jayne again about his difficulties and he found himself sleeping with Jayne behind Yvonne's back.

Deception was not something that William took casually or enjoyed — neither did Jayne — yet it seemed impossible to open the topic with Yvonne. Just to make things harder, Yvonne suddenly found herself pregnant. You or I might think this didn't matter very much, with a wedding around the corner. But Yvonne thought it mattered dreadfully. Her wedding dress might not fit. Her pregnancy might show. Then she miscarried and all went on as before.

Finally, with the wedding only a few weeks away, William realized that he must grasp the nettle or he would be saddled with a life of intolerable deception. He told Yvonne, for the second time, that all must end between them. There was no hope of their making a life together. He told her about Jayne and that he was going to have to find out whether life with her would be possible.

Yvonne was understandably furious. She had lost a boyfriend and live-in lover the first time round. Now, after another five years together, printed wedding invitations had been sent out; caterers, dressmakers and church functionaries were all primed for the big rite of passage; and still she was to be jilted at the altar. There was real public humiliation to face this time, as well as private pain. To make it worse, she had just miscarried his baby! The immediate injury quite overruled her ability to consider the certainty of future unhappiness if she forced an unwilling man into marriage. Yvonne did her best to force him.

But William was not weak. He knew well what he was now doing was right, however wrong it might have been to deceive Yvonne with Jayne over the previous couple of months. He insisted that it was over. The wedding must be cancelled and Yvonne would have to move out of Broat's Farm.

Yvonne went, but she did not take her things with her. She hoped this was not really the end.

A few months later, Jayne moved in and took her place. Yvonne still didn't remove her things until Jayne

had been there three months. Then, in a chilling little
scene, Yvonne drove up and collected her property. She
hardly spoke to Mr Smith and Miss Wilmore; she drove
away and out of their lives, they hoped.

William and Jayne found that they worked together
perfectly. In May 1988 they married and they were
supremely happy. Jayne went on nursing. William went
on working the farm and enjoying his weekly football.
Yvonne was forgotten.

That is until the threatening telephone messages began.
They were anonymous calls making horrible remarks like,
'I'm going to kill you, you bitch'. Could it be Yvonne?
There was nobody else they knew who hated Jayne so
much. Yet the break-up of her engagement was months
ago, and William and Jayne were not the sort of people
who would themselves have indulged in telephone games.
Perhaps they were getting crossed lines and wrong
numbers?

Then there was the mysterious fire in the barn. William
found it blazing one night and it took him an hour and a
half to put it out. Had he failed, it would have been a
major catastrophe. He tried to puzzle out how it had
started. He could find no explanation.

Could it have been Yvonne? Was desperation driving
her to arson? It seemed almost beyond belief, but . . .
The funeral wreath wasn't beyond belief. And it couldn't
have been a mistaken delivery. It came for Jayne, with a
card saying, 'Jayne – I'll always remember you'.

This time the Smiths had no doubt it was Yvonne. This
time William went to the police and complained. Yvonne
comes out of things pretty badly from this point on. So
perhaps we should take our last chance to consider her
point of view: her reasons for jealousy rankling until it
became literally murderous hatred.

She clearly wanted desperately to be married and she
clearly thought William would be a suitable husband, and
that she had won him. She was utterly devastated and
humiliated when she had to announce that she'd been

turned down after half a decade's cohabitation and public
plans for a grand wedding. And it was her supplanter who
first gratuitously interpreted her 'leukemia' as sheer
fraud, and so described it to William; then slept with
William behind Yvonne's back; and finally encouraged
and supported William in forcing the public break and
showdown with Yvonne. After which she quietly slipped
into Yvonne's place in Broat's Farm and William's bed,
openly enjoying the proper marriage to him that she,
more than anyone else, had denied Yvonne. I think St
Agnes would have found it difficult to forgive Jayne. I
think Dame Julian of Norwich would have suspected that
Jayne had planned the whole thing from the start. I think
no woman but a saint could have failed to hate Jayne, if
she had suffered Yvonne's experiences.

The police found the complaint about the wreath a
tricky problem. It was not a serious crime in itself; very
much a private, domestic incident. Still, something had
better be done, especially if there was any chance that
Yvonne had started arson. Two policemen went to
interview her at her father's farm.

Yvonne was friendly, forthcoming and charming. She
denied all responsibility for the hate campaign and she
was persuasive. The policemen had never seen anything
less like the twisted, spinster poison-pen letter writer of
popular legend, and they were convinced Yvonne had
nothing to do with the Smiths' problems. When William
and Jayne remained doubtful, the police assured them
that Yvonne was obviously a law-abiding woman. If she
had just possibly made the phone calls and sent the
wreath, she would certainly stop now that she knew the
law had been informed.

It seemed they were right. Shortly after the interview,
Yvonne took a break from the district. She moved to the
Scottish border and rented a holiday cottage. She found a
new boyfriend, ambulance driver Anthony Berry, and she
enjoyed his companionship out of sight in Scotland, far
away from the wagging tongues of North Yorkshire. By

12 December 1989, the past was so satisfactorily behind her that she sent a Christmas card to William's parents, with a note telling them she was now happy with a new man. Nobody could imagine she had anything to do with any troubles down south after that.

With that card safely in the post, Yvonne got in her car and drove down to the North Riding. It was a Tuesday evening and she knew that William would be off to his five-a-side football, leaving Jayne on her own in Broat's Farm when she got home from work.

Yvonne knew the Dales perfectly. A little distance from the farm she turned off the road and parked where she could observe passing traffic without being seen. She wanted to be sure William really did go to his football. It was raining stair-rods and there was just a chance he might give it a miss.

She didn't have to wait long. William's familiar car drove past. Yvonne waited another ten minutes in case he should find he had forgotten something and make a surprise return visit to Broat's Farm. When he didn't, she knew that she was safe for a good long time. If sportsman William could face the appalling rain sheeting down in the icy night, avenger Yvonne would match him.

She parked her car in front of the farm and strode to the door. There was a shotgun under her anorak. Jayne answered the door, still in her nurse's uniform. She was startled to see Yvonne. She was terrified when Yvonne put the gun to her head and made her come out into the rain. Miss Sleightholme marched her across the farmyard, pointed the gun at the back of her head and killed her with one neat shot. Then she set out to disguise the murder as a man's work.

In the pouring rain, she knelt over the body and ripped Jayne's blouse open and down over her shoulders. She tore her bra off. And with strong, fierce fingers she squeezed and mauled her rival's breasts to leave scratches and bruises suggesting a sadistic male.

Then she pulled up Jayne's skirt, exposing her nurse's

black stockings and suspenders. She ripped off Jayne's knickers and took them away with her. Using her hands, she thrust and scrabbled in Jayne's pudenda to leave every indication, except the unfakeable semen, that the nurse had been raped.

The rain streamed down on the body, drenching and washing the strangely exposed private parts. Yvonne did a good job, and her handiwork might well have passed as a man's savage sexual assault had she not been determined to do one more thing: one thing which showed William that this was no man's crime and which brought suspicion straight home to her.

She tore off Jayne Smith's wedding ring. It was difficult in the driving rain − much harder than the savage pseudo-sexual assault on the warm body. But, pulling and tussling, Yvonne got it away. The little bitch would not go to her grave ringed and banded as William Smith's!

Had it not been for the missing ring, Yvonne might never have been questioned at all. Nor had she lost her old manipulative charm and skill. The officers who interviewed her in Scotland reported that she was open, friendly and helpful: nothing at all like a potential murderess.

But the CID didn't stop at that report. They discovered that Yvonne had been away from her Scottish cottage on the night of the murder. They found bloodstains matching Jayne Smith's blood group in Yvonne's car. They had the evidence to bring charges. Yvonne's hysterical temperament asserted itself after her arrest. She went blind.

Her defence was an extraordinary story. Stressing that she had lived with William for six years, while Jayne had only been married to him for seven months, she claimed that soon after the marriage William came back to her and they started an adulterous liaison. She said that divorce seemed imminent, and William feared that Jayne would be able to claim half the value of Broat's Farm under Britain's divorce laws. To avoid this, he hired three assassins whom he had met in a drug deal. To cast suspicion on Yvonne, he sent her a false message to come and visit him at the farm that night, and purloined the murder weapon from her father's farm.

The judge at Leeds Crown Court in May 1991 characterized this as 'a wicked, untruthful story', and sentenced her to life imprisonment.

In 1993, now forty years old and registered completely blind, Yvonne turned up in the Appeal Court with fresh evidence to support her case. Documents, she said, proved that Jayne's and William's marriage was tottering. And she herself had been assaulted on the night of the murder, which proved she hadn't been involved. The judge hadn't summed up properly, and the police had withheld evidence, her lawyers pleaded. But the appeal was rejected.

Yvonne still hasn't given up, however. She wants a new appeal. Furthermore, she declares that she will refuse parole when she becomes eligible for it, as it will be conditional on her acknowledging guilt.

John Tanner

Rachel McLean was an Oxford success. She came from a soundly supportive middle-class family. In studying for an English degree she carried out their hopes and expectations. Malcolm and Joan McLean and the University of Oxford cooperated, without knowing each other, in the work of maturing and educating a lively, gifted, interesting girl.

The McLeans were well satisfied with Rachel's progress. The ancient university did not transform their daughter into a snob or a pedant or a half-baked progressive who looked down on her aeronautical engineer father and school teacher mother. Her broadening intellectual experience was associated with greater tolerance for her parents; a growth beyond the sulks and demands of adolescence; a maturation that good parents well deserve, and deserve to see enhanced by their children's professional educators.

The McLeans lived in Blackpool. Rachel went to Hodgson High School and then on to Blackpool Sixth Form College to take A' levels in English, French and Ancient History. She read voraciously — the absolutely necessary basis for academic success in the humanities. She took a bronze in the Duke of Edinburgh Awards.

Her Blackpool teachers managed to sound sober and unsensational in the aftermath of her death, not over-excited by the remembered performance of a schoolgirl who had been composed and serious; assertive without being unduly outgoing; possessed of opinions and prepared to defend them.

But anyone involved in education will know that they

must have been absolutely thrilled in 1989 when Rachel was accepted by St Hilda's College, Oxford. The pupil who wins an Oxford place is a real feather in the cap of any teacher — and justly. Even the most innately brilliant schoolchildren have to be properly prepared if they are to satisfy the Oxford admissions teams. Rachel went up in the autumn with the good wishes of everyone behind her. She didn't let them down. Over the course of the year she blossomed, developing the outgoing personality that one Blackpool teacher felt she lacked.

She had dark auburn curly hair, a pretty face and a slim, well-developed figure. She was unobtrusively active in unimpeachable good works, helping to staff the telephone for the Samaritans and Christian Aid. First-year students have rooms in their colleges, or a hostel. Rachel came to know well the delightful lawns of St Hilda's, leading down to the River Cherwell on the south side of Magdalen Bridge. She made friends and influenced contemporaries to such good effect that the following year she was elected Vice-President of her College Junior Common Room.

The National Union of Students — that curious training ground for politicians and educated unionists — is less important in Oxford and Cambridge than the other universities of England. This is because the NUS represents students at a university level, and the ancient universities are truly collegiate institutions. The thirty or so colleges comprising Oxford are more important to their members, individually and collectively, than the overall University. That august body organizes the final examinations and awards the degrees. It sets the syllabuses. It arranges scheduled lectures. The University holds formal sway over everything academic. It admits students *in statu pupillari*. It awards them degrees in long Latin ceremonies that are a peculiar form of incomprehensible entertainment for proud parents.

But for dons and students alike, the true basis of Oxford life is the college. There, first-year students and some award-holders and unmarried dons enjoy full bed and board, and all students must take some meals to prove their presence in residence. There the tutors do the University's real teaching: hearing students' essays read out every week and discussing them with them – ideally in an individual one-to-one tutorial, the perfect liberal teaching instrument. College tutors recommend lectures and reading lists. Most undergraduates row for college boats or play sports for college teams; only the really outstanding can expect to be called to the Blue squads.

Each college also has its Junior Common Room: both an actual room, with a club-like assortment of armchairs and daily papers, and a collective term for the student body of the college (or as many as can be bothered to turn up!) assembled in the room to discuss arrangements and grievances, and elect representatives to negotiate with the college dons in their Senior Common Room. Becoming JCR Vice-President proved that Rachel was popular, responsible and articulate in the eyes of her peers.

She was not a goody two-shoes. She was as fun-loving as the next young person. She enjoyed the normal healthy young woman's experiences of meeting men and falling in love and finding out about sex.

At the end of her first year she was back in Blackpool for the long break when she met John Tanner in a club where he had taken a holiday job. John is a New Zealander. Twenty-two years old when he met Rachel, he was a classics student at Nottingham University. Tall, slim and good-looking, with shoulder-length hair and finely chiselled features, he was an obviously acceptable boyfriend. They dated. They wrote to each other over the following term. They slept together.

And – amazingly – not even the tabloid press has suggested that this represented any shocking immorality on their part. Perhaps English sexual ethics really are moving to an adult post-contraceptive phase at last!

Over the Christmas break, John came up to Blackpool and stayed with the McLeans. Rachel's parents were delighted with him. An educated and intelligent boyfriend was just what they might hope for their daughter to find, and John fitted in well with the family, including Rachel's two younger brothers. Rachel's Christmas present to him was a red paisley patterned tie.

The relationship continued over the Hilary term. (Like the law courts, Oxford gives its terms antiquated names: not Autumn, Spring and Summer, but Michaelmas, Hilary and Trinity.) But over that time it changed subtly. John became increasingly convinced that Rachel was the girl for him – indeed, in a very special way was *his*. Rachel, privately, became increasingly convinced that theirs was *not* to be an intense and eternal love.

The troubles began in January when John fell ill. It appears to have been some peculiar abdominal virus. But John feared he had cancer in the groin, and it affected his sexual performance. Previously, he claims, he had been able to make love up to seven times a night. Now he found his performance faltering, and he felt that Rachel's dissatisfaction amounted to taunting him over his occasional impotence.

Rachel, for her part, was far more concerned by John's increasing possessiveness. Like many women of her age, she kept a private diary in which she recorded her emotions. We all learn about falling in love, and college students are particularly inclined to examine and re-examine their early amatory experiences. Jean Cocteau has a delightful moment in his film *Testament d'Orphée* when he wanders through a room full of young people who are embracing, kissing each other and immediately scribbling notes on pads before returning to kiss again. 'Intellectuals in love,' he comments tersely.

On Valentine's Day, Rachel came to a decisive and accurate conclusion about John. He was, she told her diary after receiving his card, 'a selfish bastard who hoped his romance with himself would never end'. How right she was! But how tolerant and forgiving, too. She wrote a letter telling John he didn't own her. Then, perhaps aware that his delusions would never let him accept such plain truth, she didn't post it.

Still, she knew enough about her own feelings to let herself start testing the water for other possible relationships. She went out occasionally with other men in Oxford. If everything seemed right, she occasionally slept with them.

Rachel did not tell John. There was no reason to break off the relationship terminally simply because she now knew it was unlikely to be permanent. They were young people who might both be assumed to be acquiring sexual and amatory experience; might both be expected to find somebody more appropriate and move forward. They weren't engaged, they were just 'going steady'.

The short Easter break ended with Joan McLean driving Rachel back to Oxford on Saturday 13 April. Mother and daughter had gone shopping together and cleaned out Rachel's fridge. They wanted to be in Oxford in reasonable time, because John was coming to spend the weekend with her.

Rachel was residing out of college by now, sharing digs with four other girls in a house in Argyle Road. The large brick semis of East Oxford are especially convenient for Magdalen and St Hilda's students, whose colleges lie at the bottom of the High, a quarter of a mile away from the city centre.

John wanted to kick off the summer term by securing Rachel to himself positively. He arrived in Oxford asking her to accept formal engagement. This was quite out of the question. Rachel's diary showed that in extreme moments she found John's emotional demands utterly intolerable. He was 'a sick, childish bastard' and she dreaded the 'vampire-like way he leeches on my affection'.

John had no idea she ever felt these things. To one of her room-mates, the two seemed happily in love. But young love is an unstable emotion: easily aroused to an intense flame by sexual arousal or the ego-trip of a desirable partner; easily doused by unexpected differences in taste or an immature lover's failure to grasp one's deep private needs.

John had totally failed to accept Rachel's need for a life of her own on her own terms. He explicitly resented her success in becoming JCR Vice-President as her duties took up time he wanted to spend with her. Rachel was right — tragically right — in seeing that he would not, in the long run suit her: that his wish to possess her wholly, like an elegant car or a beautiful pet, left no room for her own personality.

She didn't put it cruelly when it came to the showdown in her room. She told him it was impossible. She told him she wanted a life of her own and he clearly did not and could not respect and accept that. She told him that he was not the only man in her life; she had slept with others since meeting him. John snapped.

We have only his own account of how he came to kill Rachel on the spot, although his immediate conduct was so self-serving and deceptive that he cannot be trusted. But there is no doubt that as soon as he learned that Rachel did not regard herself as his personal property — that she rightly saw her body as her own, and its pleasures to be shared with partners of her choosing — John grabbed her by the throat and squeezed.

I don't know whether, as he claims, his rage was such that he didn't really know what he was doing. But it is clear that he was determined to see her dead rather than alive and with another man, because when she passed out he put a ligature around her throat and tightened it until she was strangled. His confession suggested that this may have been a tea towel: he couldn't remember for sure. The police and the pathologist were certain it was nothing so broad. In their view, the bruising shows that John strangled Rachel with a narrow piece of cloth: almost certainly the red paisley tie Rachel had given him for Christmas and which he thereafter used to hold up his jeans.

The deed done, John sat on the bed, his mind in turmoil, and wondered what to do. Had he given himself up immediately, he might have entered a successful plea of diminished responsibility. But he did nothing of the kind. He hid the body and set out to cover his tracks.

On his way back to Nottingham, he stopped in Oxford station buffet and wrote a letter to Rachel. He pretended he was writing it on the train, complaining that the bumpy journey made writing difficult. He invented memories of their affectionate farewell on the platform at Oxford.

When he got back to Nottingham he wrote to and telephoned Rachel again, implying that he 'knew' her to be alive and well when he left her.

Rachel was quickly missed. The term opened with 'Collections' — internal college examinations which have no bearing on students' degree results, but indicate to tutors how well in command of their work they are. Rachel didn't show up. She was a sensible and reliable student. The college principal assumed she must be ill.

But, no. Her room-mates did not know where she was. A telephone call to Blackpool confirmed that she had not gone home to her parents. Rachel was simply missing.

This is something every college dreads. The institution is *in loco parentis* for students away from home, and no guardian wants to be held responsible for the loss or death of one of their charges. But no reasonable explanation for Rachel's disappearance could be found, and the police had to be informed.

They made inquiries at Argyle Street and searched the house. Nothing seemed to be amiss there. Rachel's flatmates were bewildered by her disappearance, but certainly didn't associate it with John. There was no body hidden in any closet; no signs of disturbed floorboards or freshly turned earth in the garden. Rachel, it seemed, must be somewhere else.

High in everyone's mind in the late 1980s was the disappearance of estate agent Suzy Lamplugh, abducted and presumed murdered by a mysterious client whose name she recorded as 'Mr Kipper'. The Lamplugh Trust, founded by Suzy's mother, tried to keep girls and women alert to the danger that strange men who offered them lifts or made sudden dates with them might have evil intentions. The press highlighted Rachel's disappearance and the public fear was that she had fallen prey to a wandering killer-rapist.

The police didn't think so for one moment. Their investigations had led to John Tanner as the last person to positively see Rachel alive. And John's story just didn't ring true. He had left her, he said, on Oxford station. They had sat drinking coffee together in the buffet and Rachel had recognized a man at a neighbouring table, who offered to drive her back to her digs. He was a tall young man with long hair, wearing leathers. When a photofit was assembled under John's direction, the resulting image was surprisingly like himself!

Rachel's parents were dismayed when John's story appeared in the papers. It just didn't match details of the account he had given them of his parting from Rachel. The police went through the motions of following up John's story and asking for the young man in leathers to come forward. They brought John back to Oxford to lead them through his and Rachel's movements at the time when he said he left her. They watched him appear on television, angrily denying any responsibility for the disappearance of the girl he loved.

But privately they were sure John had killed his girlfriend and hidden the body. The question was, where? Nothing really suggested that Rachel had ever left Argyle Street. No witness testified to seeing Rachel and John together at Oxford station, and John did not have transport to hump a body around the city. No taxi-driver or delivery firm had taken a suspicious trunk from the Argyle Street student digs. The house would have to be re-examined.

By the crudest detective test it seemed impossible that

the body should still be there, eighteen days after her disappearance. An odour of decomposition should be spreading through the house by that time, and there was none.

The first police search had gone through Rachel's bedroom; through the cupboards in the house; through the loft under the roof where a body might have been hidden. The initial police concern had been to ensure that the body had not been successfully concealed or removed for ultimate untraceable disposal in a rubbish skip. So evidence of dissection in the house had been sought, and waste land and scrub nearby had been searched. All had proved unsuccessful. It remained to see whether the house contained a concealed cellar.

On 2 May, PC Colin Wood was back in Argyle Street with instructions to look under the flooring in Rachel's ground-floor bedroom. The constable carefully raised some boards and found a cool, airy under-floor crawl space. He flashed his electric torch toward the house front and played it around. Nothing. He flashed it back toward the kitchen area and played it around . . . an unmistakable human foot.

There was Rachel's body, partially unclothed, and tightly bound to hold it compact under the floor. The excellent under-floor ventilation had kept the house free of any malodour.

John Tanner's lies about Rachel's seeing him off from Oxford station were completely incompatible with innocence. His careful planning — changing Rachel's trousers and tying her body, writing false letters to her and making telephone calls — went far beyond a sudden rush of blood to the head. He might, as he claimed, have been an impromptu murderer. But he was a very cunning and calculating accessory to himself after the fact. His story that he hoped to persuade himself, by hiding the body and going on writing to Rachel, that it hadn't really happened and he hadn't really lost her, convinced no one.

John was found guilty of murder at Birmingham

Crown Court in December 1991. His case illustrated unusually clearly the possessiveness that mistakes itself for love but is in fact jealousy. Rachel had complained of it to her diary before she died; she had explained it was her reason for refusing his proposal of engagement; she had been killed by a man who could not bear the loss to his own ego of letting anybody else share her love.

Stormy Passions

'lust
Is perjured, murderous, bloody, full of blame,
Savage, extreme, rude, cruel, not to trust'
Shakespeare *Sonnet 129*

John Kerr and Morris Brewer

As 1949 yielded to 1950, the police in Melbourne, Australia, noted with surprise that they were dealing with more murders than usual in their placid community. Half a dozen cases on the books at any one time was distinctly abnormal.

They seemed unrelated. They included armed robberies that went wrong and a rape-murder, as well as the standard domestic disputes. Two were, however, freak cases. The murders of young women by young men in what police and prosecutors termed the frenzy of jealous rage.

John Kerr

Beth Williams came to Melbourne from Hobart, Tasmania, early in 1949 with her friend Patricia Street. The two nineteen-year-olds were typists, improving their opportunities by starting new lives in the big city. They shared digs together; they found good jobs; and they enjoyed the normal, carefree lives of young women without family responsibilities, dating and going to dances with young men. The port of Melbourne, and a rather high contingency of servicemen in the aftermath of the Second World War, enabled them to satisfy their young women's thirst for uniformed escorts. Beth went steady for much of the year with a soldier from the barracks.

That relationship broke up two weeks before Christmas. Beth suffered normal, but not devastating heartbreak, and drew on her resilience to look for other fish in the sea once Christmas was over. She went on her own to a dance at the Trocadero on Boxing Day and there she met and liked seaman James Stevens, who saw her home. She was different from the party-girls who sometimes came aboard his vessel, the Swedish freighter *Citos*, and he made a date to take her to the theatre the following night. The pair arranged to meet under the clock in Flinders Street around 7 p.m.

At about 7.20 p.m., Beth was waiting under the clock when a man she knew named Grimstead saw her and said good evening. He recalled later that she was wearing a red coat and a red and yellow tartan dress. She told him she'd been stood up and wondered hopefully whether he would like to take her out. He regretted that his purse was too light, but stayed chatting until a man with an overcoat and suitcase came out of the Flinders Street station. Beth recognized him and called, 'John!' adding to Grimstead, 'See you later!'

John Bryan Kerr, a twenty-six-year-old junior civil servant in the Immigration Department turned to see who had called him. Beth's face was familiar, and with a little effort he recalled that he had met her in Tasmania the previous year. But he could not remember her name, as he explained with an apology.

Beth was not offended. They had only met once or twice, and she cheerfully explained that she and Patricia (whom he had also met in Hobart) were now living and working in Melbourne. She explained less cheerfully that she was waiting in Flinders Street because her date had stood her up.

John Kerr was in a good humour. He had been to the races and his fancy, Laimell, had come in at 20 to 1. He invited Beth to come and have dinner with him to spend his winnings, and after an unsuccessful attempt to get a Flinders Street hotel to serve them a drink, the two went to Mario's restaurant.

Ten minutes later James Stevens arrived in Flinders Street to find the space under the clock deserted.

Beth and John enjoyed their meal together. He was a former radio announcer who had worked for station 3GL at Geelong. His rather British sounding accent might have seemed highly appropriate for radio work. Unfortunately, it didn't make him popular with fellow broadcasters, who sometimes called him 'Mr 3LO', parodying the BBC's original call-sign, 2LO, and suggesting that he thought himself the cat's whiskers among the broader Ozzie announcers. Kerr had a short temper and on at least one occasion he started a fight when taunted. In 1949, studio manager Walter Gray decided that he was more trouble than he was worth and dismissed him with a cheque to pay for his services up to date. Kerr was hurt, but found his civil service post without too much difficulty. And he enjoyed minor celebrity status as an ex-radio person in those days before television.

After dinner, John and Beth decided to go to the 'No-Hopers' Club'. This very informal drinking spot in the suburb of Parkville was just a tenement owned by a man called Edward Penno. Australia's appalling licensing laws in the 1950s meant that anywhere one could enjoy a drink in the evening was welcome. The No-Hopers wasn't really a formal club, and at any time might declare itself to be a private party. The activities were just dancing to gramophone records and buying drinks.

The spot was popular with singles. Both John and Beth had been there before. But it was certainly not what later came to be known as a 'singles bar', and neither Mr Kerr nor Miss Williams were the sort of people who cruised for casual pick-ups or went 'Looking for Mr Goodbar'.

The club's name was a private joke among members, who shared a liking for the racetrack. The notion was that they came to drown their sorrows after losing their shirts on spavined nags. But, as John's win that day proved, a 'No-Hoper' might equally turn up to celebrate the transfer of bookies' cash into his or her own pocket by converting it to refreshing liquid.

The character of the No-Hopers was of some importance, as it would later be suggested that John and Beth showed themselves to be slightly unsavoury or despairing individuals by their attendance at this unlicensed watering-hole.

In fact, it was a common acquaintance called Leslie John Wood, whom they met at Mario's, who suggested they join him in going to Parkville for the No-Hopers' 'party' that night and he drove them there. John spent part of the evening drinking and dancing with another No-Hoper friend, saleswoman Mrs Barbara Robertson. Both Mrs Robertson and Penno, the 'club's' owner, observed that Beth was wearing a blue dress.

About ten minutes after midnight, Patricia Street came home. The door to Beth's room was open and Beth's light was on, but Beth was not there. This suggested that she had come in during the evening to change her clothes — something she often did during the close summer and autumn nights.

But it was not until about 1 a.m. that Wood was ready to leave the No-Hopers and offered John and Beth their lift back to Albert Park. Beth directed him to stop at a point from which Kerr would be able to follow the tramlines back to his own house. The two thanked Wood for the lift and got out for Kerr to see Beth home.

He felt a little sick after the evening's entertainment, however, and tactfully retreated to Middle Beach to alleviate his discomfort. When he rejoined her, Beth encouraged him to sit down and recover. They kissed and cuddled a little. Then at some unspecified time, a man called Petersen recognized Kerr walking away from the area of the beach changing sheds on his own. It was an unsalubrious place. Drunks, eccentrics and dossers frequented the beach huts and local residents frequently complained about 'goings-on' there.

By 2.45 a.m. Kerr was at home and sleeping in his bed as his father saw when he woke up and checked that John had come home. At dawn next morning Beth's body was found lying at the water's edge with the tide lapping over her. Her blue dress was ripped down the front and much of her underwear had been pulled off. One garment lay on the beach, but her knickers were missing. Despite this, police said she had definitely not been raped or engaged in sexual intercourse the previous night.

A trail through the sand suggested that she had been dragged to the water from one of the beach huts. A few drops of blood suggested that she had been killed there before being taken to the tideline. Her broken hyoid bone showed that she had been forcefully strangled; bruising on the neck suggested that a man's hands had killed her. Time of death was estimated as not earlier than 11 p.m. or later than 2 a.m.

James Stevens was traced by the police, and suffered a nasty interview until he established a solid alibi for the estimated time of death.

John Kerr was arrested in a rather over-dramatic dawn raid on 29 December and taken to the police station where he very soon made a confession to manslaughter.

He had taken Beth to walk on the beach some time after 1 a.m., he said, and then realized he had 'a turn' coming on. This often happened, especially after he had been drinking. He believed he had attacked Beth. He couldn't think why. And that, you would think, would be that. The simple end of a simple case.

But no. With his statement allegedly taken down by four senior police officers, Kerr refused to sign it, remarking that he thought he had said enough for them. And by the time he came to trial he denied having made it at all!

Kerr was defended by Mr R. Monahan KC who, for reasons that have never been explained, fought his case with such ferocity that he won Kerr two retrials and pursued appeals up to the Privy Council. In the process, Mr Monahan elicited protests from prosecuting counsel and mild reprimands from the judges, since he seemed willing to attack witnesses and jurists alike with scant regard for decorous procedure.

The heart of Kerr's case was that his alleged confession had been entirely made up by Senior Detective J. Adam, whose forgery was endorsed by three other policemen. Kerr claimed he had consistently denied all responsibility for Beth's death, as the frustrated detectives well knew. He had left Beth, alive and well, in the lane at the bottom of her street at about 1.30 a.m., and walked home to go to bed. He couldn't have been in bed by the time his father saw him if he left any later. And he had not gone into the beach hut at all: just walked very briefly on the beach.

All three judges pointed out that Kerr and Monahan were charging the police with something far worse than murder in a frenzy of jealous rage: the wicked and calculated railroading of a man to the gallows in order to clear their case file.

Monahan also cast aspersions on Beth's character, hinting that she and Patricia were habitual party-girls, and Beth might even have been soliciting on that night when she invited Grimstead to entertain her and then went off with John Kerr. He did his best to make the No-Hopers' Club sound like a sleazy house of assignation, despite the disinterested assurance from Grimstead that it was a respectable place where racing men and women liked to mingle under the jocular pretence that they always lost to the bookies.

The barrister also made desperate (and unsuccessful) attempts to force medical witnesses to agree that Beth might have drowned accidentally. And he brought out the oddity of Beth's apparent change of clothing and Patricia's initial belief that she had been to change her clothes during the evening. Patricia changed her mind when she realized that Beth had been at the No-Hopers well before her own arrival home after midnight. But she confirmed Beth's possession of the tartan dress Grimstead saw. Kerr confused things further by suggesting that she was wearing black when she was with him!

Essentially, both he and Mr Monahan wanted it to be believed that she had gone home after leaving him near the beach, and then came out again in new clothes to look for another man.

The Crown, without pressing the point, wanted the jury to infer that Grimstead was mistaken about Beth's clothing. But their reference to a man's fit of jealous rage suggests that the original police theory must have been that Beth went home and changed her clothes between going to the Flinders Street hotel and Mario's with Kerr, presumably wanting something more suitable for party-ing — this leading Kerr to anticipate later sexual favours, and an uncontrollable possessive fury when they were not forthcoming.

Monahan's own frenzy of forensic eloquence drove Patricia Street to repeated tears, and back to Hobart to live safely with her parents. It confused two juries into disagreement. But the third jury enjoyed two new pieces of evidence. The belated discovery of Beth's knickers under the flooring of the beach hut lent weight to the prosecution submission that Kerr had taken the girl to this well-known squalid trysting-place, only to be frus-trated by her ultimate virtue. And the evidence of a doctor that Kerr had been under treatment for years as a victim of recurrent insane fits of uncontrollable rage both supported the confession he had refused to sign and allowed the jury to add 'a strong recommendation to mercy' to their finding of guilty.

So, after the failure of his appeals, John Bryan Kerr was sentenced to twenty years' imprisonment.

Morris Brewer
By a remarkable coincidence, no sooner was Kerr's third trial over, than Mr R. Monahan KC for the defence and Mr H. Winnike KC for the Crown confronted each other once again in the same courtroom, to pursue the ends of justice in a strikingly similar case.

Once again a nineteen-year-old girl had been found strangled a quarter of a mile from her home. Once again it was immediately announced that some man had killed her but not raped her. Once again his motive was declared to be frenzied jealousy even before he had been certainly identified. Once again the defendant was a clerk in his early twenties and the verdict would hinge on his mental state.

Morris Brewer met Carmen Walters on a herd-testing course at Burnley Primary Agricultural College in October 1949. He was twenty-three; she was nineteen. They were a good-looking couple, he with long fair hair that he combed straight back, despite its tendency to stand up spikily in front; she with well-groomed, long, dark wavy hair. He was a clerk; she was a portress on the railway.

They got on well and became engaged. Their wedding, they decided, would take place in October 1950. And – this was an important consideration – it would take place under the auspices of Morris's family and not Carmen's, for the Brewers were Plymouth Brethren.

In 1950 the sect had not undergone the schism of the 'Exclusives' which damaged them so gravely in public esteem, with families splitting permanently on points of theology, and schismatics refusing to speak or have any dealings with anyone – including their own children – who did not share all their beliefs. The Brethren were an awkward extremist persuasion, but their difficulties with mainstream society resulted from an exaggerated respect for integrity and self-denial rather than any fear of damnation if they associated with unrepentant outsiders. Though they didn't wear peculiar clothes, the Brethren were like eighteenth-century Quakers or present-day Pennsylvania Amish in believing that many forms of worldly pleasure were a harmful distraction from man's proper spiritual concerns. So they did not stop at eschewing tobacco, alcohol and gambling. They barred dancing, theatre-going, the cinema and all games of chance. They preferred, rather than enforced, social mixture with each other rather than those who might lead them astray.

It went without saying that the moral codes to which other Christians paid lip-service were treated with the utmost gravity by the Brethren. They simply did not lie, steal, cheat or defraud. They were rigid in their enforcement of traditional sexual chastity. Two years before Morris Brewer found himself in the dock, Mr Justice Humphreys in England had been rightly disgusted by defence submissions that acid-bath murderer John George Haigh's character had been warped because his parents were Plymouth Brethren, and roundly declared that he would listen to no more pernicious attacks on a body whose reputation stood effectively as high as the Quakers.

Carmen Walters' father was not an especially religious man. A war-blinded ex-squadron leader in the RAAF, he demanded some concessions on his daughter's account. Carmen did not care for dancing, but there should be no question of her giving up the cinema which she enjoyed. And since she would be barely twenty when she married, he insisted that the young couple should put off having children for a few years while they settled into the other responsibilities of marriage.

The Brewers were not unreasonable bigots. They accepted these points gracefully, and in return were grateful that Mr Walters was happy for the marriage to be carried out in Hampton Hall with Mr Clayton, an elder of the sect, officiating.

The most unhappy parent was Mrs Walters. She felt that her daughter was being refused a proper marriage in a proper church and there wouldn't even be a proper minister of religion to give it validity. But Mrs Walters and her daughter didn't see eye to eye over a number of things. Mr Walters, who unashamedly liked Morris Brewer, tried to reassure the young man by telling him that her mother counted for little more than 'the dirt under the hearth' to Carmen.

It was an unfortunate bluff hyperbole to put before a sheltered boy who thought that 'Honour Thy Father and

Thy Mother' really, truly and literally had been sent down graven on stone tablets as a special directive from Jehovah. It raised more questions about Carmen than Mr Walters could ever have imagined.

But since his social points had been accepted, the blind ex-pilot was quite unworried by his future son-in-law's religion. Indeed, he took it as good fortune for his daughter to have found a fiancé whose integrity was guaranteed and whose intentions (in the quaint phrase of the time) were indubitably honourable.

The first difference between the young couple was a minor point of taste which would worry no mature person. Carmen, an outdoorsy Australian girl, wanted a hiking-tour honeymoon. Morris, more of a townee, didn't like the idea. The more serious differences arose in 1950. Morris noticed that he was hearing differing accounts from Carmen of a period she had spent in Darwin. She told him it was six months; she told him it was six weeks. One of these times must be wrong. That meant, for Plymouth Brother Morris, one of them must be a lie. And Morris was a man who had never knowingly been lied to in his family; a man who regarded the capacity to lie as a mark of the devil.

He took his anxieties to Roy Walters again. (Presumably he could predict that his own parents would have demanded that he write off this dangerous Whore of Babylon at once!) The former squadron leader repeated his error of thinking that the young man had the normal wordly wisdom of a twenty-three-year-old. Carmen didn't always tell her parents the truth, he explained. She liked travelling and always wanted to be dashing off to strange places, whereas they wanted her to keep them informed of exactly where she was at the very least. Why, once she had even stayed out overnight without letting them know she was going or where she went!

The fact that Carmen hadn't always kept her parents precisely posted of all her movements probably didn't matter very much to Morris Brewer. But the fact that they casually accepted her as having lied to them in the past seemed horrifying. He confronted his fiancée again with renewed questions about that mysterious trip to Darwin. And Carmen then gave him information that absolutely shattered him.

While she was in Darwin, she had slept with a man. She was not a virgin.

Morris broke off the engagement instantly. But despite the strict code of sexual morality he had been taught, he was really an awfully nice young man in his way. He went to see Mr Walters yet again to explain to him. He carefully did not reveal Carmen's 'shame', which no doubt he thought would upset the girl's father as much as it did him. Instead he attributed the break to Carmen's inconsistencies and the difficulty he had in knowing how to believe what she said.

Mr Walters was impressed by the young man's straightforwardness. He confirmed that her parents had often found Carmen 'wilful'. He shook Morris's hand warmly as the respectable Christian took himself out of the Walters family.

Nobody seems to have told Mrs Walters about these events. She was placidly writing invitations to an engagement party when Carmen burst in and told her she could stop that immediately: it was all off. Only it wasn't that simple. Morris Brewer had taken a very big step in falling in love. (Roy Walters, the most normal and mature figure observing the whole business, had no doubt the young couple were both very much in love.) Morris couldn't just step out of the engagement on principle and carry on as if nothing had happened. He stopped sleeping. Tonics and medication did nothing for him. And his doctor sent him for a short stay in hospital.

The Walters didn't know it, but this was his second nervous breakdown. The rigid ethics of the Plymouth Brotherhood were a dreadful strain on a young man who was too scrupulous to fudge his way round them, yet had definite needs — including a real and deep attraction to

Carmen — which they could not countenance.

Carmen also loved Morris. When he came out of hospital in April and went to visit her he discovered, to his surprise, that though she had vehemently thrust his ring back in his hand when he rejected her, she wanted to re-establish the engagement. Now he was in turmoil. At a deep level he wanted to build on their love. Yet his intellectual morality would not permit it. He couldn't resist seeing her again. Yet he wanted nothing more to do with her.

She worked at Hampton Station, and he would go there and visit her and drink tea in the buffet. They talked round and round in circles about their hopeless conflicting aims. On 12 May, Carmen left a note at his workplace asking him to take her to tea that night. He went to Hampton to tell her family that he was not taking her to tea that night or any other. But as she said she was going away shortly, he relented and agreed to see her the following night. Strangers who overheard parts of the conversation jumped to the entirely wrong conclusion that he was asking her to elope with him to Adelaide and she was refusing.

On 13 May, the couple went to Mordialloc together for a meal. They came back by train to Moorabbin and took a bus to Glencairn Avenue, where Carmen lived. All the time, all the way, they talked about their problems. Carmen blamed his upbringing (obviously enough) which distressed him (equally obviously). As they started to walk the final stretch to Glencairn Avenue, he reproached her for apparently criticizing his parents during the evening. She responded, 'I have caused my parents a lot of worry in the past, and I think you will do the same.'

And that did it. Those words caused her death. Morris Brewer seized her throat, forced her to the ground, and pressed the life out of her. Then he went to Moorabbin Station and took a taxi to Oakleigh. There he bought a glass of sarsaparilla, before hitch-hiking up the Dandenong Road to Drouin. He hitched on through the bush to Warragul and Yarroun where he made a half-hearted attempt to cut his wrist with a razor blade. He was in hospital when the police caught up with him.

The facts were not in dispute at his trial. The hearing was all about Morris Brewer's mental state, since he (or Mr Monahan) submitted an insanity plea.

Mr Monahan conducted his defence with refreshing calm and decorum after the *Sturm und Drang* of John Kerr's trials. Psychiatrist Dr Alexander Sinclair argued persuasively that Brewer had never grown out of his natural infantile attachment to his mother. But this, coupled with his upbringing and its focus on rigid sexual morality, made it a terrible strain for him to find himself attracted to any other woman. At a deep level, he felt that he betrayed his mother by loving anyone else. He could give surface support to this denial of his natural instincts by appealing to his anti-sexual code of ethics. But, most tellingly, his writing and conversation showed that, without realizing it, he equated his mother with God.

When Carmen told him he would one day displease his mother, she was telling him he would wilfully offend God. And Dr Sinclair felt that all Brewer knew he was doing was silencing this appalling accusation. He did not think or know he was killing a real person. He was shutting up the suggestion that he might ever betray his profound, immature and irrational principles.

The prosecution expert witness was less persuasive in suggesting that this man, twice hospitalized by breakdowns, clearly knew what he was doing and that it was wrong. Even he admitted that Brewer had a schizoid personality. The jury found Brewer not guilty by reason of insanity.

Brewer's mad jealousy lacked the normal egocentricity. His jealousy tried to preserve his mother's primacy in his emotions, which he madly equated with the divinity he wanted to worship with his whole heart and soul and being. I don't agree with Oscar Wilde that 'Each man kills the thing he loves'. But I'm sure Morris Brewer was one who did.

Pamela Smart

Pamela Wojas and Gregory Smart were wild kids. Pamela's high school career at Derry, New Hampshire, was one of high achievement: cheerleader and class president, with good grades. She went on to university in her natal state of Florida, where she had lived until she was thirteen.

Greg, at high school in nearby Londonderry, achieved little that his pastors and masters thought useful. But both were famous among their peers for their active sex-lives. Pam's main boyfriend proudly reported their wide range of erotic acrobatics. She was also known as 'Wham-Bam-Thankyou-Pam' because she went through so many lovers. Greg was a notorious schoolboy stud, who would take bets on how many girls he could make out with at parties. (Three and four were reported.) Both Pam and Greg were heavy metal fans. Pam's favourite band was Van Halen: Greg's was Motley Crue.

When Pam first met Greg at the 1985 New Year's Eve party he threw in his parents' absence, she was immediately struck by his resemblance to Jon Bon Jovi, the Van Halen singer. Greg had long, shoulder-length hair and a wide-eyed, open, boyish face. He dressed like a rocker and Pam fancied what she saw.

Greg liked the look of slim, petite Pam, too, with her wavy, light-brown hair. But then, Greg fancied so many girls. It was Pam's way to go get the man she wanted, and hold him against all comers. Even so, few expected her to prise Greg away from the competition to move down to Florida with her during term time.

They seemed like a free-time couple. Pam was majoring in media studies and, as was always the way with the Wojas family, working extremely hard earning money and garnering useful professional experience. As well as normal student jobs – clerking, serving behind shop counters and waitressing – Pam worked unpaid as a reporter for a local television station and hosted a weekly heavy metal radio programme on the university's station. 'Maid of Metal' was her name for herself, and in her leathers and chains she looked at her most companionate for Greg.

He, meanwhile, was doing nothing promising at all. Just working as a labourer for a landscaping firm, enjoying rock music and living with Pamela.

The young, rocking couple had one other thing in common. Both used ordinary diminutives of their names, but spelled them in unusual ways to draw attention to themselves: 'Pame' and 'Gregg' instead of Pam and Greg.

In January 1988, Gregg proposed to Pame, offering her an engagement ring as she came out of her shower in a cloud of powder. Surprise, surprise! Such formality was not at all anticipated! But she made him go on one knee and accepted. Then an utterly unpredictable change came over the young man. The wild heavy metal punk, whose randy promiscuity had been tamed for Pame's personal possession, settled down further to the responsibilities of future matrimony. His father was a successful insurance salesman, and Gregg passed the necessary exams to go into the business. He cut his hair short, and adapted himself to the formal suits and ties necessary for earning a living in the middle-class world of commerce.

He had another change in view that was not really to Pame's taste. She loved Florida and had never really liked her father's move north in 1980 when he felt that increasing crime in Miami made it an undesirable location for a young family. She was, in Gregg's words, a real 'sun-bunny', happiest on the beach in a bikini, burning up a smooth and striking tan.

But Gregg was a natural rural New Englander. He enjoyed the New Hampshire countryside and winter sports, though his preferred recreation of careering around in four-wheel drives was not exactly Wordsworthian. It's probable, too, that Gregg felt a special closeness to his family. His boyish wildness was never a rejection of their love and standards. And it was well worth living near his father, whose established professional position helped a young man starting out in the insurance business.

Why didn't Pame break off an engagement which was moving in directions so different from their steady live-in love-life? Probably because she shared some of Gregg's ambitions. Though her attention-seeking nature steered her to the media, and she wanted to be a presenter, she knew that becoming a local television princess entailed a more sober image than the 'Maid of Metal'. She was prepared to put on smart conventional clothes and a toothpaste ad smile if that was the price of glamorous adult success. Indeed, some remarks about herself as a 'qualified professional woman' suggest that she was more stiffly converted to bourgeois ambition than Gregg. That is on the surface, for inside Pame was still an immature person whose sense of identity depended on the adulation and support of outsiders.

Anyway, the young couple moved to a condominium at Derry, New Hampshire, close to their parents. Gregg immediately set about building his career in the most promising way. Within his first year of serious work, he won his firm's trophy as their most successful new agent.

Pame was less clearly on target. She lacked the experience for instant employment by the main New Hampshire television station. The state's small population did not support enough local TV companies to give her a minor station to work for while she established herself. Professionally, she would have been better off in a bigger city or a more densely populated state. Her ambitions, in fact, demanded a different early lifestyle from Gregg's. She needed to move around the country snapping up any opening that came, whereas Gregg was best off in his home territory where people liked buying policies from a nice local bad boy making good under his father's reassuring eye.

But Pame was a Wojas. She wouldn't sit around being unemployed because she couldn't get exactly the work she wanted. She found a post as Media Centre Director for School Administrative Unit 21 in Hampton. She had an office opposite Winnecunnet High School, and her administrative job entailed PR work with the news media on behalf of the board.

Miss Wojas was only twenty-one but she enjoyed her professional standing. She hoped, ultimately, to teach occasional media courses for Winnecunnet High: teaching, after all, supplies an audience as well as a useful occupation for those who enjoy the limelight.

Her parents were uneasy about the engagement to Gregg. He was not a college graduate, and they wondered whether he would be able to keep their daughter in the manner to which she wanted to be accustomed. But the Smarts were reassuring, and in May 1989 the full white Catholic wedding was celebrated. It was not a good omen that Gregg and his best man arrived somewhat plastered.

Mrs Pamela Smart, as she always had done, expected her man to be her possession. Gregg's former girlfriends were dropped from the marital social scene for a bit, and Gregg took to masculine recreations with men friends. Drinking and gambling, specifically. He and his father both enjoyed slipping down to the casinos in Atlantic City for a weekend from time to time, and Gregg enjoyed a night out on the beer with the boys.

If Pame got sore, and wanted the rowdy company cleared out, Gregg had the distasteful habit of spitting a mouthful of beer all over her face. It made her furious. It made her rush away to clean up. And it was a handy way for Gregg to get rid of her if he saw she was about to lose her temper and get in the way. Not surprisingly some of their friends wondered how long the marriage would last.

Pame found her own social circle in the autumn. An unsuitably juvenile circle of high school kids. Chubby, fifteen-year-old Cecelia Pierce came to work as her student assistant in the media centre. Pame was so young that she accepted Cecelia pretty much at her own level. She never appreciated that the age and status difference between the two meant that Cecelia could not give her the supportive checks and balances we can all use from friends. Indeed, it's likely that Pame enjoyed having an automatic yes-man as her closest ally.

But Pame's schoolgirl girlfriend was a harmless acquaintance compared with her schoolboy boyfriend. She met Billy Flynn when she accepted the role of facilitator in some confidence classes which were part of Winnecunnet High's anti-drugs programme. Billy, a tall, marmoset-eyed fifteen-year-old, with long black hair, was a student facilitator. And he wasn't the only high school lad to notice Pame's trim, petite good looks and fancy her rotten.

No harm in that, until the end of the year, when Pame and Gregg had a marital row. It was far from their first and not obviously their worst, for it did not lead to Pame's storming out to her or his parents as had happened previously.

But it was their most serious. Not for what caused it, but for what Gregg said in the course of it. He shouted, or confessed, or made known to Pame somehow, that on a recent business trip he had enjoyed a one-night stand with another woman. It had no emotional charge on either side; it held no promise for the future nor was it an intrinsic threat to Gregg's wobbly adherence to Pame. But it had happened.

Coming just six months after the two married, I'd call it a pretty serious occurrence. It was a real signal that their relationship was not one of lifetime commitment, and the choice before them was either to get their act together or cut their losses and split. Pame made the worst choice possible. She stayed with the marriage, using Gregg's infidelity as a weapon in their future rows. She went on and on about it until Gregg (reasonably) wished he'd never told her. But he, like Pame, was too young to recognize the dangerous evidence of possessive jealousy her obsession represented.

When a jealous person's *amour propre* is highest on the list of emotions threatened by their partner's infidelity, when the victim of jealousy fears that his or her sexual desirability has been shown to be fading, the temptation to assuage the pain by starting one's own reassuring liaison is very strong. A tit-for-tat sense of retribution provides spurious moral justification. And some poor third party is likely to get dragged in as a lover-by-invitation, never realizing that they are only wanted to shore up some hurt pride. Not that most boys of Billy Flynn's age would care twopence what motivated a pretty, sexy, willing partner.

Pame saw more and more of Billy as she pulled him in to help her and Cecelia make a video for a competition, sponsored by an orange drink company. Billy's friends were originally also involved, but they quickly dropped out. They didn't share Billy's fascination with the media administrator. And they weren't interested in the wet, boring and callow activity of standing around being filmed spouting the praises of orange squash between bursts of rap and metal music.

The most familiar photographs of Billy and his friends show tense and frightened adolescent kids in deep, deep trouble. Billy, in particular, has a waif-like little-boy-lost look. But as Pame first saw him, he was a tough kid from the dodgy side of the tracks. He was from the Seabrook community: a blue-collar residential district that Winnecunnet High saw as the worst part of its catchment area. Billy and his close mates Vance 'JR' Lattime and Pete Randall had built up a respectable little record of delinquency between them: handling drugs and nicking the odd car stereo. Pete had vague ambitions to enter a

serious life of professional crime, and was vaguely
encouraged in this by their two-years-older friend Raymond 'Rayme' Fowler, who had dropped out of education and moved into drifting and petty larceny.

To respectable Mrs Smart, houseproud bourgeoise in
her spick-and-span new condo, sharing with her husband
a fastidious passion for cleaning up her home as
sedulously as they scoured their bodies, Billy, in his
leathers, looked like the real thing middle-class heavy
metal lovers imitated: a tough, punk, street-smart rocker.
She set out to seduce him.

He was easy prey. The toughness of a fifteen-year-old
lad offered no resistance to the determined pressure of a
pretty, twenty-two-year-old sexy lady coming over him
with class and status as controlling weapons. When Pame
slipped him an envelope of photos she and a girlfriend
had taken of each other posing on a bed in string bikinis,
the boy was awestruck and lust-smitten. Clearly this most
desirable creature wanted him to enjoy her.

The opportunity was created in February 1990 when
Pame invited him to come to her place to watch videos
and sleep over. Cecelia would come too; a chaperone who
was equally under Pame's adult and authoritative thumb.
Both kids could easily get away for the night from the
mothers who single-parented them, although Mrs Pierce
was already unhappy about her daughter's growing
devotion to her boss at the media centre.

The video Pam picked was *9½ Weeks*: torrid Hollywood soft-core erotica, with Kim Basinger and Mickey
Rourke displaying their charms and playing discreetly
edited erotic ice-games. The three watched the movie.
Then Pame asked Billy if he'd like to see the rest of the
house and took him upstairs to her bedroom. She
changed into a revealing turquoise-and-white negligée she
had bought for the occasion and danced to Van Halen's
sexy *Black and Blue* to tantalize Billy.

Then they made love. In bed; out of bed; standing up;
sitting down; Billy on top; Pame on top. It was a wild

initiation into the multifarious joys of sex for the virgin boy. At one point he went down to the kitchen for ice-cubes in imitation of Mickey Rourke, and no doubt learned that you can go further with them than the movie allowed in the relatively decorous tracing of Kim Basinger's bikini line.

Later in the evening, Cecelia came upstairs with a warning cry, 'I hope you guys are dressed!' A glance through the open bedroom door dispelled that hope. Pame's and Billy's naked bodies writhed, entwined, on the floor beside the bed.

Next day, as she drove the kids home, Pame tearfully told Billy it could never happen again. Not that she didn't want it. Only Gregg was so rarely away overnight. The only hope for their love, she told him, would be if he killed Gregg. Billy didn't think she was serious.

But Pame found opportunities for sex by reverting, immaturely, to a teenage-style love-life. She and Billy made out in her car and in semi-public places. Pame's position was really untenable. A professional woman employed by the school board, she was sleeping with one minor for whom she was responsible and using another (Cecelia) as her principal confidante and cover.

The Smart marriage was getting worse. Gregg seems to have been aware that Pame had levelled the score and taken a lover of her own. He didn't have a seriously jealous and insecure personality, however. He took it in his stride. It was the constant quarrelling and bitching that made him say to friends, 'Everything sucks. I'll be divorced by the summer'.

Pame's view of their disharmony was fiercer. She intended Gregg to be dead by summer, and she told Billy so. She told Billy he'd have to do the killing. She built up a deep jealousy in the lad by telling him that Gregg abused her, and dwelling on one incident before Christmas when their bitter quarrel led her to run from the house in dressing-gown and slippers, taking refuge with Gregg's parents after her husband slapped her.

Billy was obsessed with Pame and came to feel he really must carry out her lethal orders. He found difficulty in explaining, later, whether his obsession amounted to being in love – he was an inarticulate adolescent. The smooth lawyers who probed his condition couldn't use the obvious crude slang term: pussy-whipped. It was not the same thing as mature adult love but it was a contributory factor, and one which may prove as urgently commanding to a very young man.

Fake a burglary, was Pame's command. Break in with some friends before Gregg gets home from work. Steal anything they liked. Kill Gregg when he comes in. JR Lattime couldn't take this stuff seriously when Billy approached his mates. Pete Randall was a little more impressed.

But it was Raymond Fowler who gave the idea real credibility. Rayme welcomed the idea of breaking into a house left open for him; taking what he liked; maybe knocking off the owner if he came home – maybe not. Rayme mattered to Billy because he could drive. Billy and Pete couldn't. And JR, who did drive and often had the use of his grandmother's car, still saw the whole idea as ridiculous.

So when, at the end of March, Pame said flatly the time had come for the hit to be made, it was Rayme and Billy who constituted the team. Pame had a school board meeting to give her a cast-iron alibi. She left her car in the parking lot with the keys in it for Rayme and Billy to take.

As the would-be assassins got in and Rayme turned the ignition on, the stereo blasted out Van Halen's *Black and Blue*. Pame had deliberately left a tape in the system advanced to the tune she and Billy first made love to.

But despite this encouragement, Billy became sure the idea was crazy as they approached Derry and he deliberately gave Rayme wrong directions. They drove aimlessly around for some time until they reached the Smart condo to see Gregg's Chevy station wagon parked outside. He was home and they were too late. Mission aborted.

The relieved teenagers drove back to the Hampton school board building where Pame waited in her darkened office so that no one should know she had stayed around without her car after the meeting. She made no fuss about the failed murder while Rayme was present. But when he had been dropped off, Billy got an earful. He'd better let Pame know right away if he wasn't going to do the job, because their affair would end there and then! The lad meekly promised they would try again, and this time it would be for real.

Actually, a rather unreal month followed, in which three or four high school kids wrangled about whether and how to carry out a murder. In the end Pete decided it was something that mattered to Billy so much he'd better help him. JR realized his friends couldn't even start without him to drive, and he doubted whether they'd go through with it in the end, anyway. So he agreed to drive them there and back. Cecelia was hearing about it all from Pame's end.

The planning became more complex. Pame proposed the mock burglary which Gregg should interrupt when he came home. The car could be parked at the shopping mall near the condo. They mustn't use her car again as it might be identified. She would drive them to JR's grandmother's to borrow her car before the board meeting and the murder.

The hit team, wearing latex gloves to leave no fingerprints, should come over the open space at the back of the building: Pame would leave the basement door unlocked for them. They could take all her jewellery and all the stereo equipment in the house and anything else they liked. They were not to frighten the dog, who should be shut in the basement as soon as they arrived. They must not leave a light on when they were waiting for Gregg, as he was 'such a wimp' he wouldn't go in if he thought someone was there. And they should use a gun, not a knife, as she didn't want blood over her good white sofa! Even in planning a brutal murder Pame Smart was fastidious.

The kids thought her gun preference was baloney. It would be needlessly noisy and difficult to get hold of. Nor were they satisfied with jewellery and stereo equipment as payment. Billy's accomplices wanted money from Gregg's insurance, which Billy knew would be coming in to Pame. They demanded $1,000 each.

Pame baulked at that. The police might suspect such a large sum drawn from her bank account. She offered $500 apiece, paid slowly by instalments. And she refused pointblank to pay $300 for a gun − the asking price from a drug dealer they approached. Even in planning her personal fastidious murder, Pame was cheap.

In the end, JR purloined a ·38 handgun from his father's collection. He didn't want to. It couldn't be dumped after the killing because his father would miss it. And Vance Lattime Sr would be able to tell if it had been used. But there was really no alternative.

And so, on 1 May, Vance Lattime Jr drove Billy Flynn and Pete Randall to Derry. He parked at the shopping mall and waited at the car park, while Billy and Pete sellotaped their fingers under latex gloves and made their way to the Smart condo. They put the dog in the basement, and raided Pame's jewellery box in the bedroom. All they got was worthless costume jewellery. Pame was dripping with gold at her school board meeting. She had carefully extracted all her valuable pieces before the pre-planned burglary. Even when her hit-men included her own lover, she was *very* cheap.

Pete stuffed the jewellery into a cushion cover ripped from the sitting room and left it with the stereo speakers beside the back door for a quick getaway. Then the two hid in the darkened hallway waiting for Gregg.

The plan was that Billy should stand by the door to pull Gregg in if he backed off. Pete would wait by the stairs with the gun to come forward and kill Gregg quietly when the door was closed. But they managed to be in the wrong positions when Gregg's Chevy pulled up, and it was Billy, with the gun in his waistband, who lurked on the stairs.

Gregg came in and was promptly seized by Pete. Gregg was a very decent young man, and confronted by sinister hooded intruders he asked immediately if his dog was all right. The flabbergasted Seabrook yobboes assured him that the Shih-Tzu was safely shut in the basement. Then followed the amazing exchange revealing the extent to which Pame's possessiveness dictated her men's actions. Billy demanded Gregg's wedding ring.

'You can't have that,' gasped the young husband. 'My wife would kill me!'

He knew his wife very well. Pame's substitute for committed love was dedicated possessiveness, and the wedding ring Gregg wore was the symbol of her possession. She would feel deeply (and absurdly) betrayed if he failed to fight to the death for it!

But Billy, sent by that same wife for the actual purpose of killing this man, couldn't believe what he was hearing. He shot Gregg behind the ear and the two boys ran out of the back of the house, taking the cushion cover of jewellery, to JR's waiting getaway car.

Young Lattime was surprised that they had actually carried out the murder, but he put friendship first. Their tense terror needed some relief and he led them in a ludicrous off-key singsong as they drove homeward, starting with *Shoo-fly Pie*.

Pame played her part well. She came home all innocence, knowing the deed had been done, and her convincing screams persuaded the neighbourhood that Gregg had indeed been killed, as she said, by burglars he interrupted. The police were a little puzzled. The burglars were professional enough to leave no fingerprints and no signs of forced entry. Yet they picked the most unprofessional time for their robbery: just when commuters would be predictably arriving home from work.

Still, there was nothing to cast suspicion on Pame.

Gregg's heavy insurance was appropriate for a man in his occupation, and Pame did not show the avaricious murderess's premature eagerness to lay hands on it.

The story broke because it relied on teenagers to keep quiet, and because Mr and Mrs Vance Lattime were outstandingly fine Christian people.

One of JR's friends was a drop-out called Ralph Walsh. His family were among the poorest in Seabrook, and he lived in an over-crowded shack without proper indoor plumbing. The Lattimes recognized Ralph's pleasure in the baths and showers he could take at their place; realized that he could be reintegrated into society if it looked willing to give him normal, basic facilities; and arranged with Ralph's mother that the boy should come and live with them. Ralph returned to school, deeply grateful to the family that had given him security and the opportunity for a fresh start.

He was no part of the plan to support Billy Flynn's love-life by murder. So he was deeply shocked when he overheard Pete and JR discussing their involvement in the death of Gregg Smart, and hinting at the possibility of another killing to maintain their cover. He feared they might kill him. But he was still more disturbed at the thought of a villain like Pete Randall hanging around JR's little sister, whom he adored. The next time Pete came over, Ralph peremptorily ordered him off the premises and started a fight with him and JR when he refused.

It was quite extraordinary for these lads to fight. Mrs Lattime hauled Ralph indoors to ask what was going on and the boy burst into tears and told her what he had heard. Mr Lattime checked his guns, found that the ·38 had been fired recently and took it straight to the police.

Pame's hope was that the boys would say nothing, knowing that if they were convicted as juveniles they would be released on their eighteenth birthdays, after which she could pay them off and go scot-free herself. When it became clear that the District Attorney was seeking permission to try them as adults, she still assured Cecelia that she would be all right. Pame would deny anything they said about her, except, if absolutely necessary, the fact that she had slept with Billy. As she was a respectable professional adult of twenty-two from a middle-class residential township, and they were working-class delinquent adolescents, she had no doubt her word would outweigh theirs.

It might have worked. The police were hopelessly hampered by the lack of solid evidence against Pame. That was until Cecelia told her mother and Mrs Pierce saw that she told the police. Then, with Cecelia assured of no charges being brought against her, the cops listened in to her phone calls to Pame and twice wired her for sound when she went to chat to her mentor.

Pame was cunning. She tried to keep up a front of denying things Cecelia knew full well, without definitively contradicting the girl. But there was enough on the tapes to provide firm evidence against the skilled and trained communicator. And with the boys charged as adults, but given reduced sentences in return for their testimony against Mrs Smart, the jealous lady found herself in the dock.

Convicted as an accomplice to first degree murder, she received a life sentence without possibility of parole. Her last words to her counsel revealed the amazing amoral egocentricity of the possessive murderess: 'I can't believe Billy,' she said. 'First he took Gregg's life. Now he's taken mine.'

Margi Dunbar

Miss Whiplash knelt beside a bathroom mirror laid flat on the floor. Miss Whiplash, owner of the mirror, knelt opposite her. Miss Whiplash placed her fingers on the upturned wineglass resting on the mirror. Miss Whiplash did so too.

Miss Whiplash said a prayer that they be protected from evil. Then she said, 'Is there anybody there? My name is Christie. Will you speak to me?'

Both Miss Whiplashes waited in silence, as nothing happened. Christie repeated her appeal. Still nothing happened. Christie kept trying, until, after ten minutes, the glass started moving toward the Scrabble tiles placed around the mirror to turn it into a makeshift ouija board.

'SETH', said the silent wineglass. Both prostitutes felt a thrill of excitement as the spirit world opened its communication with them.

'Who are you?' asked Christie, the more experienced of the two in conjuration and psychic matters.

'A disciple of Jesus,' Seth replied.

The other Miss Whiplash (in public life, Lindi St Clair, among a host of other aliases) immediately put the question that had brought her to accept Christie's offer of spirit guidance. What was going to happen to her relationship with a third lesbian prostitute?

'Beware they will kill you,' said Seth.

Lindi thought the spirit had gone over the top. But her lesbian lover had been proving very difficult. Only that day she had pushed Lindi off the platform at Ascot as the two waited to return from the races. Lindi's new, expensive hat had rolled onto the rails to be destroyed. So she determined there and then to break off the affair.

Christie was having her own problems with her own lesbian lover. But Seth had nothing helpful to say about Margi Dunbar. Instead he broke into uttering dirty words – a surprising thing for a disciple of Jesus to do. It frightened Lindi more than the threat to her own life, and she broke her contact with the glass. Christie, aware that spirits can get tired too, said, 'We're going now. Will you speak to me again?'

'Yes,' said Seth.

Then Christie uttered a short blessing to protect the two women against any demonic possession and reassured Lindi about the fell warning.

'Spirits tell lies sometimes,' she said. 'It was probably a mischievous one hanging around with nothing better to do.'

Both of them then went to bed and made love, the start of a brief affair to fill the time while Christie's lover, Margi, was away.

It was the AIDS scare that threw Lindi St Clair into the lesbian world in 1985. A prostitute since her teens, she claims to be a bi-sexual nymphomaniac who gets a great deal of satisfaction from her work. But she was always careful of her health, and insisted on clients using condoms from her early days in the profession. When she heard of several colleagues dying from AIDS, she doubled her precautions. Punters had to wear two condoms before penetrating her; she donned latex gloves if they wanted her to fondle them; they had to put a sheet of clingfilm over their lips if they wanted to kiss or suck her!

Not surprisingly, she lost virtually all her 'straight' trade and became heavily dependent on the whippings and bondage market, in which, like Christie Offord, she operated under the trade name 'Miss Whiplash'.

She also turned her private love-life lesbian. Since she had always disliked the smell of semen and loathed it clinging to her body after penetration and ejaculation, one suspects that she was turning to a form of sex that appealed to her far more than that she purveyed.

But she also found there was a serious snag to lesbian love. Jealousy. The lesbians she knew were far more competitive, suspicious and threatening than men. Men didn't mind that other men enjoyed her services or paid to be her slaves. Lesbians did. One lesbian lover made Lindi get rid of her favourite 'slave' — a train-driver who loved to do her menial housework clad in purple crutchless panties — because Lindi seemed too fond of him. Another, a butch clippie (not a bus conductress: a fraudulent prostitute who takes money from punters as a 'deposit' and then fails to turn up at the appointed place) raised frightful scenes if she ever detected that Lindi had let one of her clients penetrate her, no matter how thickly the man's member was buried under layers of stout condoms. Lindi had even hired a heavy to put the frighteners on another lesbian: not something she had done in many years of heterosexual love.

But by indulging herself in the little dalliance with Christie Offord, Lindi St Clair ran a real risk of being beaten up by heavies herself.

Christie Offord was thirty-five and had been on the game since her divorce, eight years earlier. She had two teenage children, Damon and Denise, and her earnings from the 'torture dungeon' she ran in a little flat in Queens Gate supported them comfortably. She had a £100,000 detached house in Hounslow with its own swimming pool, and she could send the children on skiing trips to the continent if she felt like it. Until she copped a conviction in 1984, her neighbours had no idea that her daily tube journeys to the West End culminated in her donning fetishistic black leatherette corsets and boots, tying squirming men to racks, and whipping them till they screamed — with ecstasy.

But the neighbours did know she was a lesbian. One year after the divorce, twenty-year-old prostitute Margi

Dunbar moved in with Christie. Margi was a pretty, plump, round-faced blonde girl with long silky hair – the fem in the relationship. Big, square-jawed, butch Christie's earnings were quite enough to support them both as well as the children, so she insisted that Margi come off the game and live at home as a kept woman, looking after the kids. The pair were responsible and affectionate parents. But their love was tainted by jealousy, and it was well known in the neighbourhood that they sometimes had terrible rows.

Four years is long enough for anybody to sit around like a household pet and by 1982 Margi wanted to add a new and exciting element to her life. She and Christie agreed that it would be good for them and the household if they became joint parents rather than mother and stepmother. Margi had herself artificially inseminated and gave birth to a little boy, Jake, in 1983.

Jake's birth brought a change over Christie. She was now a father. She carried out the role admirably from a caring point of view. She got up at night to bottle-feed and change the baby. She proudly pushed him out in the pram. She was everything most wives and mothers wish their men would be.

But she also tried to become something Margi didn't want. She tried to make herself increasingly like a man. She cut her hair short. It didn't harm her trade: the masochists accepted any amount of ferocious androgynous appearance in their 'mistress'. She wore men's clothes. Jackets, trousers and even underwear. Margi drew the line at Y-fronts! She wanted a love-life with a woman and she didn't like fondling baggy underpants that might conceal a penis instead of silky knickers that clung to a vulva. Moreover, Christie smoked cigars and drank pints of beer and behaved in completely unladylike ways that her lover found a real turn-off.

Their rows built up to outrageous levels, until Margi stormed out of the house. That was when Lindi St Clair telephoned her friend Christie to weep on her shoulder about her own difficult lesbian lover. That was when Christie went round to Lindi's place with a couple of bottles of wine and the expertise to seek spirit help for their troubles. That was when Lindi and Christie became lovers.

Lindi learned that Margi was notorious for her jealous tantrums and scenes. She was rumoured to have chopped up her mother's poodles when she grew jealous of the affection lavished on them. She was known to slash her wrists lightly or put her head in the gas oven when enjoying a heroin-enhanced rage. And on her frequent disappearances, she slept with as many people as she could, hoping to provoke Christie's jealousy. But she had a fabulous figure and Christie, whose mannishness apparently extended to being pussy-whipped, just said, 'If you want someone and they're full of shit, you just have to put up with it'.

Lindi and Christie broke off their liaison when Margi came back. Only Margi knew about it. And Margi was jealous. She was also infuriated that Christie didn't change her masculine habits. The tension built until, once again, Margi was out of the house.

This time she did something she knew Christie would hate. She went back on the game and opened her own 'torture den' in Cornwall Gardens, just a couple of blocks away from Christie's work-place as Miss Whiplash. She stocked it with heavier whips and severer racks, as the dominatrices even managed to be competitive over who had the kinkiest equipment and punters. She hoped Christie would feel she was taking trade away from her.

She also threatened Christie's life. She had done this before, but Christie had accepted it as one of the brickbats people fling in quarrels: raging sound without literal meaning. But this time their friends were worried. Christie and Margi had been leading lights of the little clique of lesbian prostitutes who foregathered in late-night cafés around Earl's Court, and the other girls decided that if Christie wouldn't look after herself, they'd better do it for her. They went to Acton police and reported that they feared very serious threats were being made against Mrs Offord.

The police dismissed them out of hand – a bunch of toms coming round to report a domestic between two dykes! The prostitutes weren't satisfied, but what could they do?

Later that summer, Lindi St Clair was getting ready to take one of the long foreign holidays her lucrative profession permitted. A minder she sometimes hired was in her Earl's Court flat, waiting to drive her to the airport, when two men turned up at the door asking for business. Lindi was busy packing and probably wouldn't have turned a trick anyway. But there was no question of her taking two men at once. Most sensible prostitutes refuse multiple clients out of hand. The danger of being beaten up and gang-banged, with no hope of redress from the police, is all too real in their occupation.

The two men, however, didn't want to take no for an answer and hung around disconsolately outside the door for some time, until they caught sight of the burly minder and scarpered. When Lindi came home from her holiday five weeks later, she learned that the men were Robert Casaubon-Vincent and Barry Parsons. She had had a lucky escape.

Margi's jealous rage and hatred had built up as she, perhaps, lashed herself into finer frenzy while lashing punters to their curious climaxes. She wanted revenge on Christie and Lindi. She was also missing Jake, who stayed with Christie and the respectable suburban roof over Mrs Offord's head, rather than his mother, who was somewhat unprofessionally living at her working premises.

Margi went for the sort of revenge sadly common in the demi-monde of prostitution. She turned to the heavies. Parsons and Casaubon-Vincent were Sussex men: out-of-towners who would not be recognized by their victims. Margi wanted them to go to Christie and Lindi, presenting themselves as punters. When admitted, they

were to beat the hell out of the treacherous former lovers.
It would never be suspected as anything but sadistic
clients getting out of hand, and the police could be relied
upon to do precious little about another couple of
prostitutes getting a going-over, so the heavies would be
perfectly safe. They were welcome to rape their victims if
they felt like it. There was £40 apiece for Parsons and
Casaubon-Vincent in this, and Margi would enjoy revenge; she might even find Christie crawling humbly back
to her, needing her little blonde friend to lick her wounds.

Lindi escaped unharmed and might never have known
she was threatened had not Christie, foolishly and
unprofessionally, worked on her own without a maid to
summon help if necessary, and, compounding her folly,
let the two men into the Queens Gate flat together.

They went enthusiastically about their revolting task.
They raped Mrs Offord and sodomized her. They tied her
up so that she could not move. They pressed an iron bar
from her torture equipment against her throat to force
her into the bathroom. Then they threw her, face down,
into a bath full of water. But they had already killed her.
The iron bar had crushed her throat, so that she
suffocated before any water could be drawn into her
respiratory passages. Christie Offord was found trussed
and submerged, face down, a grisly corpse in a tub of
bloody water.

The police immediately jumped to the conclusion
Margi had predicted. They assumed a punter had gone
over the top after Christie had let herself be tied up for
bondage games. They appealed to any of her clients to
come forward, so that they could be eliminated from the
inquiry and any information they could offer about
Christie's professional practices could be made known to
detectives. Even those who didn't remember her name or
recall her address from several they had visited might
identify her by her striking tattoos: a snake on her right
foot and a spider's web on her left shoulder.

Remarkably, over thirty men immediately contacted

the police. They clearly recognized that the way they conducted their sex-lives was utterly unimportant compared with the duty of helping the police solve a cruel slaying. Once upon a time, all those men would have kept their heads down and hoped nobody ever imagined for one moment that they enjoyed Mrs Offord's services.

But the working girls were contemptuous of this line of inquiry. 'There's no way Christie would let anyone tie her up for bondage,' declared 'Madame Busty' Stevens. 'None of the girls who knew her believe for one moment a punter has done it.'

Before long the police were compelled to accept the truth of their argument. Margi found herself forced to make declarations of her innocence to the press, which loved the story. And once Parsons and Casaubon-Vincent had been traced, she found herself arrested and charged with murder, along with her hit-men.

The public gallery at the Old Bailey was packed with prostitutes as the three came to trial in 1986. Not all were unsympathetic to Margi: 'It was all a terrible mistake,' as her counsel explained. 'She was high on drink and drugs, and she only wanted them to hurt her a bit.'

The jury evidently agreed. They convicted the men of murder and rightly so. They had gone to Queens Gate with the intention of committing the crime of actual bodily harm, in the course of which they accidentally killed their victim. Accidental death caused by a felon in the course of perpetrating his felony is, in law, murder. Parsons and Casaubon-Vincent were given life sentences.

Margi, who had not overseen the brutalization of her former lover, had only conspired to encompass her rape and beating, in the course of which, agents, over whom she had no further control, accidentally killed her. Margi was convicted of manslaughter and sentenced to seven years. Even that was overturned by the Appeal Court the following year, and Margi Dunbar headed for Spain in the company of a lesbian warder whose embraces she had enjoyed in prison.

Bibliography

Anspacher, Carolyn, *The Acid Test*, Dawnay, London, 1965.

Begg, Paul and Keith Skinner, *The Scotland Yard Files*, Headline, 1992.

Bogdanovich, Peter, *The Killing of the Unicorn: Dorothy Stratten*, Morrow, New York, 1984.

Camps, Francis E., *Camps on Crime*, David & Charles, Newton Abbot, 1973.

Clarkson, Wensley, *Hell Hath No Fury*, Blake, London, 1991.

Cotes, Peter, *Trial of Elvira Barney*, David & Charles, Newton Abbot, 1976.

Englade, Ken, *Deadly Lessons*, Grafton, London, 1993.

Fido, Martin, *Murder Guide to London*, Academy Chicago, Chicago, 1990.

Murders After Midnight, Weidenfeld, London, 1990.

Hell Hath No Fury (audio-cassette), Bookpoint, London, 1992.

Furneaux, Rupert, *Famous Criminal Cases 3*, Wingate, London, 1956.

Gallagher, Mike, *Lovers of Deceit*, Doubleday, New York, 1993.

Gaute, J.H.H. & Robin Odell, *The New Murderers' Who's Who*, Headline, London, 1989.

Godwin, John, *Murder USA*, Ballantine, New York, 1978.

Goodman, Derek, *Crime of Passion*, Becker, Antwerp, 1958.

Goodman, Jonathan, *Murder in High Places*, Headline, London, 1989.

Hancock, Robert, *Ruth Ellis: The Last Woman to be Hanged*, Weidenfeld, London, 1985.

Harris, Jean, *Stranger in Two Worlds*, Macdonald, London, 1987.

Home Office Archives, CRIM 1/160, PRO, London.

Honeycombe, Gordon, *More Murders of the Black Museum*, Hutchinson, London, 1993.

Huie, William Bradford, *The Crime of Ruby McCollum*, Jarrolds, London, 1957.

Jackson, Robert, *Francis Camps*, Hart Davis, London, 1975.

Lustgarten, Edgar, *The Chalk-Pit Murder*, Hart-Davis MacGibbon, London, 1974.

MacKenzie, Drew, *Sunday Bloody Sunday*, Blake, London, 1992.

Marks, Laurence and Tony Van den Bergh, *Ruth Ellis: A Case of Diminished Responsibility*, Penguin, London, 1990.

Murder Casebook (part-issue, passim), Marshall Cavendish, London, 1989–92.

Nash, Jay Robert, *Encyclopedia of World Crime*, Crime Books Inc, Wilmette, 1990.

World Encyclopedia of 20th Century Murder, Headline, London, 1992.

Real Life Crimes and How They Were Solved (part-issue, passim), Eaglemoss, London, 1992– .

St Clair, Lindi with Pamela Winfield, *It's Only a Game*, Piatkus, London, 1992.

Sawicki, Stephen, *Teach Me to Kill*, Avon, New York, 1991.

Scotland Yard Archives, MEPO 3/167, MEPO 3/680, PRO, London.

Sifakis, Carl, *The Encyclopedia of American Crime*, Smithmark, New York, 1992.

Steiger, Brad, *Bizarre Crime*, Signet, New York, 1992.

Taubman, Bryn, *Hell Hath No Fury*, St Martin's Press, New York, 1992.

Trilling, Diana, *Mrs Harris: The Death of the Scarsdale*

Diet Doctor, Harcourt Brace Jovanovich, New York, 1981.

Whittington-Egan, Richard, *William Roughead's Chronicles of Murder*, Lochar, Moffat, 1991.

Wilkinson, Laurence, *Behind the Face of Crime*, Muller, London, 1957.

Wilson, Colin, *The Mammoth Book of True Crime*, Robinson, London, 1988.

and Donald Seaman, *Encyclopaedia of Modern Murder*, Pan, London, 1989.

Journals and Newspapers

London
Daily Express, *Daily Mail*, *Daily Mirror*, *Daily Telegraph*, *Evening Standard*, *Mail on Sunday*, *News of the World*, *Observer*, *People*, *Sun*, *Sunday Express*, *Sunday Mirror*, *Sunday Pictorial*, *Sunday Times*, *Times*.

Elsewhere
Crime Beat, *Master Detective*, *True Detective*, *Western Morning News*, *Sunday Post*, *Yorkshire Post*, Melbourne *Argus*, Los Angeles *Times*, New York *Times*, San Diego *Chronicle*.

Index

More True Crime from Headline:

FRANK JONES

MURDEROUS WOMEN

TRUE TALES OF WOMEN WHO KILLED

As Madame Fahmy stalked and killed her husband in cold blood at the elegant Savoy Hotel, what thoughts were in her mind? Could Louise Masset have thought that murder would open the way to a respectable marriage? What led Myra Hindley to participate in the grisly torture and murder of ten-year-old Lesley Ann Downey, photographing and tape-recording her death agonies?

In *Murderous Women* Frank Jones delves into the psyches of fifteen notorious females, from Victorian times to the present. With wit, insight, suspense and compassion he grippingly reconstructs their gruesome crimes from beginning to end.

NON-FICTION/TRUE CRIME   0 7472 3798 0

A selection of non-fiction from Headline

THE *INDEPENDENT* BOOK OF ANNIVERSARIES	George Beal	£8.99 ☐
MEAN BEANS	Cas Clarke	£5.99 ☐
ENCYCLOPEDIA OF FORENSIC SCIENCE	Brian Lane	£7.99 ☐
JUST THE ONE: The Wives and Times of Jeffrey Bernard	Graham Lord	£6.99 ☐
MALE SEXUAL AWARENESS	Barry McCarthy	£5.99 ☐
BURNS: A Biography of Robert Burns	James Mackay	£8.99 ☐
WORLD ENCYCLOPEDIA OF 20TH CENTURY MURDER	Jay Robert Nash	£8.99 ☐
PLAYFAIR FOOTBALL ANNUAL 1993-94	Jack Rollin (Ed)	£3.99 ☐
HEART AND SOLE	David Sole with Derek Douglas	£5.99 ☐

All Headline books are available at your local bookshop or newsagent, or can be ordered direct from the publisher. Just tick the titles you want and fill in the form below. Prices and availability subject to change without notice.

Headline Book Publishing PLC, Cash Sales Department, Bookpoint, 39 Milton Park, Abingdon, OXON, OX14 4TD, UK. If you have a credit card you may order by telephone – 0235 831700.

Please enclose a cheque or postal order made payable to Bookpoint Ltd to the value of the cover price and allow the following for postage and packing:
UK & BFPO: £1.00 for the first book, 50p for the second book and 30p for each additional book ordered up to a maximum charge of £3.00.
OVERSEAS & EIRE: £2.00 for the first book, £1.00 for the second book and 50p for each additional book.

Name ....

Address ....

....

....

If you would prefer to pay by credit card, please complete:
Please debit my Visa/Access/Diner's Card/American Express (delete as applicable) card no:

Signature .... Expiry Date ....